ID0983590

Literacy
and the Nation's
Libraries

Literacy and the Nation's Libraries

HELEN HUGUENOR LYMAN

AMERICAN LIBRARY ASSOCIATION
Chicago 1977

The research reported herein was performed
pursuant to a contract with the Office of
Education, U.S. Department of Health, Education
and Welfare. Contractors undertaking such
projects under government sponsorship are
encouraged to express freely their professional
judgment in the conduct of the project. Points of
view or opinions stated do not, therefore,
necessarily represent official Office of Education
position or policy.

Library of Congress Cataloging in Publication Data

Lyman, Helen H   1910-
    Literacy and the nation's libraries.

    Bibliography: p.
    Includes index.
    1. Libraries and new literates. 2. Illiteracy--
United States. 3. Reading. I. Title.
Z716.45.L9314   021'.24   77-4450
ISBN 0-8389-0244-8

Printed in the United States of America

Contents

Figures

Tables

Literacy and Libraries: An International Perspective

According to the most recent estimates of the United Nations Educational, Scientific and Cultural Organization (UNESCO), there are at least 800 million adult illiterates in the world, more than one-third of the entire adult population. Almost half the children in the developing countries are not attending school. For many of them, there are no schools and no teachers. A considerable number of those, who do have access at least to primary school, attend for only a few years, not long enough to acquire permanent literacy. So the total number of adult illiterates is constantly augmented by youths who have never learned to read.

The highest rates of illiteracy are in the areas having the fewest libraries. Most communities in these regions have no libraries at all. In some places, efforts are being made to create libraries for the general public even in the face of problems that are almost insuperable, problems such as the crucial and increasing paper shortage. If libraries are to be provided in such areas, buildings must be constructed or adapted, staff must be trained, and stocks must be built up, sometimes through the cooperation of local publishing houses that are also in the process of development. Mobile libraries, in some places called "book vans," are frequently proving to be a practical alternative.

A major problem for organizers of literacy programs has been the danger, and indeed, in too many cases, the inevitability that the new literates will revert to illiteracy. Another is that there have been varying concepts of what constitutes literacy; although through the years, international groups of experts have phrased carefully worded definitions. Now, at last, we can see the emergence of a universal consensus that literacy is a phase of life-long education and a human right that should be available to all. It should provide each individual with command of the tools or reading and writing which will enrich his own cultural, social, economic and civic development. From this point of view, it appears that the dichotomy between the literacy needs of the highly industrialized countries and the developing countries may be more imagined than real.

Internationally, the knowledge base, concerning what probably will or will not work effectively in reducing illiteracy rates, has been considerably expanded during the last decade through the Experimental Literacy Program of the United Nations Development Program (UNDP) and UNESCO. The objective of the experiment was "to test and demonstrate the economic and social returns of literacy and, more generally, to study the mutual relations and influences which exist or may be established or strengthened between literacy training, particularly among the working population, and development." Careful evaluation of the program led to the conclusion that literacy training designed primarily to help individuals contribute to their countries' economic development is not always in harmony with their own personal needs and aspirations. The concept of functional literacy, per se, long regarded as the panacea, is now more often seen as "only a technical solution to a problem that is not only technical."

Having recognized the validity of this hypothesis, a number of the developing countries are now making remarkable headway in breaking the illiteracy barrier. From them, other nations are learning to approach literacy education in terms of the learners themselves rather than through foreign models aimed mainly at economic development. It has been found that such models may lead to alienating the very people they were designed to serve. This has important implications for librarians.

Today, there is a universal trend toward adapting the library to the needs of its particular locale, including the whole spectrum of citizens in its community. Library services are being expanded as an aid to literacy education in a growing number of regions of the world. In general, libraries have become more education-oriented, utilizing a wide range of communications media. This is especially important in areas where the great majority of the people are illiterate and where literacy education must begin and often continue indefinitely to operate at the pre-book level. In such regions, literacy is still not necessarily considered to be the first stage in the process of education, and the oral tradition still prevails. Audiovisual media make a natural bridge between customary and new ways of learning. Accordingly, library services are being developed which capitalize on this phenomenon, services which can respond flexibly to the varied and changing needs of an expanded readership.

All over the world, wherever literacy activities are under way, libraries, however limited their resources, now have an opportunity to accelerate their efforts to rise to the challenge of providing the literate environment so necessary for the promotion of the reading habit and the maintenance of the literacy skills.

ELLA GRIFFIN
Education Program Specialist
U.S. Office of Education

Introduction

In our complex society, the fact that one of seven American adults is functionally illiterate can no longer be considered merely a troublesome but tolerable problem. Eradicating illiteracy must be a pressing priority. As the publication of this manual demonstrates, it is a top priority of the American Library Association (ALA) and of the many librarians across the country who collaborated in the creation of the book.

The purpose of this manual is to guide librarians in their efforts to assist people of all ages and all reading levels to become competent, habitual, and independent readers. By bringing together, organizing, and disseminating information on literacy training, the manual is designed to stimulate librarians to start literacy programs and to guide them along the way with concrete suggestions and ideas.

Librarians launching literacy programs do not need more platitudes about the evils of literacy. They need the kind of down-to-earth practical information this manual offers—information, for example, on how to plan the training sessions necessary to teach staff to run literacy programs. Once these programs are started, librarians need to know how to evaluate them. They also need to know how to identify groups within their communities who need literacy training, and how realistically to assess the library's resources for initiating or supporting such training. They even need answers to questions as basic as "What is literacy?"

The National Advisory Council on Adult Education estimates that 28.5 million people require basic literacy training. The problem of illiteracy is obviously such a huge one that libraries must not repeat work already being done by other groups and individuals. So this manual is also a guide to cooperation. It offers concrete suggestions on how to plan and implement joint programs. It helps librarians determine the scope, nature, and effectiveness of already existing programs.

Although in the history of libraries and literacy training this manual is new, the link between libraries and literacy training is not new. Historically, the path American public libraries have followed has been one of participation in the education of the adult. The ALA Commission on Library and Adult Education was formed 53 years ago, in 1924. And our colleagues then were asking many of the same questions we are asking today.

> What is adult education? It may mean the teaching of reading to illiterates. To some, it means the Americanization of the foreign-born; to others, it signifies vocational training. But adult education goes far beyond all these. It is based on a recognition of the fact that education is a life-long process, and that the university graduate, as well as the man of little schooling, is in need of further training, inspiration, and mental growth, that the training secured in school and college is necessarily limited to fundamentals, and that the real development of the individual lies in the independent effort of later years. [*Adult Education and the Library* (Chicago: ALA Board of the Library and Adult Education), 1, no. 1 : 1.]

In the months ahead, as you use this manual, think about the long participation of libraries in adult education. But also think about the problem of illiteracy in concrete terms. Think about the fact that 28.5 million people read so inadequately that comprehending a want ad or directions for long-distance dialing is beyond them. Think about the fact that thousands of young people drop out of school before becoming literate adults. And think about the fact that thousands pass from one grade level to the next and out the doors of high schools grasping diplomas but not grasping the most basic reading skills.

The gap between our ideal of a totally literate adult population and the reality that one of every seven adults is functionally illiterate is one that libraries, with the aid of this manual, are uniquely equipped to fill. The publication of *Literacy and the Nation's Libraries* is, we believe, a milestone on the road to the ideal. But reaching the ideal will depend on librarians' successful implementation of the programs outlined in the pages that follow. In other words, it is the imagination, commitment, and hard work of librarians that can turn the ideal—an adult population in which everyone can read and write—into a reality.

Eight units of ALA contributed to planning and writing this manual.

The project was funded by the Bureau of Library and Learning Resources, the U.S. Department of Health, Education and Welfare, Office of Education.

Our thanks to all whose input, time, and dedication made the publication of this manual possible.

ROBERT WEDGEWORTH
Executive Director
American Library Association

Author's Introduction

Literacy and the Nation's Libraries is addressed primarily to librarians. It also can be of use to adult educators and others who are concerned with literacy in the United States. Chapter 1 reviews briefly the literacy goal and the role of libraries and librarians in support of the national literacy effort. Chapter 2 looks at the value of literacy and points out recent studies and a few of their findings. Chapter 3 discusses the specific role of various types of libraries and the role of librarians. Chapter 4 suggests steps in the planning process that are considered essential to a successful literacy program. The essential first stages of preplanning, planning, the assessment of the community, and the client and the environment are outlined.

Chapter 5 continues the discussion on the planning of a literacy program for various types of libraries—public school/media centers, public library, academic, and state. Chapter 6 identifies the population groups that are potential clientele. Such groups include: age groups, rural and urban, ethnic, cultural and language, disadvantaged by a particular handicap, participants in lifetime learning programs that range from preschool through college.

Chapter 7 presents profiles of selected client groups and outlines some library responses to their needs and interests. Six major groups that may be developing literacy abilities are: the independent learner, the ABE learner-client, the early childhood group, the student in higher education, bilingual and bicultural clients, and the imprisoned and incarcerated client.

Don A. Brown has contributed chapter 8, "The Nature of Reading and Reading Instruction." As a member and consultant of the Literacy Manual Project Board, he worked closely with the board. He is a reading specialist, researcher, and teacher—a professor at Northern Colorado University. He has had special experience with beginning readers in inner city ghettos and with residents of prisons who are developing literacy skills and knowledge. An active member of the International Reading Association and Adult Education Association, he has also worked closely with libraries and librarians.

Some questions that are raised frequently by librarians and that often are controversial are answered in chapter 9, the final chapter.

The appendixes contain material for use in developing literacy programs. "How-to suggestions" include a checklist and forms for use in community analysis; a preplanning, clientele assessment; a program profile outline; and a list of "real world" materials. The resources section provides funding sources, lists of literacy programs and organizations, a list of handbooks for tutor training, and resources for school libraries.

Six library project profile reports are included. Project directors describe the projects at Bay County (California), Dallas, Denver, Brooklyn, Mountain View (Florida), and Santa Fe (Florida), that add an extra dimension, the reality of practice. They are gratefully acknowledged. The list of objectives defined in the National Assessment of Education Programs and Adult Functional Competency studies is reproduced. The objectives are not only informative but also practical. They suggest interest and needs in reading that are relevant to the selection of materials.

The Literacy Manual Project Advisory Board wished to avoid the weight and interruption of footnotes, and so they are not used. However, the sources named in the text are cited fully in References at the end of each chapter. Suggested Readings are included in the text where they seemed most appropriate. For example, sources for selection and acquisition of materials are part of Material Resources section. The General Bibliography at the end of the book lists additional reading suggestions.

Two important aspects of library literacy programs—collaboration and initiation—are emphasized throughout this book. The importance of cooperation and collaboration is stressed because of the breadth of the literacy problem, the necessity of efficient use of resources, the great number of other agencies and organizations that are part of the literacy efforts, and the distinctive functions that libraries have. Initiative is stressed because libraries are considered to have a major educational responsibility as well as unique services and resources to contribute to the development and maintenance of lifelong literacy skills and knowledge. Such services are a part of the history of the development of libraries in the United States.

Acknowledgments

In the development of this manual, *Literacy and the Nation's Libraries,* the Project Board, the Project Resource Board, and the Project Director and Associate Director, have had a deep and continuing involvement. Their advice and assistance, their sincere criticism and support has been of the greatest encouragement and practical help. I am deeply grateful to each member of the two boards and to Gerald Born.

Donna Curtis, who assisted in bibliographic searching and organization, also contributed ideas from her own experiences.

At any time, day or night, Jean Coleman was there to give invaluable help in analysis of the manuscript, the collection of data, and perceptive review and criticism. Her assistance and support, encouragement and patience, and contributions made it possible to complete the manual.

It is a pleasure to say thank you to all these librarians and adult educators and others who contributed from their knowledge and experience as well as time and effort. At the same time, they were never restrictive and gave the author full freedom. In the final analysis this author takes full responsibility for the content of this manual.

HELEN HUGUENOR LYMAN

PROJECT BOARD MEMBERS

Jean E. Coleman, Project Director; Director, Office of Library Service to the Disadvantaged, ALA

Gerald M. Born, Associate Project Director (formerly Executive Secretary, Public Library Association)

Margaret A. Richek, Project Evaluator; Assistant Professor, College of Education, University of Illinois at Chicago Circle

ALA Representatives

Neva L. Bequette (LSD), Kennewick, Washington

Elizabeth C. Breting (CSD), Director, Children's Services, Kansas City Public Library

Patricia Gaven (PLA), Director, Englewood Library, Englewood, New Jersey

Peggy Glover (RASD), Coordinator, Office of Work with Adults and Young Adults, Free Library of Philadelphia

Phyllis M. Land (AASL), Director, Division of Instructional Media, Indiana Department of Public Instruction, Indianapolis

Helen Huguenor Lyman, Professor, School of Library Science, University of Wisconsin—Madison

Doreitha R. Madden (HRLS), Coordinator, Library Outreach Service, New Jersey State Library, Trenton

Rebecca Olson (YASD), Study Unlimited, Chicago Public Library, Portage-Cragin Branch (now Perry County District Library, New Lexington, Ohio)

John S. Page, Jr. (ACRL), Department Head, Technical Services, Federal City College, Library and Media Services Division, Washington, D.C.

Educators

Don A. Brown, Reading Center, University of Northern Colorado, Greeley

Jinx Crouch, Associate Director of Field Services, Literacy Volunteers of America, Inc., Syracuse, New York

Ann H. Drennan, Chief Investigator, Library Project, Appalachian Adult Education Center, Morehead State University, Morehead, Kentucky (now Executive Director, Literacy Action, Washington, D.C.)

George Eyster, Executive Director, Appalachian Adult Education Center, Bureau of Research and Development, Morehead State University, Morehead, Kentucky

PROJECT RESOURCE BOARD MEMBERS

Librarians

John A. Axam, Program Director, Reader Development Program, Free Library of Philadelphia

Linda Bayley, Librarian, Industrial and Business Training Bureau, Division of Extension, University of Texas, Austin

Jean Brooks, Learning Center Project Director, Dallas Public Library

Geraldine Clark, Director, School Library Service, New York Board of Education, Bureau of Libraries, Brooklyn

Willye F. Dennis, Supervisor, Loop Program, Jacksonville Public Library, Jacksonville, Florida

Mary-Jo Di Muccio, Director, Sunnyvale Public Library, Sunnyvale, California

Daniel F. Duran, Doctoral Student, Library School, University of Wisconsin—Madison

Melissa Forinash, Materials Librarian, Reader Development Program, Free Library of Philadelphia

Stephen E. James, Doctoral Student, Library School, University of Wisconsin—Madison (now Assistant Professor, School of Library Service, Atlanta University, Atlanta, Georgia)

Katherine Keathley, Head Librarian, Arkansas River Valley Regional Library, Dardanelle, Arkansas

Richard L. Keller, Chief, Reading Improvement Program, Brooklyn Public Library

Clayton E. Kilpatrick, Adult Service Coordinator, Anne Arundel County Library, Annapolis, Maryland

Bernice MacDonald, Coordinator of Adult Services, the Branch Libraries, New York Public Library (now Assistant Director, the Branch Libraries)

Lowell Martin, Professor, School of Library Service, Columbia University, New York City

William Miles, Deputy Librarian, Buffalo and Erie County Public Library, Buffalo, New York

James B. Nelson, Director, Cabell County Public Library, Huntington, West Virginia

David Reich, Director, Chicago Public Library

Norma Richey, Bookmobile Coordinator, New Mexico State Library, Santa Fe

Susan Schmidt, Librarian, Appalachian Adult Education Center, Bureau
for Research and Development, Morehead State University, Morehead, Kentucky (now Director, Mideastern Ohio Library Organization, Louisville, Ohio)

Eleanor T. Smith, Library Services Program Officer, U.S. Office of
Education, Region 2, New York City (now consultant)

José Orlando Toro, Director, Office of Library Independent Study and
Guidance Projects, College Entrance Examination Board, New York
City

Kathryn D. Wright, Readers' Advisor, D.C. Public Library, Watha T.
Daniel Branch, Washington, D.C.

ALA Staff Members

Peggy Barber	Patricia Harris
Herbert Bloom	Howard Pasternack
Ruth Frame	Irene Wood

Educators, Publishers and Others

Sven Borei, Philadelphia Adult Basic Education Academy, Philadelphia

Bayard Clark, Coordinator, Clearinghouse on Adult Education, Adult
Education Division, U.S. Office of Education, Washington, D.C.

Lee Collins, Associate Director, Literacy Council of North Virginia, Inc.,
Alexandria

F. Priscilla Gipson, Consultant to Program Development, Laubach
Literacy International, Syracuse, New York

Joseph A. Gray, Director, Literacy Volunteers of America, Syracuse,
New York

Ella Griffin, Education Program Specialist, Bureau of School Systems,
U.S. Office of Education, Washington, D.C.

Connie Haendle, Director of Field Services, Literacy Volunteers of
America, Inc., Syracuse, New York

Ruth Love Halloway, Superintendent, Oakland Unified School District,
Oakland, California

John A. Hurst, Consultant, Adult Basic Education, Elgin, Illinois

Carol Kemmel, President, National Congress of Parents & Teachers,
Chicago

Martha A. Lane, Coordinator, Volunteer Reading Aides, Lutheran
Church Women, Philadelphia

Tom Lawrence, Executive Director, Education Service Center Region 14,
Abilene, Texas

Margaret McNamara, National Chairman, Reading Is Fundamental, Inc., Smithsonian Institution, Washington, D.C.

Virginia Mathews, Consultant, Literacy and Libraries, Stamford, Connecticut

Robert A. Palmatier, Associate Professor, Reading Department, College of Education, University of Georgia, Athens

Samuel B. Ross, Jr., Headmaster, Green Chimneys School, Brewster, New York

Marjorie Rutiman, Coordinator, FILMS PLUS, Modern Language Association of America, New York City

Leslie Sandy, Dean, Non-Traditional Programs, Institute for City-Wide Programs, Chicago

Ralph C. Staiger, Executive Director, International Reading Association, Newark, Delaware

Ronald B. Szcypkowski, Professor, Bronx Community College, Bronx, New York

Sandra Timmermann, Associate Dean, Institute of Lifetime Learning, Washington, D.C.

Tim Wells, Division of Adult Basic Education, Indiana Department of Public Instruction, Indianapolis

Statement of Purpose

This manual is intended to:

Encourage and assist librarians in helping
people learn to read and become competent,
independent readers
Suggest ideas and methods for librarians
who wish to:

determine the scope and nature of literacy
programs in their communities
identify literacy needs not being met
assess the library's resources for supporting
or initiating programs in or out of the
library
collaborate with others with literacy
concerns or objectives in joint planning and
implementation of programs
develop appropriate programs of action
evaluate and adjust programs.

ALA LITERACY MANUAL PROJECT BOARD

1
Literacy–
A National Priority

Literacy is not an end in itself. It is a fundamental human right. It is not merely the ability to read and write, but a contribution to the liberation of man. Thus conceived, literacy creates the conditions for a critical awareness of the contradictions of the society and of its goals.

National literacy has long been a priority in the United States. A common school system and publicly supported libraries of many types testify to this fact. The proportion of Americans completing a high school level of education or beyond has increased steadily, so that the nation now has attained a median grade level of 12.3 years—the highest such figure in the world. In view of these facts, why the concern? Why is literacy a national priority? Many persons find this emphasis on literacy surprising and even unbelievable in a nation with millions of highly educated people who have high school and college degrees. Many predictions foresee the end of literacy, print, and reading; nevertheless, the ability to read and write are recognized as among the most important skills anyone can have. They have an extreme social significance and an importance as vital tools for lifetime learning and career success. During the last decade, however, the phenomenal emphases on reading and national literacy has resulted in reaching only a small number of the millions of people who require literacy skills to solve even everyday problems. They need not only to learn to read, but also to comprehend what they read.

This introduction to the significance of literacy and lifetime learning for everyone as a national priority and as a priority for the libraries of the nation reviews briefly the relationship between national goals and library goals. After a brief look at some background facts and at the meaning of literacy, specific ways are outlined for support by libraries and librarians of the learning activities and literacy goals of all people of the United States.

A GOAL FOR LIBRARIES AND LIBRARIANS

Librarians have before them the invigorating activity of joint venture and the unparalleled opportunity to collaborate with many groups and other libraries already involved in a total national commitment. They are in a unique position to concentrate their attention on and take an active role in the achievement of national literacy. Every library in the country—no matter what its size, function, purpose, and resources—has a place in the national literacy effort. Every library in the country can work with other libraries and other educational agencies in the community, region, or state. Librarians will find many people to relate to: teachers, researchers, reading specialists, citizens, volunteers from many fields, other librarians, and interested families, friends, and neighbors of the new literates. In fact, throughout the nation, many public and private groups and volunteers, unpublicized and unfunded, have worked for years and continue to work in literacy and language programs. They are found among the members and staff of churches, high schools, colleges, universities, international houses, armed services, and in the Laubach Literacy and Literacy Volunteers of America programs, as well as many local volunteer programs. Libraries' unique functions can be marshaled to support and extend these activities.

The responsibility that libraries and librarians have for developing and interpreting collections of communication media places them in the forefront of the nation's effort. Only teachers, administrators, and researchers in curriculum-oriented study have a closer and more active role. Librarians have a real responsibility to identify, find, even produce, the written materials that can be matched with various levels of reading skills.

Librarians have had a long and deep commitment to adult and continuing education. Their support of reading activities for children, young adults, and adults is implicit in their professional organization—the American Library Association. The major goal of ALA is "the promotion of libraries and librarianship to assure the delivery of user-oriented library and information services to all.... Emphasis is on *service* which includes delivery as well as access to *all* people." A first objective of this ALA goal is to provide "information services and resources for all the people of the United States of America in order to increase their opportunity to participate in society, to learn, to achieve self-fulfillment, to pursue careers, and to obtain information needed for research." A second objective stresses the "provision of leadership for interlibrary cooperation. . . ." Various professional standards established for libraries also commit librarians to action in the provision of such services.

These goals imply delivery of information and freedom of access to everyone. Although they do not emphasize direct intervention and instruction in the use of information and library resources, such activities may be implied. The development of library networks and systems enables all libraries to broaden and extend services and intervene directly in the community's and the nation's literacy effort.

The American Library Association, reinforcing its long advocacy of improved literacy and recognizing its responsibility to provide leadership and coordination for developing literacy programs, has launched a nationwide effort to focus librarians' attention on their active commitment to the achievement of national literacy.

The importance of a totally literate population is agreed upon by more and more segments of that population. The recognition is widespread that a large part of the population is not adequately literate; that is, many people do not have the knowledge and reading skills necessary for daily life. The world in which we live today is one great communication network. Language holds it together. A sound, a picture, a word, a letter, a sign—any and all such symbols are vital to each person's survival, alone or with others. Each needs to be able to get and to give messages, to make sense out of what is in the message, to use it in making decisions on what to do and why, and to get practical help and pleasure in living. For some, this means knowledge of only one language; for others, knowledge of two or more languages.

Furthermore, lifetime learning is becoming an important part of today's society. Commitment to the education of adults and the right of every person in the United States to attain literacy skills and knowledge has been supported by legislation and funds. For over a decade, federal partnership with state and local education agencies has made possible adult basic education programs.

The federal government is one source of financial support and technical assistance for the nation's schools and colleges. As a major component of the U.S. Department of Health, Education, and Welfare, the Office of Education administers programs at every level and for every aspect of education, including literacy education. Office of Education program regulations recognize the value of libraries and information science in providing activities designed to bring together the total information, educational, and cultural resources of communities and organizations into patterns of service to special target groups such as the underemployed, undereducated, culturally or geographically isolated groups, and others who have been unserved or minimally served in the past.

BACKGROUND OF THE LITERACY PROBLEM

Although the impressive achievements in education in the United States would seem to assure a highly literate population, statistics and performance do not bear this out. At one time in the past, little schooling was needed.   In modern society, however, it seems necessary for everyone to have the equivalent of a secondary or high school education. Against this background of increased school attainment, it is essential to note:

> In 1975, in the United States, 57 million adults 16 years of age or older, and not enrolled in school, had not completed a high school education.
> In 1970, there were more than 27 million workers 16 years of age and over with less than 12 years of school.
> Projections for 1980 show that the same number of workers will not have completed high school.
> In 1976, it is estimated that 28.5 million people need basic literacy training.
> More than 80 percent of the nation's prisoners—adult and juvenile—cannot read or have reading problems.
> Each year about 1 million students leave school before completing high school. Projections indicate that this will continue through 1982.
> Projections for 1990 show that there will be about 22 million workers with less than a high school education.
> The problem of illiteracy will continue at least to the year 2000.

The 1974 report of the National Advisory Council on Adult Education presents vital statistics about the literacy and adult education needs of the United States population in general and of specific groups among the younger and older populations, the ethnic and minority population, the labor force, and the very poor. A detailed review of these facts is not possible here, but they present overwhelming evidence that:

> There is an urgent need to increase the national effort in delivering adult education services.
> The increasing demands of a technological society are raising the educational requirement levels for employment and general living.
> The future will bring new educational requirements as new standards and new needs arise for the high school diploma, and new programs are adapted to meet the human needs of the time.

People with little education can experience severe limitations on their ability to perform as citizens, to realize their full potential as individuals, to take advantage of leisure-time activities, and to serve as economically active members of the work force.

The rather startling results of several recent reports center attention anew on literacy as a national priority. If "literacy" means that adults must have the ability to use communications skills and knowledge of subjects and information needed to do the things they need and want to do, then many Americans are not literate. The University of Texas 1975 study *Adult Functional Competency* reported that one out of five adults in the United States lacks the skills and knowledge needed to function effectively in the basic day-to-day struggle to make a living and maintain a home and family. Most alarming were the difficulties encountered in the field of consumer economics, where almost 30 percent of the population was found to be functioning with difficulty, and an additional third of the population to be functional but not proficient.

The 1975 study amplifies a 1970 National Reading Council survey that measured tasks such as reading classified advertisements, leases and credit forms, and Social Security forms. Literacy was defined in terms of "survival thresholds," measured by the reading ability necessary to fill out these forms and others in common use. The results of the study indicate that from 4.3 to 18.5 million adult Americans were functionally illiterate.

General literacy has developed slowly, and mass literacy is a major concern of the twentieth century. For centuries illiterate people had a highly complex, sophisticated life without written languages and formal schooling. Printing made mass literacy possible. The development in scientific knowledge, the changing economic, social, and technological framework of modern society, urbanization, and the need to know and adopt new ideas have made literacy necessary. It is imperative for political development and informed citizen participation. Literacy is essential for coping with daily problems and for improving the quality of life for persons of all ages, particularly for middle-aged adults, who have responsibility for the care of the young and the old as well as of themselves.

The modern world shares the concern. In 1975 the International Symposium for Literacy met in Persepolis (that fabulous Persian city built by Cyrus the Great about 530 B.C.). A result of the symposium of international delegates was the *Declaration of Persepolis,* which said in part:

> The number of illiterates is constantly growing.
> In spite of the progress . . . there are close to one thousand million illiterates in the world, and many more under-nourished people.
> Successes were achieved when literacy was linked to meeting man's fundamental requirements, ranging from his immediate vital needs to effective participation in social change.
> Literacy, like education in general, is not the driving force of historical change. It is not the only means of liberation but it is an essential instrument for all social change.

Standards of measurement vary within cultures and between countries, as is seen in the most recent studies in the United States. Age is not a criterion. Literacy figures change with population changes and according to the standards of measurement. The dimensions of the problem vary accordingly.

Individuals and nations recognize the close connection between social and economic development, between job competencies and incomes, and between cultural development and the quality of life. The concept of functional literacy moves far beyond earlier definitions. It means that one is able to perform competently in activities normal for the culture and the group in which one lives. Illiteracy inhibits or prevents the effective exercise of human rights that are dependent on literacy skills. Because of ignorance men and women suffer discrimination. Ignorance prevents choice of work, prohibits productive income, makes exploitation possible, and favors political mismanagement.

Literacy can mean many things: to be able to do what one might want or need to do, to perform daily tasks, to meet new work requirements, and to understand new techniques. Literacy makes it possible to review and augment what is seen and heard in the more pervasive communication media of movies, radio, and television. Literacy skills affect seemingly simple daily matters as well as complex learning and study, and thereby have tremendous influence on a person's life. Specifically, literacy means that:

For the first time a man is able to sign his name when he gets his paycheck at the plant where he works.

An old man and woman waiting for a bus on a country road can read the destination sign. It is possible for a young man in a metropolitan city to leave the neighborhood where he lives because he can, for the first time, read street signs and maps.

For the first time a mother and father read a story to their child, help with school lessons, and demonstrate in various ways the values of reading and writing.

An adult can find a number in a telephone book; open a bank account; read labels on grocery products and add up their cost; compute income tax and Social Security benefits; pass a driver's test; fill out forms for job application and Medicaid; learn about legal rights.

People can easily read the Bible, a newspaper, a magazine, or a restaurant menu in their own language; and it is possible to read about one's own heritage and culture and to read books written in the language of one's choice.

A person knows how to use the dictionary and encyclopedias, find the way around a library, prepare for and pass a high school or college level examination, pursue self-directed independent learning, and help others to read and write.

It is recognized that almost everyone's reading efficiency can be improved. Developmental reading programs frequently are continued from sixth grade through college and beyond. Individual capacities, abilities, and problems must be considered. Cultural and ethnic differences, attitudes, and values are major considerations. They should be seen as strengths on which to build. Such distinctions and difficulties should be assessed realistically by teachers and librarians; each teacher and librarian should also assess his or her own personal attitudes, values, and differences.

LIBRARIES' AND LIBRARIANS' SUPPORT OF LITERACY GOALS

Librarians not only are creating a new clientele of adult readers, but also are assisting readers in the maintenance of basic literacy skills and in broadening the application of those skills. Librarians should create an awareness of the multiple resources, range of subjects, and variety of communication media that can enrich the lives of their clienteles.

Libraries can support the learning activities of adults and young adults, of children and youth who are learning to read and are developing the basic literacy skills, and of those persons who are involved in programs for independent learners.

Today many options are open to the library that sets a policy of focusing resources on a literacy program. Much depends on the initiative of the librarian and the library board. Every library, regardless of size, can conduct a full-fledged program. The library will provide the necessary services as determined by assessment of the community or particular group needs. The full range of services will be provided, from development of reading and related media collections to training of staff and evaluation of what is done, from serving other literacy programs to organizing and conducting the library's literacy program, from advice and counseling to teaching. The program would include such services as these:

1. The library should serve as an information source about learning opportunities—local, state, and national—should assemble and interpret materials, develop a referral service, and collaborate with other agencies. Libraries can and should be information centers for literacy programs. They should maintain an up-to-date reference and consultant collection

about local, state, and national literacy programs. Librarians should be prepared to provide adults with advice and counsel on selecting courses, program activities, and materials, and give encouragement and support to those taking examinations and tests. The library often is a neutral agency, whether within an academic, private, or public library community, which can act as a facilitator of information and as a referral agency.

2. Libraries can and should be resource centers for materials both for the client and for professional personnel. It is almost imperative to have an adequate number of authors and titles so that the material is readily accessible, and not even the smallest library is exempt from this requirement. If it is not possible for a library to provide the needed material, it is essential that it provide purchase information, rental service, interlibrary loan, or referral to a dependable source. Literacy programs will require workbooks, textbooks, and pamphlet materials not usually acquired by libraries. Librarians must be familiar with the study materials and guides, and provide them or help the student find other sources for obtaining these materials through loan, purchase, or rental. The library staff should be able to assist personnel from literacy programs in optimum use of the collection. The large public library and the university library have a special responsibility to develop teaching and research collections. They can support and collaborate with education and library science departments in developing curricula, institutes, seminars, and staff orientation programs. The state library, with or without the collaboration of public and university education departments and libraries of the state, should develop study collections and provide learning opportunities for librarians and teachers. The state library and central or regional library of a system should make materials from reading development collections available to individuals and libraries, in ways most convenient to the learners' demands. The library board and library staff may need to redirect selection and acquisition policies toward collecting and organizing different types of material, to find new publishers, and to discover new sources.

3. Librarians should assist in the recruitment of participants in formal and informal educational programs, and promote and publicize these programs.

4. Librarians can encourage the potential learner or reader who is reluctant, fearful, or uninformed. They should be able to suggest alternative activities—courses with other learners, or study with a tutor or independently. Librarians can develop a network to introduce individual learners to one another and bring them together in library-sponsored activities, such as study groups, discussion programs, storytelling, reading aloud, and problem solving, in which learners use their newly acquired skills and knowledge. Librarians should develop

information files on resource persons, tutors, speakers, and specialists who can assist the learners and serve as resources for library activities.

5. Libraries and media centers, as public facilities, have space and physical facilities that should be used to the maximum by being open as many hours as possible and at the times most convenient to the various user groups. All libraries will want to provide the best possible study conditions, suitable hours, and individual attention to the client.

6. Librarians should produce information bulletins, guides to the libraries, and media presentations on radio and television as aids in teaching the individual, the class, or the group how to use the library, the reference aids, and the required study material.

7. Libraries, schools, and other agencies and organizations with literacy programs should sponsor and conduct training seminars, institutes, and workshops for professional and volunteer staff. Librarians and volunteer staff should be trained and become skilled in assessing the needs and resources of the community served and in planning and developing services. They also should have training in how to assess the needs and interests as well as reading abilities of the individual learner. Librarians and volunteer staff should be trained and become skilled in teaching when the situation makes it advisable and desirable. In most situations such teaching is neither needed nor advisable; but when it is, and when the staff has the interest and the qualifications, such an opportunity to extend and to reach out from the traditional service should be seized.

8. In many instances, librarians may serve as liaison between literacy programs and the library, or between students and teachers or tutors, and report on problems, changes, and evaluation.

9. The library and other agencies will need to make periodic assessments, evaluate services, keep relevant records, and exchange information about learners.

10. Libraries should place their skills and knowledge, their science of evaluation, organization, and interpretation of reading and audiovisual media at the service of the teachers and administrators of literacy or relevant adult education programs.

It can be seen that no really new functions or services are suggested. What may be new for a library is the decision to focus on an effort to achieve a totally literate population within its community. If no library program in this area of service exists, this doubtless will entail a redirection and setting of different priorities, and possibly less support for existing programs. It is important to make a reassessment, to reevaluate policy, and to redirect efforts. Where a literacy program and services already are in progress, the effort may be mainly toward strengthening or improving the services.

Let no one be deceived. Literacy and reading development at any level present a very sensitive problem. The involvement by the libraries of the nation requires a dedicated and sustained effort. It is a long-term effort that must be made quietly, without fanfare, and with a conscious effort never to expose or exploit the needs of the clientele.

Admittedly, it is not easy to determine the exact role of the library. The appropriate role will vary. It is a primary assumption here that libraries *do* have a role—and that their role is a positive, active one.

What does it mean for a library to give priority to the literacy effort?

The initiation, improvement, or expansion of any library program has an effect on every other aspect of the library's operation. If the new or expanded activity is to be undertaken with present resources, it means that some staff members will have to work harder than they have been working, or that they will have to drop some of their other activities. It means that if the library is to select and acquire special materials, selection and acquisition of other materials will have to be postponed—perhaps indefinitely. It means that money spent on the new activity will never be available for anything else.

When an appropriation is made or a grant secured for the literacy activity, the impact on the total library program is not eradicated. Although new staff may be employed, they will have to be supervised; and their presence will involve many people in the library, from the fiscal officer to the custodian, in additional work. Rarely do grant funds cover the processing and cataloging of additional materials. If old space is not required for new activities, the acquisition of new space is a time- and effort-consuming activity.

The question then arises: Can any library—operating as efficiently as possible and making full use of all its resources in the operation of its present program—afford to initiate, improve, or expand a literacy program?

The answer is that the libraries of the United States have no choice. They exist to make it possible for the people they serve to have access to the information they need to survive and to the records of the past and the creative thinking of others, which they need for substance and guidance in the pursuit of the satisfaction of living. Any person who cannot read competently has no such access. Every library has an obligation to participate in the national effort to break the barriers of illiteracy and to admit all of the people of the country to full use of the materials and services they need.

A high-priority program like this requires a review of the library's present program and a determination to eliminate less important activities to make room for the new. Organizational patterns and routines may show need for change. The consolidation of scattered duties may release some supervisory personnel for program activity. It may be possible to eliminate units that are performing only minor functions. Of course, in establishing new priorities, it is often difficult to eliminate older programs that have created their own supporters among staff and users.

The percentage of library income spent on materials has declined steadily through the years, but the nature of the purchases that are made should be assessed for their contribution to the quality of life and the needs of the members of the community. Academic and special libraries may find it necessary to eliminate general recreational materials from the collections to release funds for reading development materials. Public libraries may have to decide to what extent they will meet the requests of their most demanding patrons at the expense of those in greatest need. All libraries that are not engaged in some program of cooperative purchasing, reciprocal borrowing, or other cooperative enterprises with the other libraries in the community, state, or region may have to be more flexible in purchasing procedures to release funds for literacy materials.

If every community agency with an educational or humanitarian purpose turned all of its resources to the elimination of illiteracy, the full result would probably not be accomplished in this generation. Literacy programs must be given top priority, not only for a year or two but also for the foreseeable future. As far as libraries are concerned, opening access to knowledge for everyone has to be a first and continuing concern.

References

"A.L.A. Goal and Objectives, Revised Draft," *American Libraries* 6, no. 1 (January 1975): 39–41.

International Symposium for Literacy. *Declaration of Persepolis.* Symposium held in Persepolis, September 3–8, 1975. Paris: Distributed by the International Co-ordination Secretariat for Literacy (42 bis, Avenue de Saxe, 75007 Paris).

Northcutt, Norvell, and others. *Adult Functional Competency: A Summary.* Austin: The University of Texas, Division of Extension, 1975.

Survival Literacy Study (ERIC-ED 068 813). Conducted for the National Reading Council by Louis Harris and Associates, Inc. Study No. 2036. September 1970.

"Survival Literacy Study." *Congressional Record,* 91st Congress, 2d sess., 1970, 116, no. 184.

United States. National Advisory Council on Adult Education. *A Target Population in Adult Education:* Report of the National Advisory Council on Adult Education. Economic Perspectives and Prospects. A Focus on the Client State Demographic Data. Washington, D.C.: U.S. Government Printing Office, 1974.

2
Understanding the Value and Nature of Literacy

THE VALUE OF LITERACY

For centuries cultures and nations have come and gone with only a small number of literate people in the population. In the modern world, however, with its powerful electronic communications media, the importance of the skills of reading, writing, and computing, and of comprehension of knowledge through these skills pervades the whole of life. Visual literacy in an age of electronic communication is critical, but at the same time reading and computation skills are fundamental, and print is not replaceable. Only the literate person can meet the demands of a highly organized, complex, and changing society. The gap between the ideal of a literate society and the reality is great.

This chapter relates to the value and nature of literacy as it has been defined by educators and researchers. Some recent studies are discussed: the National Reading Council *Survival Literacy Study* by Louis Harris and Associates, the *Adult Functional Competency* findings at the University of Texas at Austin, and the conclusions of the Human Resources Research Organization (HumRRO) research on literacy and work conducted by Sticht and others. In the future, new studies and additional findings will no doubt modify and influence planning. At this time these recent studies and others add specific data to the rhetoric. They are discussed here because of their implications for the nation's library service and for interpretation by librarians.

Literacy (as the International Symposium for Literacy, *Declaration of Persepolis* declared) is:

> ... not just the process of learning the skills of reading, writing and arithmetic, but a contribution to the liberation of man and to his full development. Thus conceived, literacy creates the conditions for the acquisition of a critical consciousness of the

contradictions of society in which man lives and of its aims;
it also stimulates initiative and his participation in the creation
of projects capable of acting upon the world, of transforming it,
and of defining the aims of an authentic human development.
It should open the way to a mastery of techniques and human
relations. Literacy is not an end in itself. It is a fundamental
human right.

Why do people want and choose to read? Reasons are as diverse as
are readers. Traditionally, major reasons given for reading have been:
instrumental or informational effects, reinforcement of attitudes and
beliefs, vicarious enjoyment, aesthetic pleasure, respite from the struggles
of daily life, and escape. People read for jobs and for survival. Reading
is basic to survival: it is a tool that provides the chance for success and
meaning (although it is not a guarantee). "Teach me to read" and
"Learn me to read" are pleas and commands testified to by reading
specialists and tutors. Near the end of Warren Miller's *Cool World* are
these lines: "Readin'... that the beginnin of ev'ry thing. . . . When
you can read an write why you can do any thing. Do any thing. Be any
thing." "Find me a book to help me" and "Find me one I can
understand" are familiar appeals from learners to teachers and librarians.

More specifically, people choose to read:

For survival needs—to read street and road signs, written directions,
labels, recipes, application forms

For such useful purposes as comparison shopping, figuring sales and
income taxes, filling out job applications or driver's license applications, reading Social Security directives

For fulfilling important roles as parents in relationships with their
children

To earn a living, to get legal and civil rights, to vote

For academic purposes such as getting high school diplomas and
college course credits

For love of learning and extending horizons, for pleasure and
enjoyment, for spiritual enhancement, for self-esteem

For individual control over one's own life, to make possible action
and direction.

Not everyone chooses to read. Some young people and adults have
been discouraged so completely that reading seems an impossibility for
them. Many persons are not totally illiterate but have limited reading
skills. Some have found that they get along quite well without reading.
Some use a language or a dialect that is ignored and neglected by the
schools and libraries. Some, before they can learn to read easily and

well, must find reasons and results that have real meaning. Quite often, before skills can be attained, attitudes toward reading and toward one's own ability must change. The individual must have a reason for wanting to learn to read, and must soon find a growing pleasure and satisfaction in the activity. Where personal motivation is high, the individual's ability to organize and direct his or her progress in learning is apt to be high also.

Nor is the vital fact to be ignored or unrecognized that some, even many, people feel that they have more important and productive things to do. They may choose to use, exclusively or extensively, other communication media, such as radio, television, and recordings, and to be occupied with innumerable activities, such as jobs, sports, hobbies, and travel.

Today, however, literacy is no longer limited to a person's ability to read or write or to compose a simple sentence. The approach is more selective, functional, and work-oriented.

New measurements for literacy result in new definitions. Quoting the words of David Harman, Harvard's Graduate School of Education, in an unpublished paper, "The 'Right to Read': An Assessment":

> What is commonly referred to as reading level bears only incidental relation to the actual act of reading—of deciphering a code of letters into meaningful words and phrases. Rather, reading level relates more directly to the comprehension of what is read. Clearly, comprehension is associated intimately with one's experience, environment, and interests. Social, cultural and economic realities combine to form a context to which comprehension is bound. ... It is for this reason that there cannot be a universal definition of literacy. ... Reading is not a static skill in that once acquired it needs no further development. The individual is required to keep abreast through constant adaptation.
>
> Reading is not, in and of itself, an objective. The real aim is that of social participation and reading is but a tool—one means— for its attainment. Nor can reading be narrowly confined to the decoding and understanding of written messages. Rather, it entails also the substance that makes its use as a tool meaningful; the content which makes social participation in a much broader sense possible.

DEVELOPMENTAL STAGES

Educators and reading specialists define certain developmental stages in reading levels. Librarians must be aware of these different stages when they assist learners. Equally important is the consideration that individuals learn and progress in different ways and modes. Broadly, the four developmental stages are:

1. *Total illiteracy,* the stage where a person is unable to read and write. Because few persons beyond early childhood are thought to be completely illiterate, the term usually is applied to those whose ability to read and write is so limited that it cannot be used for communication. However—it may be hard to believe, but it is true—many persons are totally illiterate. They have the greatest need and present the greatest challenge.

2. *Functional illiteracy* includes those persons who read to some degree, but cannot read well enough to function in society without assistance from others who read.

3. *Limited literacy* includes those persons who are functionally literate, but unable to read well enough to handle materials outside their immediate functional needs, and those who are unable to read well enough to become all they might through additional technical, vocational, or high school and college-level training.

4. *Literacy* includes the mature reader who is able to read and understand virtually all materials that everyone is expected to read, plus materials within his or her special interests, excluding only esoteric or technical materials outside the individual's interests. (See figure 1.)

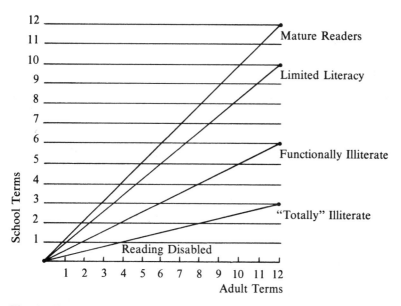

Fig. 1. Developmental Stages in Reading Levels

Table 1. Kohl's Four Stages of Literacy

Level	Skills
Beginning	1. Knowing print 2. Known words 3. Words that connect and words that place 4. Alphabet 5. Sounds and combinations of sounds 6. Simple sentences
Not bad	1. Combinations of sounds 2. Complicated words 3. Complex sentences 4. Everyday reading 5. Paragraphs and stories
With ease	1. Unfamiliar words 2. Different forms of writing 3. Voice 4. Test taking
Complex	1. Knowing about language 2. Special uses of words 3. Special languages 4. Critical analysis

Source: Herbert Kohl, *Reading, How To* (New York: Dutton, 1973), p. 133.

Kohl's definition of the four stages of literacy is shown in table 1. These nongraded stages have particular meaning and appeal to persons who find the grade-level correlations rather meaningless.

SOME STUDIES OF LITERACY

Recent studies provide concrete data on the nation's literacy problems. The findings are useful for guidance and in making decisions regarding librarians' understanding of the needs and interests of potential clientele. They may seem to reinforce stereotypes or point out lower levels of reading abilities in certain areas or among individual groups, but it is imperative to realize how quickly situations change. Trends are evident. A constantly changing society points up the need for constant assessment and evaluation. For example, young adults and farm workers who comprise a major part of the migrant group may move rapidly into permanent settlements within communities. Black youths who have formerly had lower education completion levels than whites, have narrowed the gap so much that little difference exists in such areas as high school completion.

Awareness of and interest in the research findings about literacy and reading—the knowledge of current assessments and practices—serve as the foundation for decisions about libraries' objectives, activities, and innovative programs designed to meet the needs and interests of rural and urban clienteles. Theory and practice can suggest alternative approaches to the problem and assist in assessment of the local library situation.

National Assessment of Reading

The National Assessment of Educational Progress (NAEP), an information-gathering project, regularly conducts a reading assessment survey of the educational attainments of four age levels—9, 13, 17, and 26–35—in ten subject areas—art, career and occupational development, citizenship, literature, mathematics, music, reading, science, social science, and writing. It assesses vocabulary skills and people's abilities to extract significant facts from passages, interpret charts, read forms and signs, follow directions, use reference materials, identify main ideas and modes of organization, draw inferences, and read critically. The assessment reports on reading of printed materials and on reading skills taught in the schools. Reading objectives developed in NAEP's assessment are useful to librarians. (See appendix 4, "National Literacy Studies," under the subhead "Reading Objectives—National Assessment of Educational Progress.") The assessment reports data on reading tasks representing eight themes: word meanings, visual aids, written directions, reference materials, significant facts in passages, main ideas and organization of passages, influences from passages, and critical reading of passages.

The NAEP functional literacy assessment prepared for the National Right to Read effort reported that nearly all 17-year-old groups did moderately well on all questions in the assessment.

In only a few instances did fewer than 80 percent make a correct response. All did best at reading tasks involving drawings and pictures.

The poorest performance was shown on reference materials and reading exercises involving forms. It was also found that parental education makes a significant difference in school-age children's reading performance, and that there is some relationship between low income and low reading performance.

Three exercises on which no group, including superior readers, performed well were an automobile insurance policy, an application blank with instructions for enrolling in a book club, and a traffic ticket.

School-age boys consistently had percentages of success that were significantly below those of girls at the same age level.

Whites as a group consistently performed better than blacks as a group on various measures of reading skills.

The Southeast has a lower level of reading success than other parts of the nation.

Literacy for Survival

The *Survival Literacy Study* conducted for the National Reading Council by Louis Harris and Associates defined literacy in terms of "survival thresholds." The tests used were facsimiles of simplified applications and instructions, ranked according to increasing difficulty. The tests included forms of identification and applications for personal loans, a driver's license, public assistance, and Medicaid. The study was designed to measure the extent of reading deficiencies in the United States and the "survival literacy" rate, and to determine the percentage of Americans who lack the reading skills necessary to survive. *Fundamentally, it tested functional, rather than by-rote, literacy.*

The average range of illiteracy was from 3 percent (low survival threshold) to 13 percent (marginal survival threshold), which, projected to the population, indicates that from 4.3 million to 18.5 million Americans are functionally illiterate. It was found that:

Reading ability is increased in direct proportion to years of education.

Practical literacy seems to decrease in direct proportion to income in the United States.

The average range of functional literacy for rural residents was 4 to 16 percent; for city residents it was 4 to 13 percent. Fewer people living in small towns and cities had difficulty reading forms, and suburban residents filled them out most easily.

The South had the highest average range of functional illiteracy, from 4 to 15 percent. People in the West tended to have fewer reading deficiencies than those in other regions.

The age group from 16 to 24 proved the most literate; the group aged 50 and over was the most deficient in reading ability. The old and the poor each have serious reading problems, but the elderly poor must struggle most for "survival."

Women had fewer deficiencies than men.

The illiteracy range of immigrants to the United States was 7 to 16 percent, compared with a range of 3 to 13 percent for the native-born.

FUNCTIONAL READING COMPETENCY

Why is reading important? This is the fundamental question answered by the long-awaited summary of the Adult Performance Level Study (APL) conducted at the University of Texas and supported by the United States Office of Education. The report, *Adult Functional Competency,* adds further dimensions to the definition of literacy and indicates what is needed in terms of learning opportunities for adults.

(See appendix 4, under subhead "Adult Performance Level Study—Objectives for Functional Competency.")

The study defines functional literacy competency as "the ability to use skills and knowledge needed for meeting the requirements of adult living." The skills that have been identified as important to adult functional competency are: the communication skills of reading, writing, speaking, and listening; computation; problem solving; and interpersonal relations. These skills are applied in everyday life situations, which are classified into five broad general knowledge areas: occupational knowledge, consumer economics, health, government and law, and community resources. These knowledge areas may be considered as the *content* of adult literacy.

Five national surveys of adults were conducted using this two-dimensional concept, and sixty-five requirements for functional literacy were defined. The study developed a general index of literacy that classifies adults into one of three categories:

1. Those adults who function only with difficulty because of their unsatisfactory mastery of the requirements of functional literacy
2. Those adults who are functional but not proficient
3. Those adults who are proficient.

The criteria chosen as the index to success were income, level of education, and occupational status.

An important contribution to the concept of literacy that the general theory of the APL study states is that persons are functionally competent only to the extent that they can meet the requirements that exist at a given point in time. If the requirements change and the individual does not adapt by acquiring either more or different knowledge and skills, that person becomes less competent.

The study has based its interpretation of functional competency on communications skills and essential knowledge categories.

The results of the study, indicating the competency levels by knowledge area and skills, are summarized in table 2.

What, according to APL findings, are adult education needs?

In terms of general knowledge, the greatest difficulties encountered by adults are in the area of consumer economics—money management, comparison shopping, and figuring sales and income taxes. Thus, nearly two-thirds of the United States population may need to acquire skills and knowledge in consumer economics.

About one in five adults in the United States functions with difficulty on occupationally related performance indicators.

A greater percentage of adults appear to be in need of educational assistance in the South than in other parts of the country.

Table 2. Competency Levels

Knowledge areas and skills	APL competency levels		
	1 *Function with difficulty*	*2* *Functional but not proficient*	*3* *Proficient*
Occupational knowledge	19.1	31.9	49.0
Consumer economics	29.4	33.0	37.6
Government and law	25.8	26.2	48.0
Health	21.3	30.3	48.3
Community resources	22.6	26.0	51.4
Reading	21.7	32.2	46.1
Problem solving	28.0	23.4	48.5
Computation	32.9	26.3	40.8
Writing	16.4	25.5	58.1
Overall competency levels	19.7	33.9	46.3

Source: Norvell Northcutt and others, *Adult Functional Competency: A Summary* (Austin: University of Texas, Division of Extension, 1975), p. 6.

Rural areas have the greatest estimated percentage of persons who need assistance in developing the basic skills.

The trends among age groups show the older persons having difficulty in adult areas of competency; this is also true of persons in the lower income group whose income depends on skills and occupational knowledge.

Literacy and Work

Another approach has been the study of literacy qualifications for specific job performance. The Human Resources Research Organization (HumRRO) has produced considerable information about literacy in relation to job performance. The HumRRO research and development for the Department of Defense have focused on the study of literacy in relation to work and parallel studies by civilian educators. Similar efforts for the United States Office of Education (USOE) have resulted in the Right to Read program, the National Reading Council, and the University of Texas studies. At the same time, the Civil Rights Commission, the Equal Opportunity Commission, and the Department of Labor have been concerned with identifying literacy demands for jobs.

The conclusions of HumRRO research reported in *Reading for Working,* edited by Sticht, are that people want job-related skills and knowledge, and that literacy skills are perhaps the most salient of formally acquired skills demanded by varied occupations in our complex, technologically based nation. If, as a nation, literacy training programs that will enable children and out-of-school adults to find rewarding careers are to be developed, understanding of the reading requirements of jobs and methods for teaching job-relevant reading skills are needed. Equally, if libraries are to be an active part of this effort, librarians must acquire well-designed job manuals, career information, job requirement information, and written study materials for preparation for jobs.

Because of the focus on job-related literacy demands, *functional literacy* was defined as "possession of those literacy skills needed to successfully perform some reading task *imposed by an external agent* between the reader and a goal the reader wishes to obtain." For example, to get a job as a mechanic ⟶ to earn money ⟶ to eat ⟶ to survive requires reading skill (as defined by the employer) to perform successfully the reading tasks found in the mechanic's job. The reading skill is an enabling skill to help the reader reach the goal ⟶ to eat ⟶ to survive. The organization is not concerned with reading tasks required in reading for enjoyment. Their definition of *functional literacy* depends "on the nature of the reading *task*—whether it is self- or externally imposed—and *not* on a person's skill level."

The evidence is overwhelming that many adults can neither read nor easily use many of the written materials needed to function in today's society. Evidence is also clear that the writers of the written materials fail to match the literacy skills of the intended readers.

Sharon reports on a recent national survey conducted by the Educational Testing Service for the U.S. Office of Education that concludes that more people (42 percent) spend more time (61 minutes a day) at work-related reading than at any other type of reading. Most people read newspapers (74 percent) but for only 35 minutes a day. Daily newspapers are written at ninth- to tenth-grade level. Articles in many magazines—*Reader's Digest, Popular Mechanics, Harper's*—are at a twelfth- to thirteenth-grade level of difficulty. Job manuals in seven army career fields are of eleventh- to twelfth-grade level in difficulty. The HumRRO simple, easy-to-administer formula for estimating reading grade level, *FORCAST,* produced an accurate estimate of the reading difficulty of army job reading materials.

Schools emphasize the teaching of reading and interpreting novels, plays, and poetry; little emphasis is given to the reading and writing of job manuals, technical directions, and job-related materials. In this context, it is to be noted that only some 13 percent of the jobs within the army are strictly military; 87 percent represent civilian occupations.

The HumRRO data present some important conclusions and findings, drawn from studies of military- and industry-based reading training programs, that can be valuable in developing library reading collections. They are as follows:

1. It appears possible to improve reading skills to a modest degree in about 100 hours in any number of programs.

2. Programs that relate directly to the students' job interests and involve direct tutoring in the tasks needed to accomplish the job-related reading task appear to be highly motivating; they are also more powerful in attracting and retaining students.

3. Skills for performing specific job-related reading tasks can be taught in a fairly short time, but this does not mean that the general educational development needed to read and learn from a variety of materials will be much improved.

4. Follow-on reading training is needed to maintain the impetus achieved in the relatively brief job-related programs and to produce literacy skills flexible and extensive enough to enable the students to accomplish a wide range of reading tasks.

5. The principles involved in applying instructional technology to program development, and the orientation of reading training to the specific job-reading tasks to be encountered by students, seem to underlie any particularly successful literacy training programs in the military or industrial setting. Hence, transportability lies not in the particular program materials, but in the principles behind the programs.

6. A critical problem for job-related (and all other) ABE [Adult Basic Education programs] is the recruiting and retention of students (the "outreach" problem). We call this the "delivery system" problem—specifically, the problem of getting a program to the intended users and keeping them in it long enough for it to work. This problem frustrates practically all current ABE, manpower, and employability programs. Thus, there is reason to anticipate this as a major problem that will be encountered in any program aimed at providing basic education for employment access and entry for out-of-school, "hard-core" unemployed adults.

In summary, it can be said that the mounting evidence documents for the first time what literacy means to the life of individuals and to the nation. The skills needed to manage and direct the daily demands of living and to perform in jobs are obviously essential. The social, political, and psychological implications are numerous. The various studies indicate that millions of people in the United States would gain economically, mentally, and spiritually from literacy programs. A new confidence originates with the abilities attained at whatever level from early childhood to old age.

References

The Adult Education Act, P.L. 91-230, and all of its amendments, including P.L. 93-380, through August 21, 1974 (20 U.S.C. 1201-1211a).

"The APL Report and Some Reaction," *Adult and Continuing Education Today* 5, no. 23 (November 10, 1975): 98–105.

Comptroller General of the United States. *The Adult Basic Education Program: Progress in Reducing Illiteracy and Improvements Needed.* Report to the Congress. Office of Education, Department of Health, Education, and Welfare. Washington, D.C.: U.S. General Accounting Office, 1975.

Educational Programs That Work. Vol. 1: A Catalogue of Demonstration Sites of Successful Educational Programs Disseminated through the New Jersey Elementary and Secondary Education Act, Title III, IV-C Program. Trenton: Division of Research Planning and Evaluation, Department of Education, State of New Jersey, 1975.

Harman, David. "Illiteracy, an Overview." *Harvard Educational Review* 40, no. 2 (May 1970): 226–43.

————. "The 'Right to Read': An Assessment." Mimeographed. September 1975.

International Symposium for Literacy. *Declaration of Persepolis.* Symposium held in Persepolis, September 3–8, 1975. Paris: Distributed by the International Coordination Secretariat for Literacy.

Kohl, Herbert. *Reading, How To.* New York: Dutton, 1973.

"Literacy and World Population." *Population Bulletin* 30, no. 2 (1975): 3–28.

Miller, Warren. *The Cool World.* Boston: Little, Brown, and Co., 1959.

National Advisory Council on Extension and Continuing Education. 9th Annual Report. *Equity of Access: Continuing Education and the Part-Time Student,* March 31, 1975.

National Assessment of Educational Progress. *Reading Objectives.* Denver, Colo.: National Assessment of Educational Progress, 1970.

————. *Reading Objectives: Second Assessment.* Denver, Colo.: National Assessment of Educational Progress, 1974.

————. *Reading Reports 02-R-01-09, 02-R-00, and 02-R-30.* Washington, D.C.: Superintendent of Documents, Government Printing Office, 1973 – 75.

————. *Reading: Summary Data (Report 02-R-00).* Washington, D.C.: Superintendent of Documents, Government Printing Office, July, 1974.

National Center for Health Statistics. "Development of the Brief Test of Literacy." In *Vital and Health Statistics.* PHS Pub. No. 1000, Series 2, No. 27. Washington, D.C.: U.S. Government Printing Office, 1968.

————. "Literacy among Youths 12 –17 Years: United States." In *Vital and Health Statistics.* DHEW Pub. No. (HRA) 74-1613, Series 11-131. Washington, D.C.: U.S. Government Printing Office, 1973.

Northcutt, Norvell, and others. *Adult Functional Competency: A Summary.* Austin: The University of Texas, Division of Extension, 1975.

Reading Programs That Work: A National Survey. Edited by Mary Ann Lachet, Ronald L. Capusso, John J. Geyer, and Bea Mayes. 2d ed. Trenton: Office of Program Development, New Jersey State Department of Education, 1975.

Sharon, Amiel T. "What Do Adults Read?" *Reading Research Quarterly* 9, no. 2 (1973 –74): 148 –69.

Sticht, Thomas G., ed. *Reading for Working: A Functional Literacy Anthology.* Alexandria, Va.: Human Resources Research Organization, 1975.

Sticht, Thomas G., Beck, Lawrence J., Hauke, Robert N., Kleiman, Glenn M., and James, James H. *Auding and Reading: A Developmental Model.* Alexandria, Va.: Human Resources Research Organization, 1974.

Survival Literacy Study (ERIC-ED 068 813). Conducted for the National Reading Council by Louis Harris and Associates, Inc. Study No. 2036. September 1970.

"Survival Literacy Study," *Congressional Record,* 91st Congress, 2d sess., 1970, 116, no. 184.

Thorndike, Robert L. *Reading Comprehension Education in Fifteen Countries: An Empirical Study.* New York: John Wiley & Sons, 1973.

3
Libraries' Support of the Literacy Effort

THE ROLE OF LIBRARIES

What are the roles of libraries and librarians in their support of the literacy effort? What are the libraries' functions and place?

Every library in the country—no matter what its size, function, objectives, and resources—has a role to play in the national literacy effort. Every library in the country has other libraries and other educational and social agencies in the local community, the state, and the nation with which it can work. Librarians will find many other persons who are engaged in the effort: community leaders, teachers, reading specialists, and others in schools and universities and in volunteer programs.

What is the objective? It is to direct the educational resources, human and material, in the libraries of the country toward helping every child, young person, and adult to learn to speak, read, write, and compute—in brief, to learn how to learn. It is also to advise on and interpret resources, particularly materials on subjects that are necessary to the individual's or group's needs and interests. It is to reach out to each and, in collaboration with other institutions or agencies of today's society, to establish as a high priority the development of a community-wide reading and learning improvement system.

Why? Because language—whether it is a sound, a picture, a word, a letter, or a sign—is vital to each person's survival. One must be able to get the message, to give messages, to make sense of what is there, and to use it in making decisions on what to do and why.

The need is greatest among groups who have suffered poverty and the selfishness and power of interests by which individuals are disregarded, and who have been deprived of education and sufficient support for their basic needs—food, housing, clothing, health, and safety. A major handicap that confronts librarians, then, is the difficulty of developing library services directly or indirectly for what is essentially a library

25

nonuser group. Nonusers, who are found in every library community, public or academic, have the right to library service. Somehow the library must manage to link its services and resources to the needs and interests of nonusers of libraries and less skilled readers and demonstrate to them how reading and other media skills can have meaning for them. After all, libraries and librarians have a practical reason for, a vested interest in, broadening the reach of their resources.

The three primary roles of libraries in literacy efforts are education, collaboration, and community awareness. Libraries also have a unique role in the maintenance of reading skills by providing access to materials that have a variety of reading levels and meet diverse interests and needs. Equally important is the librarians' knowledge of the materials and their skills in selecting and interpreting them for the teacher and the client or student. Also, the changing nature of materials results in changed handling of materials. New media formats and relatively unused print sources require flexibility and a positive attitude toward change itself. An open mind becomes essential for the consideration and creation of new and different services for those people who are represented either not at all or minimally within the communication system.

Provision of materials is only one aspect of educational service by libraries. A more active role is the provision of educational programs and activities within the library and of reading or learning guidance service, advice, and counsel, either with the professional or volunteer educator or directly with the client or student.

The emerging philosophy of community education suggests an expanding role for the librarian. In such a role the librarian, as initiator or participant, will become increasingly active in the cooperative deliberation and planning of the educational goals and forces of the community. Through a process of collaborative planning and agreement, communities will be able best to use their educational facilities, leadership, and resources for the education of all.

Collaborative planning among educational institutions and agencies is not a simple process. Collaboration means working jointly and cooperatively, with authority for decisions being shared equally or delegated by a consensus of all involved. The collaborative process is plagued by constraints related to differences in such areas as funding sources and responsibility, administrative structures, articulation and interrelationships, operational programs, and many, many others. Collaborators in interagency planning and agreements must recognize and consider factors that inhibit or prohibit and those that support or strengthen planning and cooperation, to reach the maximum level of agreement and commitment.

The role of libraries in community education will vary in each community. Collaborative planning, therefore, must be local. It is clear, however, that the information needs of children, youth, and adults can be served at every level along the continuum of education, and that the library has a service that *cuts across every educational agency and institution.* The library is a *key* resource for every agency and for the people each serves. Furthermore, many agency programs, or agencies themselves, are apt to be predicated upon local, state, or national crises or priorities; where these priorities change or funding fails, such programs or agencies often are weakened or terminated, leaving their users without services. The library, like the school, has permanence in every community; it is the major information resource and should be linked directly with all educational services to ensure continuity of educational opportunity and support.

An urgent need exists to make both regular collections and special literacy collections not only available but also easily accessible to literacy clients. A comprehensive and highly coordinated delivery system that utilizes all available resources in the community will serve better the learning needs of this clientele. Significant collaborative and cooperative programs have been developed, but not until all types of libraries and library systems take action will the effort result in a response that is effective and successful in its impact. The internal structure of library systems and networks places them in a position to achieve this response. Librarians can serve as facilitators in the community and as information specialists and advisers. Expanded systems of information retrieval and development of appropriate collections to meet the daily needs and problems of the community can be emphasized in the same way that service is provided to the more traditional business and academic communities.

A review of how widespread the network of libraries is and how various are the major functions performed by libraries indicates what can be accomplished. The following list suggests the range of various types of libraries and possible systems of cooperation and collaboration among them.

1. Federal libraries
   Office of Education Instructional Materials Center
   Educational Resources Information Centers (ERIC)
   Library of Congress
2. State library
3. Public libraries (all units)
   Public library (independent)
   Public library system (delivery system)
      Central or regional or headquarters (County or municipal)
      Medium branch
      Small unit or neighborhood center

        Information centers
        Bookmobiles
        Books by mail
        Book deposit collections

4. School libraries
        Media centers in elementary schools
        Media centers in secondary schools (instructional materials centers)

5. Academic libraries
        Junior college
        Technical and vocational libraries
        Community college
        College
        University

6. Research centers
        Learning resource centers
        Learning library—laboratory
        Instructional materials center

7. Special libraries
        Business and industry
        Labor
        Education
        Library science
        Social sciences

8. Military libraries
        Armed services libraries

9. Institutional libraries
        Hospitals/mental hospitals
        Nursing, convalescent, or retirement home
        Rehabilitation centers
        Retardate/developmentally disabled institutions
        Correctional institutions (jails, prisons)

The basic, unique, and variable functions of library systems can support national literacy. They include:

Community understanding and assessment
Selection and acquisition, organization, and production of materials
Information and referral, educational, recreational, and spiritual
Interpretation, instruction, and diagnosis
Archival and research functions
Bibliographic and developmental functions
Brokerage and liaison
Advocacy

Supplementation and support of other agencies
Recruitment and motivation of adult learners
Innovation and outreach.

The global nature of library systems and networks service, and even of a single library service, makes it possible that all or some of these functions can be interrelated. The basic functions can be developed or improved according to priority need and resources. Some are narrow and specific. Some are unique. The variety of libraries and the variety of functions must be assessed in the individual situation. Collaborative arrangements permit agencies to help one another and divide responsibilities. As the Project Profile Reports demonstrate (see appendix 3), library functions have been developed to include different services based on recognized needs and on cooperation with other agencies. Sophisticated, advanced services result where librarians choose to provide them. Librarians need not fear the extension of service, and if staffs are unprepared, they may gain the additional knowledge and skills needed through staff development programs made available through the library system or other agencies. The library has a link directly to the client. It has all the tools and all the contacts necessary to the brokerage function. Librarians are in a position to diagnose and counsel. The advocacy function places the library in the action role. In the information-referral role the librarian serves as a link that puts the resources together with the need.

THE ROLE OF LIBRARIANS

Librarians who are competent in the selection and development of library collections are in a position to know the extent and variety of resources—facts, knowledge, ideas—contained in the collections. The range of resources within the collections of state, public, school, academic, and special libraries is immense. Librarians who supply the resources to help people learn, develop, and extend their lives have a stake in people's being able to use those resources. To be able to use them, people must acquire the skills of learning, that is, become literate. In a society that is built upon the principle of education for all, and that makes education available to more and more people, it is vital that everyone has a range of choices in suitable learning resources. The adult learner who requires materials of high interest and who is developing reading skills also requires supportive encouragement, guidance, and direction within an active literacy program.

Librarians should place themselves in the position of building a potential clientele, a clientele that has the basic skills and maturity to use the libraries' resources efficiently. The potential clientele then become mature, independent users.

4
Planning for Action:
The Process

Any library that undertakes a literacy program must be involved very early in the planning stage with those agencies that are also working in literacy programs. Preplanning or early planning with such agencies will avoid duplication of effort, misunderstanding, hurt feelings, hostility, and territorialism. It will permit a maximun and efficient use of resources and the development of mutually agreed on goals and objectives. As a result of such planning, the library may be better able to provide the services unique to its function and resources and to support the literacy efforts of the other agencies. A sharing of materials, staff, money, and facilities is possible, and mutual decisions can be agreed upon among two or more agencies. In the long run such a collaboration should result in benefits to the clients. The input from community resource people more often than not is the critical element in success. They are able to interpret community needs and interests, provide support, and serve as liaison to the community.

Each community is different and individual. The local situation must be analyzed, and in the assessment process the nature of clients and the library situation must be defined specifically. At the preplanning and planning stages, the library initiates collaborative and cooperative effort with agencies directly involved in the literacy effort. At this time, the library's specific contribution to that effort can be defined more clearly and, perhaps, be more successful than if the library were attempting to work alone.

All too often, when the librarian is approached by an individual who seeks help or by an agency that requests materials, no time for planning exists. An instant response is necessary to meet the demand. The response can be twofold: first, meeting the need of the client as well as possible, and second, recognizing the request as a sign of community need. In other instances the librarian can anticipate and, in advance, plan the part the library will take.

STEPS IN THE PROCESS

The first step is the development of awareness or consciousness of the situation and the problem among those individuals or agencies who are involved or are to be involved. An awareness common to those who are informed and those who are not must be achieved before anything else is attempted or before real interest can develop. Community leaders, educators, and librarians who are interested initially should bring general information about the local situation and literacy effort to decisionmakers—city officials, members of library boards, library and adult education directors, representatives in literacy and adult education programs, state librarians, community advisers, and potential influential participants or clients. Personal conversations, telephone calls, correspondence, individual discussions, and group meetings are necessary. As people become acquainted and work together, interest is stimulated and understanding of the situation is acquired.

The next step creates a permanent interest. Relevant facts and findings from the assessments of the community (see section on "Community Assessment," p. 33), literacy needs and interests, the existing literacy programs, and library resources are applied to program planning. The collection and analysis of background information regarding the community, the potential clientele or client groups, and the library's resources provide the information on which to base decisions. Recommendations can then be applied to the development of a program.

Librarians, teachers, and administrators need to know why, for whom, what, and how. Local decision makers, superintendents of schools, boards of education, library boards and directors, and literacy boards and administrators need to know the immediate and long-term economic and social impact of the library's focus on the literacy needs of the community. Then recommendations and support will be based on what is known and will be limited by that knowledge. Staff who bear responsibility for the service need to know what will be necessary to provide that service. The librarian takes an active collaborative part in assistance and planning. In such instances the brokerage function emerges. Planning takes place to match resources and needs for optimal educational development of the total community. Changes can be initiated where detailed plans of what is to be done serve as a guide.

The third step is a trial-run or practice stage where all concerned have an opportunity to try out in the sheltered situation of a workshop the strategies decided on in the plan. In a carefully planned learning situation with experienced advisers and educators, staff members can be involved as participants or as observers. They can gain understanding of the potential clientele, develop some basic skills in personal relations, study and evaluate materials, and plan a literacy collection and services. This sheltered, low-cost situation serves as a basis for a further trial in a demonstration project. Such a project will benefit from the preliminary sessions of discussion and practice in which both administrators and practitioners were involved. The library service can be developed in one segment at a time; for example, acquiring the literacy collection of materials and staff training may be necessary before more extensive service can be provided. Service may be focused, at first, on one group in the population and gradually be expanded to reach other groups or clients.

The fourth step will be the adoption of the service in an ongoing literacy program. Because the preceding stages of planning provide a firm foundation, a gradual extension of service according to pre-determined objectives and schedules can be managed.

The fifth step is evaluation of what has been done and what has happened. Actually, evaluation, that is, looping evaluation, is a part of each stage of the process. Each step must be evaluated as a program progresses. Questions to ask are: "What did we want to do?" "Did we do it?" Internal evaluation and measurement must develop at the same time each planning and service step is planned and developed. A well-developed schedule provides not only a guide for what is to be done but also a checklist to determine if it has been done. This process of developing awareness, finding interest, trying out a program during a learning period and trial activity, followed by adoption of a service and adaptation to the situation and clientele, concurrently with regular and planned evaluation of what happens throughout, is never clear-cut or rigid, but rather has a back-and-forth movement.

Emily Anthony, the director of the Northeast Georgia Regional Library, succinctly describes her first response when, following training workshops, she was faced with providing library services in the Library-ABE demonstration program of the Appalachian Adult Education Center:

> So it all boils down to the same thing, that it's a one-to-one contact with push coming from the public library, the reaching out saying, "Here we are. We are interested in what you are doing. We are interested and concerned about people that you are working with. May we work with you? May we help you? How can we supplement what you are doing? Is there something that you would like to have that perhaps through the library we could get for you?"
>
> And it works. It's often slow, and you have to go back and back and back. . . . [p. 39]

From the small library to the large library system it is possible to "start where we are." Study, observe, visit others, do some self-searching and analysis, assess the community and the library resources, and above all determine who is the clientele.

Many libraries will have well-developed and well-organized programs and services that reach various clienteles, and many libraries have the channels for such service. In such instances the identification of clientele and the redirection of priorities can make it possible to build a literacy program into the existing structure. Other libraries will be in the position of joining this nationwide effort when, for the first time, they focus on literacy programs for the local community. At whatever stage the library literacy program may be, either nonexistent and to be developed from the beginning or already in existence and to be extended and up-graded—at whatever point—the library will be involved in change. That change will be both within the library and in the learning opportunities for the individuals of the clientele groups. The library that is dedicated to the improvement of quality education and quality of life for people of all ages in the community it serves by focusing the library's effort and resources on the problem of illiteracy, has alternative ways to go. The planning and management of a literacy program are charged with great responsibilities and hazards and with great rewards and satisfactions. The service must be suited to the needs, interests, and abilities of a diverse and unfamiliar clientele and frequently in terms of services, skills, and materials unfamiliar or little known to librarians and administrators.

COMMUNITY ASSESSMENT

If all agencies are to be involved in planning at the outset, what are some procedures and methods to accomplish the level of involvement and agreement essential to the success of expanding library services to the disadvantaged and those not so disadvantaged, for them to gain proficiency in communication skills, in literacy content areas, and in their use of library resources?

The scope of the assessment has to be defined by the library board, the library director, other agency directors who will be involved, representatives of staff and client groups, possibly consultants from reading and literacy programs, educators, state library staff, and federal educational program staff. A first essential step is a thorough review of existing studies and assessments. The assessment of the community may be limited to one aspect or several aspects, be general or specific, be a study of the whole community, of neighborhoods, or of a specific client group. Questions to answer include: "How extensive should the study be?" "What geographic areas will be surveyed?" "What groups will be studied?" "What resources and survey instruments are needed?" "How much will a survey cost in time, money, and effort?" "What are the advantages and disadvantages of the survey and its costs?" "Who will make the assessment?"

Such an approach can create sanction and support and develop interest. It also can create hostility and competition, raise fears, and bring new problems. Both positive and negative responses should be anticipated and solutions sought.

The assessment of the library service and resources requires that a survey of the interagency or interlibrary system be made as well as a study of the individual unit or units. The various governing boards within the system of districts, counties, and cities need to be involved. The potential flexibility of the organizational structure and staff responsibilities must be considered, as well as the existing structure. Staff competencies, talents, and interests should be identified and potential interests and needs defined. It is important not to impose limitations of service and exposure to library materials on a child or adult because of personal limitations of staff. Training needs can be identified and then provided. Often teamwork of several staff members and community liaison or volunteer workers is feasible. Existing services and delivery systems, agencies served, literacy programs, materials needed, and outreach efforts must be identified. Budget and funding sources are more numerous and varied than may be realized. Appendix 2, "Resources," page 150, under the subhead "Federal and State Funding," indicates a number of sources.

The assessment of a learner-client may be part of the larger study or an individual matter at the opportune moment. For this purpose the "Clientele Assessment ... Checklist" and "Adult Learner Profile" in appendix 1 are suggested. It may become quite naturally a part of the client interview which the learner-adviser, teacher, or tutor may make.

Suggested guides for use in assessment of a community and program planning are "Community Analysis Checklist" and "Preplanning Information for Expanding Services for Disadvantaged Adults," both in appendix 1, page 139. Other aids to assessment include the Appalachian Adult Education Center (AAEC) library service guide, *Assessing Community Information and Service Needs;* Roland Warren's *Studying Your Community;* the American Library Association handbook, *Studying the Community* (now out of print); and Ruth Warncke's *Analyzing Your Community: Basis for Building Library Service.*

Tables 3 and 4, on pages 35-41, "The Client and Her/His Environment," and "Assessment of the Community," outline steps to take and sources of information.

Table 3. The Client and Her/His Environment

Definition	Objectives	Resources for Information
What is the community?	To define the community and its characteristics	Social or demographic characteristics
a people with common goals, interests, and concern plus communication	To learn about the people who live in that area and are potential clients or client groups	study and observe, analyze census, define boundaries, natural boundaries, transportation lines
a geographic area served under law by a library or library system		
a governmental structure, rural, town, city, county, region, state		mobility of population
a group having common characteristics within a larger society that does not share those characteristics		
a geographic area	To define physical characteristics— size, shape, climate	existing maps, library records
an interaction of people		
a political entity		governmental and civic reports— planning departments, schools, public utilities, banks, telephone companies, libraries
an economic base		
social institutions	To locate institutions and groups by mapping	
ethnic and national groups		
economic institutions, farming, business, industries, income level	To learn how many people work in various occupations	Chamber of Commerce; visits to town job locations; labor unions, management
educational institutions, schools, colleges, universities, libraries	To identify disadvantaged and differentiated	observe, collect data

(Continued)

Table 3. The Client and Her/His Environment (Continued)

Definition	Objectives	Resources for Information
religious institutions	To identify religious beliefs and values	use existing studies, telephone book, commercial atlas
mosaic of communities, neighborhoods	To identify and define characteristics	survey by questionnaires, interviews, spot checking
governmental institutions, governing boards— city, county, state boards of education, library boards	To identify political beliefs and values, power structure	
	To identify decision-makers	
	To determine taxes and expenditures, sources of funding	
historical background	To define heritage and events, traditions and values	older citizens, historical records, newspapers
People—individuals, groups	To identify in terms of needs and interests	Vital statistics from census, studies, school and business projections in relation to sex, age, origin, ethnic and cultural heritage, schooling, occupation, income, moving and migration, attitudes and values, literacy needs, problems
Problems		
individuals, groups, institutional	Literacy needs and abilities as a whole and individually	
Cultural groups	To collaborate and support programs	
museums and art galleries, libraries	To evaluate libraries' programs and resources	Existing records, surveys, and studies
Recreational groups		
Developmentally disabled		
Correctional institutions		
Service clubs and organizations		

Definition	*Objectives*	*Resources for Information*
Disadvantaged groups aging, farm workers, displaced persons, indigent, poor		
Literacy programs	To support ongoing programs	Library collections Share administrative duties Recruit volunteers Share costs Train staff and volunteers

What are the neighborhoods?	Study and define in the same way as total community	
ethnic occupational, business geographic people, problems		

What groups make up the neighborhoods?
What problems make up the community?

Table 4. Assessment of the Community

The library staff and others chart the way to support strongly the goals of the national and local literacy effort.

Why?

→ Libraries are educational institutions, learning, and resource centers.

They are information and referral centers for the total community, and specifically for learners within the various institutions and groups in that community.

They have a major role and responsibility to initiate action and collaborate with others in providing continuing literacy education to the entire community at levels needed.

They are able to initiate preplanning, assessment of the community in relation to local and national literacy programs, and implementation of an active program.

They are agents of social change.

They are part of the total community education resources.

They serve clients in ways to enable individual growth and development.

They serve undereducated group whether disadvantaged in other ways or not.

(Continued)

Table 4. Assessment of the Community (Continued)

How?

→ Start with those who are interested:	→ Prepare for planning and acting:	→ Assess community characteristics and needs of clientele:
on the library staff and in the community	acquire and identify pertinent facts and knowledge	→ what are attitudes toward literacy, toward learning and libraries
are already involved, such as teachers and volunteers	study and read what is known and reported	→ assess library resources and services, and users and nonusers
find leaders and decisionmakers	learn about literacy and reading techniques and content	→ define problems
develop awareness on part of others	learn about ethnic life styles	
and assist in initiating strengthening interest	analyze interest, biases, qualifications	
	do some self-searching and analysis	
	attend workshops and institutes	
	attend courses on reading and teaching and library science	
	organize training opportunities	

Whom?

→ Start with those already involved in literacy programs	→ Find out who might be learners and students; how many? At what level of literacy—adult basic, content, credential, advanced?	→ identify collaborative agencies and sources of support
		→ identify clientele
		→ have written work agreements

For what purpose?

→ Policies and overall goals

Objectives—itemize long-range, intermediate, and short-range

→ Determine policies, goals, objectives

→ Internal assessment:

→ what can the library do alone?

→ what can the library do that no other agency can do as well?

→ what can the library do with other agencies and programs?

→ what can the library do with the help of other libraries in the system or region?

Program planning

→ Initiate preplanning and involvement of other agencies at the very beginning:

→ identify collaborative agencies

→ do some self-analysis

→ assess the community

→ define needs and interests of adults

→ identify library and community resources

→ identify gaps and priorities

→ identify and develop resource collections

→ find out what the services are

→ How can the library serve teachers in ABE and other adult education and children's programs?

→ What talents does the staff have? what interests? what qualifications?

→ What is needed?

→ What is needed? from where?

→ Define specific services

→ Is reorganization of services and management needed?

→ Who in the community can assist the library to meet its objectives in the literacy program?

→ find staff

→ Are there sufficient staff qualified in meeting clientele literacy needs? What specialization is needed?

(Continued)

Table 4. Assessment of the Community (Continued)

→ conduct orientation and training programs	→ For whom? Staff, trustees, administrators, personnel and administrators in other agencies?
	→ By whom? Training schools, library science schools, literacy program?
	→ What help is needed from other librarians and specialists?
	→ Who has experience and knowledge of reading behavior and skills?
	→ Who knows content of adult education courses? ABE? GED? ESL? CLEP? Reading readiness?
→ how promote and publicize?	→ By whom and where? What formats and media are to be used?
→ what time schedule meets goals and objectives?	→ Trial period
	→ One year to five years
	→ Monthly and daily

Costs
→ How much? Specific budget?	→ Where and what are sources of funding?
	→ Who are competitors?
	→ How will literacy funds be allocated?
	→ Where are funds needed most—for resource materials, personnel, promotion, service, training?

Action
→ Hold trial demonstration, initiate services	→ Initiate services; establish procedures; develop delivery methods
→ Recruit volunteers	→ What help is needed from the community?
	→ Train volunteers
→ Evaluate program	→ What is its use? what do others think? were objectives met? what changes and developments are needed?

Adopt literacy service program
→ Extend to more groups, more clients, more agencies	→ For whom and with whom? What and how?
→ Adapt and change	→ Reassess
→ Set priorities	

Adoption means:

→ involving planners in decision about action to follow based on interpretation of findings from assessment, new interest, trial, training, and evaluation.

→ making agreements with other agencies on collaborative and cooperative service.

→ deciding on changes in service and priorities.

→ developing library collections and setting priorities on subjects, formats, types of materials.

→ adjusting, where necessary, hours of service and location of access sites.

→ developing an ongoing staff orientation program to meet client and service needs.

→ supplying information about community problems to the total community and to interested groups and leaders.

→ developing a time schedule of what the library will do.

→ continuing evaluation.

BUDGET AND FUNDS

Important considerations in program planning are the cost of the program and the sources of funds. Estimating the budget and determining the source of funds are vital to the support, evaluation, and even success of the library's literacy effort.

A cost analysis for a prospective program should be made during the planning process. Estimates will need to be made for each category in the budget. Such estimates are based on current and past costs as well as future estimates. They may include direct and in-kind costs. They will relate to such major items as personnel, materials, space, physical facilities, equipment, supplies, telephone, and transportation.

Factors to consider in budget planning are:

1. Acquisition policy, in general and specifically
2. Age, size, and quality of collection
3. Number of units to be stocked: central, branches, mobile units
4. Types of materials to be acquired, e.g., audiovisual, print
5. Subject areas requiring priority funding
6. Requirements for current additions to match local needs
7. Requirements for retrospective or new collections; additions to strengthen gaps or meet new needs and priorities
8. Special programs or activities requiring special allocations
9. Fixed and rising costs of bibliographic, informational, and reference tools and services

10. Materials to serve needs of user groups requiring collections in languages other than English

11. Specialized materials and collections for system or network services

12. Outright purchase or rental of materials

13. Equipment costs relating to use of resources; cost of audiovisual equipment for media collections.

In the initial planning stage the amounts estimated will be general. As soon as the specific literacy program is determined, a cost analysis that is detailed and as exact as possible will be done. An item-by-item budget that is based on the most accurate information possible will be made. In the budget planning process it is necessary to:

1. Review the library's literacy goals and services, and set priorities

2. Establish objectives in terms of time and needs in relation to major cost factors, such as staff salaries and benefits, material (print and nonprint), number of volumes, films, recordings, transportation facilities, supplies, publicity, evaluation

3. Determine number of staff—professional, paraprofessional, clerical, custodial, volunteer—and salaries of each

4. Determine quantity of materials needed and period of time when this will be achieved

5. Determine minimum for a new collection

6. Determine what is needed for maintenance of collection in replacements, new material, binding, repair, processing

7. Determine what is needed for provision of additional new services or extension of service

8. Determine losses or expendable or consumable materials

9. Establish priority items, time of achievement, what will be done first

10. Review all sources of funds—within the operating budget and potential sources or in-kind service in collaboration with other agencies

11. Assemble current data on anticipated income and potential sources of funds from literacy funding programs or educational grants

12. Assemble current data on costs or estimated costs of materials

13. Assemble current data on costs or estimated costs of equipment

14. Assemble current data on salary costs and benefits

15. Budget items for specific purposes, such as those above, for bookmobile

16. Prepare budget for three- or five-year period as well as current period

17. Outline itemized budgetary record.

Current costs plus estimated inflationary costs (approximately 6 percent) must be included. Average costs per volume can be figured from current average costs of paperbacks, hardcovers, films, and magazines from library or annual trade costs shown in the *Publishers Weekly* annual February analysis. Both direct costs and in-kind costs should be itemized. The sources of funds identified or suggested must be included.

With the detailed list of proposed expenditures completed, the estimated costs will be entered. If one half of the time of a paid staff member is allocated to the literacy program, one half of the salary and one half of the fringe benefits will be entered under contributions in kind or funded with another column for source. If volunteers are to be part of the staff, this should be included, or some reimbursement should be noted. Miscellaneous expenses and a contingency fund of 10 percent each year may be allowed. Some libraries have a standard overhead percentage. Others may have to determine what a fair percentage would be.

Fiscal procedures to account for each item in a budget are needed, not only at the planning stage but also in reporting. Contributions of gifts and grants, as well as regular budget allocations, must be accounted for as spent and in a final auditing. Such accounting indicates not only to what use funds have been put, but also what additional monies will be needed. A detailed budget and record serves as an evaluative measure. The cost of a program per person can be planned. The total costs as compared with those of other programs of lesser or equal significance can be figured. Benefits to the library, the community, and the new reader should be studied and needs determined.

Some of the data needed for budget planning are:

Size of book and print collections; goals for collection development; volumes added—estimate of price changes; volumes withdrawn—replacement estimates; volumes estimated—anticipated cost of expanding particular collection

Size of audiovisual collections in each media category: items added, items withdrawn, items estimated

Bindery costs

Maintenance and equipment costs and estimated price changes for audiovisual materials

Cost of acquisition and processing; contracts for services

Insurance costs; review insurance coverage

Ratio of expenditures to one another and to total budget

Attrition

New collections and new services; capital funds needed.

Staff
    Librarian   Volunteers
    Library technicians   Artists
    Clerical   Writers

Materials
    Volumes estimated addition   Maintenance and equipment costs
      books   for media
      paperbound   Insurance costs
      replacements   New collections
    Media collections (each category)   New services (needs)
      films, filmstrips, recordings, etc.   capital funds
      videocassettes,   Equipment—rental or purchase
    Binding costs   kind, number

Space (per sq. ft. cost)

Public relations
    Graphic art work   Materials
    Printing   Distribution (mail, etc.)
    Reproduction

Media production
    Production   Broadcasting, video, cable

Other

Supplies
    Paper, stationery, stamps   Machines, telephone

Overhead (percentage of total costs)

Contingency

Fig. 2. Sample Budget Form

References

American Library Association. Library Community Project. *Studying the Community*. Chicago: American Library Association, 1960.

Anthony, Emily. "The Newest Appalachian Project Library" in Fleming, Lois D., comp., *Proceedings of the Conference "Adult Basic Education and Public Library Service" June 5-6, 1974. Miami Springs, Florida*. Division of Library Services, Department of State and the Adult Education Section, Florida Department of Education. [1974?]

Appalachian Adult Education Center. Library Service Guide. *Assessing Community Information and Service Needs*. Chicago: American Library Association, 1976.

Warncke, Ruth. *Analyzing Your Community: Basis for Building Library Service*. [Springfield?] Illinois State Library and Illinois Library Association, 1974.

Warren, Roland L. *Studying Your Community*. New York: Free Press, 1965.

5
The Literacy Effort: Action and Direction

Action and direction involve several major, well-defined tasks and a program plan designed by those who are involved. The plan should include statements and agreements regarding the role of each agency involved, the various aspects of the library's collaborative effort, and support of the local and national literacy effort. To summarize, the plan will state policies, objectives, services, staff (including volunteers), collection development and organization of materials, delivery systems, budgets, funding, promotion and public relations, physical facilities, and evaluation methods and reporting. Different types of libraries have variable functions. They have some common, some distinctive, and some overlapping responsibilities. What is to be done will be determined within the specific literacy situation of each community. Methods are suggested for gaining public acceptance of the relationship of libraries that have a basic mission to serve the client population with literacy programs.

The libraries of the nation have seven, possibly more, major tasks. These are to:

1. Provide services, reading and audiovisual materials, and opportunities for anyone who needs them in the development of literacy skills and knowledge.

2. Demonstrate to adult educators, teachers, and educational administrators the support and place of libraries in an educational system that aims at a totally literate society.

3. Demonstrate to political decisionmakers the place of libraries in that educational system.

4. Extend and develop the libraries' traditional functions in service to a population that is learning to read, write, speak, and compute, developing competency in literacy skills and gaining new knowledge.

5. Take new directions, experiment, and venture into what may be untraditional ways of service to strengthen library practices.

6. Be interpreters of the communication resources and be active as educators, disseminators, and promoters of the use of those resources, and in so doing become agents to promote change.

7. Work closely with other agencies that are involved with literacy programs.

This manual suggests and recommends the design of a plan after an assessment of the community and the library has been made. It seems absolutely essential that a library system have a literacy service plan to give direction and guidance to the staff and others who are involved and to ensure greater success for the literacy program. The staffs of many libraries, and particularly the small library, may feel that planning is unnecessary and rather burdensome. They may see the service as an extension of the library's existing service and the collection of materials as a part of the everyday selection process. They may feel that they know the situation in relation to the board members' attitudes and that they have their support. They may know the people of the community who are involved in literacy projects, and know what the schools and organizations are doing. They may feel that enough is being done, that the library cannot serve people who cannot read, or that money, time, and staff deficiencies make such service impossible. On the other hand, skeptics and doubters, the sure and the unsure, may find it useful and productive to give attention to the design of a plan.

The importance of helping persons who are acquiring literacy skills and knowledge to develop behavior patterns for the use of materials cannot be overemphasized. Librarians are seeking out needs and opportunities for library services, which are ever increasing as the number of literacy and adult education programs increase. The nation's educational system is such a complex and extensive process that librarians, more than ever, must design unique services and utilize their knowledge and skills in a creative and effective use of materials, that is, the media of communication. It is evident that libraries, which are agencies for the collection, organization, and interpretation of the communication media resources of this society, have an immediate and urgent need to take active responsibility and place their services at the disposal of the people of the country who may need this stored knowledge and information.

Librarians must prepare staff and develop collections that really assist adult new readers in continuing to practice their newly acquired skills. The participants in literacy programs—Adult Basic Education (ABE), Laubach Literacy, Literacy Volunteers of America, General Educational Development (GED), College- Level Examination Program (CLEP), and others—have acquired the basic skills and immediate subject knowledge. The ABE student can attain only the elements of beginning literacy, however, and all the programs and courses are limited in time. They assist learners to improve for specific purposes. The librarian is in a position to assist the teacher with professional materials, to supply necessary and relevant materials for the student, and to offer learners advisory service and guidance. The librarian must take the responsibility for informing the teachers and the students what the library and its staff is prepared to do, and act upon it. Then, the staff may demonstrate by doing and by providing materials, advisory service, and encouragement. After a student has finished a program, the library must assist that student to continue using and developing the skills acquired.

The following design for planning a literacy program suggests some major elements that are necessary to the trial and adoption stages of the change process.

DESIGN FOR LITERACY PROGRAM PLANNING
Analyses

Analyses must be made by the library and the community representatives. They:

1. Analyze and interpret the findings of the community assessment. What was learned? Write reports in a style fitted to the audience to be reached.

2. Analyze the library's resources and attitudes and opinions regarding the library's resources and place in the literacy effort. What does the library have? Who can use the library services?

3. Obtain sanction and commitment from policymakers and library staff. The officials of the library issue a written policy statement based on advice from as many people as possible whose concern, at this point, is relevant.

4. Devise a workable plan with attention to these major components:

community involvement in planning and preplanning
collaborative agreements between agencies
the situation as interpreted in the assessment of the community and of the library or library system
a definition and profile of clientele who are students in the literacy programs and potential students and library users—their needs and interests as determined in the survey and especially through contacts with community representatives and other agencies
a statement of goals and objectives
specific, well-defined services and activities to be provided together with other agencies or alone

resources, human and material
    staff, responsibilities, qualifications, talents, needs; assign pro-
        ject staff and delegate authority
    staff development and training program to support design
        of services and activities
volunteers, their recruitment, training, and retention
collection development—what materials does the library have,
    what does it need?
acquisition and selection policies statements
organization of the collection and services to provide to the greatest
    extent possible intellectual, social, physical, institutional, and
    cost access
organization of the collection to be easily available to users through
    various delivery systems
physical facilities and equipment—what does the library have,
    what does it need?
public relations—the promotion of and publicity about the services
    and collections
budget—what is needed to achieve objectives, and what resources
    does the library have to respond efficiently? What new resources
    does it need? What funding sources are there? What collabora-
    tive methods of support?
collaborative efforts and methods—with whom? how?
trial period and timing—what will be done on a limited basis?
    when? where?
extension and adoption of service and activities—why? for whom?
    what? how?
evaluation of what is happening as the program progresses

Programming

The information collected in the assessment of the community and of
the library or library system is next put to use in translating and applying
the findings to plans for the library's action and decisions on directions to
be taken. It is possible with the facts in hand to see the community's
needs and clientele and match them with the library's ability to respond.
Again, the analysis and setting of objectives based on that analysis are
based on the combined judgments and knowledge of the professional
and community representatives.

Of first importance is the obtaining of sanction, commitment from,
and opinions of community representatives, policymakers, library staff,
and the decisionmakers within the community who are relevant to the
plan. Although the question of whose approval and commitment is
necessary and appropriate can be determined only in the local situation,
in general sanction and direction of the governing officials, policymakers,

the library staff, and the community representatives is necessary. Such a group may include library board members; government officials in local, state, even federal departments; representatives of funding sources; directors and administrators of the library, the library system, and any collaborating or cooperating agencies; library department heads who are directly involved and support staff; and representatives of potential participant groups or clients. Consideration of the political, economic, educational, and social implications of the proposed activities is important. Will a more literate group that was formerly less literate threaten or alarm those in power, in jobs, and economically better off? Such problems are avoided by preplanning. During the preplanning personal contacts, discussion with, and survey of key agencies, organizations, and client groups will indicate attitudes and the place of each in the situation. In no way should obstacles be a decisive reason for *not* establishing literacy programs. Rather, they should provide an incentive to find ways to remove them.

A statement of what has been learned in the survey is valuable as a working paper. The attitudes and talents of the staff should be noted, as well as the characteristics of the potential clients or client groups and participants in any current literacy programs. Goals and objectives necessary to attain the goal should be stated explicitly. Is the library to support existing programs; to initiate a literacy program; to advise, counsel, and provide materials?

Staff

What staff is needed? What staff is available? Professional? Volunteer? Nonprofessional? Community workers? The responsibility and authority for specific tasks are assigned and delegated. The director must have autonomy and freedom to act. If planning has been well done, agreements will have been made and leadership acknowledged.

At this point, decisions are to be made regarding staff orientation and training. It is essential that the staff have opportunities to continue to learn, to gain and develop the necessary skills, to test them in practical workshop or supervised program situations, and to evaluate continuously what is happening. There is evidence to show that the effort spent on staff development is more important than that spent on equipment. Like the planning effort, it provides the foundation for a more successful and continuing program of service.

The staff will have knowledge and skills already. Study in the needed areas of knowledge will develop further these assets:

knowledge of the disadvantaged child's environment, needs, and
   learning modes
knowledge of reading and adult learning

as complete an understanding as possible of the clients of all ages

knowledge of materials for use in the literacy efforts

knowledge of advisory and interviewing techniques

knowledge of the library and community literacy programs and
  supportive activities

knowledge of new federal and state laws to meet new service
  demands, such as consumer education, career education, child
  development, and lifetime learning, as well as earlier legislation
  such as adult education and Right to Read.

A primary effort may be needed to overcome personal, ethnic, and
professional prejudices that can nullify attempts to provide effective
service. Staff members with personal biases may want to screen
themselves out of any program. As this is not always possible, and as
biases should not be an excuse to withdraw, attitudes may be modified
by study and training so that obstruction of literacy programs does not
occur.

Knowledge of the adult learner and of learning concepts are valuable
assets. The librarian as learning consultant or adviser must know how to
assist the learner, transmit and interpret communication, administer
diagnostic tests or contract with other agencies for this service, advise on
reading courses and on material selection for courses of study, make
referrals to other agencies, and cooperate in carefully defined ways.

Training can be in the form of self-directed study, of courses at library
schools and universities, or of workshops and institutes. Consultants
from the fields of education, psychology, creative arts, and librarianship
can provide professional advice, instruction, and inspiration. Many
librarians feel qualified; some will prepare and study alone. Everyone
should be willing to learn by mistakes, but not at the expense of the
client.

A reading specialist on the staff can contribute not only assistance for
learners but also advice and instruction to librarians and volunteer staff
members.

The staff librarians must be highly sensitive to individuals and
develop skill in interviewing. They must attain a flexibility and
responsiveness to each client and situation. At the same time, they must
be able to listen and hear not only what *is* said, but also what is *not* said,
and assist the client in clarifying problems and in making choices.
Choices are necessary for deciding what problem or problems are
uppermost, what courses, study, and reading will be most useful to the
adult, what agencies can serve the client, and what the library can
contribute.

Referrals to other agencies can link the adult with adult education
programs and with others who have similar concerns and interests, and

can identify and direct the client to social agencies and organizations that are not educational or literacy programs but that serve supportive needs, such as health and housing.

As an example of what a public library can do, the Ferguson Library, Stamford, Connecticut, provides: a place for tutor training; a place for volunteers and students to work together; a telephone service that takes messages from students and tutors; ordering and distribution of materials; production and distribution of brochures, flyers, newsletters; and library public relations. All of this is in cooperation with the Literacy Volunteers of America affiliate in Stamford.

Volunteers

For successful programs the staff often must be supplemented by volunteers and community workers with other than library science backgrounds. Volunteers can serve as: tutors, liaison to the community, intermediaries between learner and librarian. They can escort and transport clients, transport and deliver materials, make referrals, support and encourage the learner, find ways to solve personal problems, and serve agencies that serve children and adults. They may assist in organizational and leadership positions; work on training and keeping records; assist with material resources; work in public relations, finances, and fund raising; be counselors and recruiters; work with children; or assist with work in the library such as collection development and organization, and in outreach programs.

The Literacy Volunteers of America has found that volunteers come from among middle-aged and young homemakers, businessmen, professionals in various fields, college students, members of ethnic groups, retirees, and librarians. Volunteers from among the literacy program graduates have proved very successful. Peer teaching is often advantageous. Also, as one student put it, "I think that you so-called educated people have a lot to learn from us uneducated." The volunteer, the librarian, the writer who speaks to adults must speak as an equal.

Volunteer workers are unpaid staff; they give of their time and energy to assist literacy organizations and libraries to conduct literacy programs or specific supportive services. Volunteers are generally part-time workers, giving time over periods of short or long duration.

Volunteers often bring to an activity and an organization a new outlook, a different perspective, added talents, a fresh approach, and a stimulating concept. They also bring a different motivation from that of the paid staff.

In considering the direct services gained by an institution from its volunteers, a library also needs to recognize two indirect benefits often derived from volunteer assistance. First, community support, community utilization, and public relations are immeasurably enhanced by the direct and personal involvement of large numbers of persons in the activity. Volunteer workers are personally involved; they are excellent liaisons to the community. Second, volunteer work experience is a major source of potential recruitment into occupations and professions. Many persons who begin work on volunteer projects continue their education and training for careers in the same kind of work.

Librarians may wish to adopt John Cassavetes' philosophy. It has been said that he mixes professionals with amateurs in his films because amateurs work amazingly hard. "What professionals can give amateurs in the way of help, amateurs can give professionals in the way of inspiration." The literacy program gains the support of special talents and knowledge of people with various backgrounds. In vocational schools they may serve as printers and secretaries. English students and others can write materials. Library science students can organize library collections and find materials for those collections. They can provide much-needed individual tutoring. This one-to-one approach permits learners to go at their own learning pace, at the time and place most convenient, and with individual attention and instruction. The personal relationship permits deeper acquaintance and assistance in solving personal, economic, and family problems.

Volunteers gain satisfaction and pleasure in the progress of the students. They also want training, supervision, and administration that will assist them in the work they do. Volunteers must have quality training and agreed-on commitments of time and effort. The library coordinator of the volunteer program must interview and know all volunteers and provide supervision and support at all times. Tutors will need to have training in techniques for teaching basic reading, practice, and continuing training opportunities. They should have rewards in recognition of their work and through well-organized library administration. The librarian, the student, and the volunteer can all work together to great advantage.

Principles for Success

The American Library Association outlines the following principles that should be borne in mind by libraries in using volunteers:

1. Basic to the success of a volunteer program are prior planning and approval on the part of the staff and the governing body of the library.
2. All the principles and good practices that relate to sound manpower administration, such as planning, training, evaluation, and development, must be applied to volunteer workers.
3. Planning for the use of library volunteers must include clarification of their status regarding such items as compensation for work-related

injuries, insurance coverage when operating a library vehicle, and related benefits.

4. Library volunteers may have work-related expenses that are to be paid or reimbursed by the library. The library's policies and procedures regarding such expenses should be established and made known to volunteers before they begin library service.

5. If it is essential that a minimum or basic library program be initiated or developed by volunteers, this use of voluntary persons should be considered as a temporary measure pending the employment of staff.

6. Volunteers should not supplant or displace established staff position spaces.

7. Recognition and appreciation of every volunteer and of all voluntary assistance is imperative. As volunteers receive no salary, other forms of appreciation and recognition are essential.

8. Volunteers should be assigned to meaningful work that makes use of their own talents, experience, training, and interests.

9. Volunteers should be assigned to those jobs that they feel competent to do and for which they have been trained and given orientation.

10. Volunteer assignments should generally be for specific time periods to enable the library and the volunteer to review, evaluate, and reassign duties.

11. There should be a staff coordinator of volunteers.

12. Continued orientation and training are essential for volunteers to keep them informed of procedures, policies, and objectives in the same way that the continued training of regular staff members is.

13. The staff should have training on the role of volunteers and should share responsibility for the success of the volunteer program.

14. Written, detailed job descriptions for volunteers are necessary.

15. Realistic scheduling of volunteers' time is essential; this may mean some overlapping or duplication of personnel schedule to cover emergencies and absences.

16. Programs and services must be planned bearing in mind the possible termination or unavailability of volunteer help.

17. Friends of Libraries, parent-teacher associations, Literacy Volunteers of America, Laubach Literacy, and other groups provide volunteer services and programs. Some kinds of volunteer assistance may best be provided through such organizations.

COLLECTION DEVELOPMENT AND ORGANIZATION

The development of library collections for literacy service and the identification within the entire collection of appropriate materials to meet the client's interests and needs is as important an element in the literacy program as is staff and staff development. The quality of the materials, the range of content and formats, and the relevancy of that content to learners' reading development, subject needs, and interests are crucial to use and success.

Unless a completely new library collection is being developed, the first step is to assess what the library collection already contains: to identify specific titles, subject areas, reading levels, potential use, and probable client use. Such an assessment, along with the assessment of prospective clientele, serves as a base for the formulation of acquisition and selection policies. Specific client groups and characteristics should be matched with resource needs. The extent and character of the collection and priority areas with objectives for use are to be stated as guides for collection development. Criteria for selection and evaluation of materials should be stated apart from acquisition policy.

Acquisition policy will define the subject areas; staff responsibilities; the extent of the collection at various levels, such as none, minimum, basic, extensive, comprehensive. The nature of the clientele, library functions, the character of materials, and the budget will be major determinants of what is acquired.

Teachers and administrators of adult education and literacy programs will suggest materials needed for courses. The objectives, curriculum, and clientele identified in the literacy programs will indicate what kind and level of material is needed. Librarians can learn from the clients or students what they would like. Personal contacts, visits to classes, and discussions with library users will suggest types of materials. Evidence indicates:

> The adult reader's interest in the material and the purpose for which the material is read are more important than low reading levels and high interest content.
> The relevance of instructional or reading material to daily survival activities is highly significant.
> Adults want to read practical, everyday material for a specific purpose, rather than for some remote or unidentified purpose.

The reading matter used can make the difference between success and failure in a literacy program. College students acquire basic reading skills when the reading material relates to the student's frame of reference. Children and adults are motivated to learn and to read when material reflects cultural backgrounds and language known to them. More and more emphasis is being placed on using materials from daily sources—"real world" reading experiences—and on using the special interest of each individual reader as a basis for selection. Such materials range from daily newspaper articles to application forms. (See appendix 1, subhead " 'Real World' Materials," p. 146.)

Librarians, as well as teachers, must be resourceful in planning curriculum and innovative in gathering materials. They should be able to collect and produce relevant materials for school-age children, youth, and adults. Learners should not have to depend entirely on the use of publishers' texts, basal readers, and spelling workbooks.

It is important to locate, identify, and review materials from regular trade publishers, alternative publishers, ethnic publishers, the review media, bookstores, paperback collections, bibliographies, and government, and in literacy lists. Many collections are chiefly paperbacks, pamphlets, and periodicals.

Examination copies are advisable because titles need to be reviewed and decisions to purchase or reject made. Because materials selection is so important to the literacy program, materials should be examined, not ordered from lists. Exceptions may be possible when the reviewing source is known to be dependable and transferable selections are appropriate.

Whenever possible it is advisable to have a review committee made up of staff directly responsible for the collection; representatives of the literacy programs, both teachers and students; and others engaged in the collaborative effort.

Professional collections for the staff are also essential. They allow examination, selection, and continuing independent study and research. They contain materials on various aspects of literacy, reading, adult education, clientele, and student groups. Also important are study and loan collections of materials useful to students and clients, bibliographies, programmed learning, and relevant reference and informational sources. In short, whatever is needed to fit the teacher's and librarian's needs should be accessible and located at a convenient library center in the community or region.

The evaluation of materials requires a careful analysis of the major aspects of a work. The *Materials Analysis Criteria: Standard for Measurement, MAC Checklist,* provides a systematic procedure for such analysis. The major components analyzed by the use of the *MAC Checklist* are: bibliographical data, content analysis, readability, and appeal. The analysis includes the use of a readability formula, a quantitative analysis, evaluation for specific use, and, finally, a summary of the facts collected in the entire analysis and a detailed annotation. The annotation should include a description of what the work is about, the objective and subjective comments of the evaluator, and comparisons with other material. The annotation then serves as a guide to selection and use and interprets the work in sufficient detail and depth to assist the librarian and reader to decide on the work's appeal and use.

The various types and formats of materials, the techniques of selection, sources for appropriate materials, bibliographies, and annotated lists are discussed at many points in this manual.   Regular acquisition and selection procedures as well as alternative and hitherto unused methods are necessary.   The needs of the clientele and the local situation must be the decisive consideration.   Selection of materials must depend on the library staff and wise use of every resource person. General sources for materials are noted under client groups, suggested readings, in the References, and in the Bibliography.   See especially Material Resources, page 158.

Librarians are quite apt to use bibliographies and lists that have been selected for some specific program or purpose.   A word of caution is necessary.   No one list can be transferred to another program.   Lists also become dated and must be checked for new editions and more current material.   Only the timeless stories, biographies, and literature can be used continuously, and even they become useless for some readers and in some situations.   Whenever it is possible, take a trip to Philadelphia, Dallas, or Chicago, or other local center where libraries have developed collections; talk with other librarians; examine the books in the publishers' booths at conferences of librarians and of adult educators.   Often it is necessary to take a chance and experiment.   Many times it will be necessary to depend on the publisher's catalog and, by trial and error, determine the most useful publications.   Evaluation of publishers' lists, reviewers' points of view, and jobbers' dependability often takes the place of evaluation of the material.   (See Material Resources, p. 158.)

Alternative Ways for Bringing Materials to Users

Once the librarian has located sources for selecting suitable materials and has become skilled in evaluating them for suitability and levels of readability, a major consideration must be given to organizing them in a manner that will make them more accessible and usable.   Should they be placed in one particular location? Should they be interfiled with other materials set aside for a particular clientele that uses such material, (large-print adult books, children's books, ethnic collections, films, or records)? How can they be located easily when needed?

There is no one answer.   The librarian must determine what arrangement will be most useful to the particular clientele and the particular library situation.   Will the materials be used directly by the client? Will a collection set apart for reading improvement be discouraging and embarrassing to users? Also, a variety of resources that are overwhelming can be discouraging and confusing.

A number of answers are possible.   The collections for both consultants' purposes and students' use can be placed in a separate area, on specially designated shelves or in a secluded area or room.   One library set aside a small room that was devoted to reading improvement.   The collection was entirely for adults and included: beginning-to-read workbooks, basic English and bilingual material, vocabulary improvement material, technical reading, and speed-reading material. Such a collection is useful to the beginning reader. It can also be popular with high school students, researchers, and teachers who are looking for usable tutoring materials. It is important to have a staff member to assist in its use.

Another library draws almost completely on the entire library collection for learners' reading material. A learning center broadens the range of materials; it includes programmed learning material, media kits, and a reading laboratory as well as a print collection. Yet another library has a collection called "Books for New Readers," which is located in a special area of the library.

The collection for the Reader Development Program at the Free Library of Philadelphia brings together many duplicate copies. Teachers and others select titles and order the quantity needed for collections that are deposited with them for student use. For maximum use some libraries interfile titles selected for literacy or adult education programs in one collection, and some libraries interfile adult and juvenile titles.

Rotating deposit collections for a limited short-term or one-year period permit wider choices. These collections may be sent to such circulation and reference places as: literacy program centers, adult education classes, learning laboratories, homes, YMCAs and YWCAs, settlement houses, and churches.

A separate card file can be developed for a particular clientele, with subject entries, reading level, and other pertinent information noted. As new books, pamphlets, documents, and other materials are acquired, additional cards could be made for those that would be helpful in the literacy program.

A color-coding system can be used to denote, in a very general way, the reading level of the literacy materials. The color notation can be placed either on the materials, which are filed among the regular adult collection, or on a catalog card, or both.

Many of the most useful items in a literacy collection include: pamphlets, products, signs, posters, articles, pictures, labels, and application forms. Vertical files are organized to hold these materials, but unless their contents are promoted, they become neglected and unused. Learning games, tape recorders, typewriters, and teaching machines also must have a place and access points.

Whatever the method of organizing the materials, once they are selected, the librarian remains the key to their usefulness. Sensitivity to and genuine interest in the client and a spontaneous, creative approach to the possibilities that exist are by far the most important factors, whatever arrangement is decided upon. Direct access within the library to open shelves and reader development collections is important.

Various alternatives and innovative means of access to materials are possible. They include the use of mobile units such as vans, automobiles, bookmobiles, and airplanes; mail delivery; delivery with meals-on-wheels; sidewalk displays; and delivery by the librarian, tutor, volunteer, or aide during home and class visits. Whatever method is closest to and most advantageous for the clientele is a reasonable solution.

ASSURING A SUCCESSFUL PROGRAM

The interpretation and promotion of materials through the usual advisory techniques and by means of publications, television, cable, or radio can provide innovative access to a library's resources. Personal consultations and guidance are of immediate value. They provide an opportunity to know the client individually and to learn the user's responses to service and materials. It is possible to identify needs and interests of the individual or group, find the right material to fit those needs and interests, and assess or diagnose reading abilities as closely as possible.

The library staff can encourage and suggest possible reading selections and alternatives with enthusiasm and critical guidance; can instruct in the use of dictionaries, encyclopedias, and reference aids; and can provide orientation and instruction in the use of the library at moments of interest or demand. The library will further promote use and interest by providing comfortable reading places, listening areas, and program activities. Clients have an opportunity to get acquainted when social gatherings are held at hours convenient to them. Librarians and clients can present book discussions, panel discussions, and interview programs in the library and outside—in homes, at club meetings, school events, and public affairs, in migrant camps, welfare offices, or detention homes.

Publicity and promotion as well as guidance is possible through exhibits and displays. Bibliographies can generate interest in subjects and individual items. Some libraries have found valuable the organization of such worthwhile experiences as visits to a grocery store or supermarket to price groceries; opening accounts at a bank; field trips to zoos, museums, plays, and movies. Above all, it is essential to use stories, histories, biographies, coping skill material, such as applications and forms, legal documents, and periodicals related to the needs and interests of the client.

The library staff member, the volunteer, and the advanced students can serve as models of success. The entire family may be involved in the literacy activities.

Literacy programs sometimes have difficulties. It is well to understand and anticipate them. They are surmountable. Poverty results in undernourished, poorly clothed, frequently ill potential clients; these conditions make it very difficult for the clients to study and read.

Unfavorable geographic conditions, migration and moving patterns, and language differences can create barriers. Previous failures and disbelief in the values of literacy may discourage participation. Lack of funds and teachers proportionate to the problem and lack of proficiency in teachers or librarians are inhibiting factors. Lack of time and daily survival problems often make study by adults impossible. One estimate concludes that nearly 200 hours a year must be given to an adult basic education class for a successful learning experience.

LIBRARIES' RESPONSIBILITIES IN LITERACY SERVICE

The various types of libraries—public school, public library, academic, state—have unique and common responsibilities that are summarized in the following discussion.

The Public School/Media Center Library

The public school/media center has an important supportive and supplementary role in the literacy effort because of its direct relationship with the educational system. Because the student is in the process of developing literacy skills, the public school is a critical point for learning the use and range of materials in a library. If at this time the library becomes a part of the student's learning experience, it is more likely that it will continue to be a resource. Media centers and learning resource libraries often have the most complete collections of all types of materials and format on which to draw. The media center librarian advisedly will:

Bring to the attention of teachers and students what library resources and services are and the fact that librarians are teachers.

Develop service to support the curricula and extend the students' opportunities for learning with basal textbooks, bilingual and bicultural materials, and supplementary print and nonprint materials.

Be an active consultant in individualized reading guidance programs for both the student and the teacher to extend and enrich reading.

Develop a reading laboratory.

Develop collections that meet the instructional goals of the school reading programs and that consider the attitudes, values, life-styles, and interests of the students, and provide them with choices according to children's and youths' interests, stages of development, and proficiency in reading.

Develop library group activities such as reading aloud, puppetry, dramatization, storytelling, and writing.

Publish a newsletter with student writings—poetry, jokes, comic strips, biographies, stories, book reviews, puzzles, and notes about favorite authors, magazines, movies, and television programs.

Instruct students in how to use dictionaries, encyclopedias, and reference aids.

Collaborate with teachers in appraisal of student skills and individual needs.

Cooperate with public libraries in every possible way.

Initiate a collaborative reading program with public libraries.

Work closely with parents and involve parents at all stages of planning and in guidance activities.

Conduct workshops and discussions on the parents' supportive role in the child's learning.

Provide, when appropriate and necessary, the same range of services and activities for adults in ABE, GED, and ESL programs.

The Public Library

The public library has always looked on itself as the "open door" for all people. It has a long history of designing programs for the expressed needs of all its users and fitting the materials to the particular user. It has only to reach out to the nonuser and broaden its communication resources to find itself a significant place in the literacy program. As an extremely important element of a community-wide reading improvement network, the public library system and each unit in the system can make a substantial contribution to the quality of service provided. Many librarians feel that to survive as a meaningful institution, the public library must work with other social and educational agencies in raising the cultural, educational, and economic levels of the disadvantaged. It must bring library services, and especially reading and audio-visual materials, to those millions of underprivileged citizens who, because of the inaccessibility of libraries, apathy, ignorance, neglect, and fear, have not made use of library facilities and services. (See figure 3, "Reaching the Client Directly or Indirectly.")

The public library has, together with the public school libraries and media centers, a key role in providing services for children and parents. In carrying out these many services, librarians will find it absolutely essential to go outside libraries to homes, migrant camps, parks, plants, churches, neighborhood centers, and many other areas of the community. At the same time it is important to bring people to the library, where the total resources and services are accessible. In developing any or all such services, the library must take into consideration and reconcile constraints of time, funds, staff, and other factors. The public library, as a community-based facility and a neutral agency, can:

Serve as a resource center for learners and personnel—facilitators, teachers, administrators.

Serve as a catalyst and take a coordinating and leadership role.

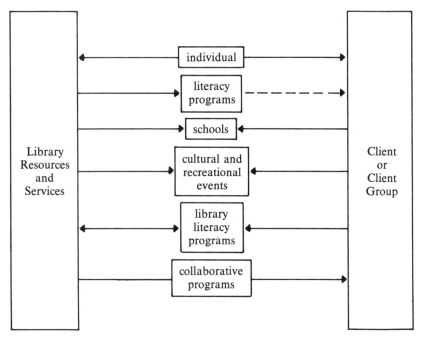

Fig. 3. Reaching the Client Directly or Indirectly

Provide information and promote interest in and understanding of literacy throughout the community.

Serve as a clearinghouse for literacy programs, activities, and resources in the community.

Collaborate in every possible way with community literacy activities.

Direct and sponsor group instruction and conduct tutorial programs.

Furnish materials for beginning readers and materials in the languages of all the clientele groups in sufficient variety to meet needs and offer a choice.

Provide recruitment programs and activities and programs that reach out to people through all the system's outlets, especially through the bookmobiles and vans but, above all, through personal contacts.

Provide staff development in the awareness of literacy needs and modes of service to meet them.

Play an important role in assisting persons who are far from mastery of reading skills and those persons who cannot easily define a problem area or a need or wish.

Follow up on reading programs and provide follow-on reading materials.

Provide meeting rooms, physical facilities, and equipment.

Bookmobiles and vans and books-by-mail can and do perform a great service to residents in rural farm areas and urban ghettos. They can help in seeking out the nonreading poor on the back roads of eastern America and on isolated farms in the Midwest, in migrant camps, mobile-home settlements, and inner-city low-cost housing and slum areas of the ghettos. Educators and librarians frequently have restricted the use of these methods to mere delivery. And indeed bookmobiles, vans, and postal service do deliver books. But bookmobile service is far more. A bookmobile or van is a small branch with trained staff to interpret the total collection and service; most of all it *seeks out the clientele*. It provides a place for tutoring and for study. A well-developed books-by-mail service brings informed advice to readers by means of annotated lists of materials and telephone guidance and reference services.

Such methods are the heart of the rural library service. In setting up a program for migrant farm workers, one library system asked the county planning board to make a map of the population density of the area so that it could determine if and where branches were needed. When the locations of the library's regular readers were placed on the population residency map, it was seen that some of the densest population areas had few readers, while in other sections 80 percent of the residents were being served. Consequently, the library focused its attention on the migrant needs in the rural areas and established a special bilingual bookmobile.

The Academic Library

The academic library, college and university, has an essential role by extension of its traditional functions and responsibilities into the area of literacy. Perhaps most important is its acceptance of this role and its active participation in a collaborative effort with other libraries. Among the contributing and supportive activities the academic library might carry out are:

Development of collections of literacy materials for teacher education and training.

Development of collections of research data and the promotion and dissemination of research information.

Support of the academic curricula through the provision of relevant materials and guidance in their use.

Assistance in developing college students' literacy skills by instruction in the use of dictionaries, encyclopedias, reference aids, and the use of the library and by advice and counsel to students on the use of media materials.

Advice to students who are tutoring individuals in ABE, GED, CLEP, ESL, and TESOL programs on appropriate materials.

Collaboration in the literacy effort with public school media centers and particularly public and prison libraries with literacy programs.

Development of instructional materials on what the library can do for the professional student and faculty.

Provision of a resource center for teachers in programs of English as a second language and for speakers of other languages.

Provision of bilingual and bicultural materials for those people whose native language is other than English, whether they be native- or foreign-born Americans, which may be a unique responsibility.

Development of reading and writing laboratories.

The State Library

The state library can assume an active role throughout the state and nationally as a major support of educational activities at the child, youth, and adult levels. State libraries can:

Take a leadership role in creating awareness and understanding of the importance of a literate population and of the libraries' place in achieving this goal among legislators, decisionmakers, and trustees, as well as librarians.

Assist in coordinating literacy activities of local and federal staff responsible for adult education programs.

Assist regional and county library systems by providing funds for outreach programs and strengthening systems in the literacy effort.

Place emphasis on the nonusers of libraries and focus on activities for adult beginning readers and disadvantaged children and youth.

Provide librarians and trustees with consultant services on planning literacy programs.

Organize and conduct training programs for trustees, librarians, and paraprofessionals on how to sustain a literacy program.

Provide funds and collaborate with library schools in workshops, institutes, and courses related to literacy.

Develop English and bilingual and bicultural collections of literacy materials for study and demonstration purposes and for long-term and rotating loan collections.

Develop media collections for use in promoting community awareness of literacy needs.

Provide direct services for small and medium-sized independent libraries in rural and isolated areas.

Inform librarians, trustees, and legislators on a continuing basis of significant developments in the field of literacy.

Initiate and support demonstration and experimental literacy projects.

Assist librarians in writing proposals for demonstration literacy projects.

References

Appalachian Adult Education Center. *Adoption of ABE Innovation Model: Awareness, Interest Trial Adoption.* Morehead, Ky.: The Center, Morehead State University, October 10, 1972.

————. *Interrelating Library and Basic Education Services for Disadvantaged Adults: A Demonstration of Four Alternative Working Models.* Annual Report, Vol. 1–2. Washington, D.C.: United States Department of Health, Education, and Welfare, Office of Education, 1973.

Colvin, Ruth J., and Root, Jane H. *READ: Reading Evaluation—Adult Diagnosis.* A Test for Assessing Adult Student Reading Needs and Progress. Administrative Guide. Syracuse, N.Y.: Literacy Volunteers of America, 1976.

Fleming, Lois, comp. *Proceedings of the Conference "Adult Basic Education and Public Library Service," June 5–6, 1974, Miami Springs, Florida.* Tallahassee: Division of Library Services, Department of State, The Adult Education Section, Florida Department of Education, n.d.

Lyman, Helen Huguenor. *Reading and the Adult New Reader.* Chicago: American Library Association, 1976.

Simpson, Edwin L., and Loveall, Philip W. *Preparing and Selecting Printed Educational Material for Adult New Readers.* Information Series no. 9. ERIC Clearinghouse in Career Education in cooperation with Department of Secondary and Adult Education. DeKalb: Northern Illinois University, 1976.

Smith, Joshua I. *Library and Information Services for Special Groups.* New York: Science Associates/International, Inc., 1974.

Sticht, Thomas G., and others. *Auding and Reading: A Developmental Model.* Alexandria, Va.: Human Resources Research Organization.

6
The Clientele

The library's literacy effort begins with the individual client; and individuals, when grouped together, make up the clientele groups in various literacy programs. The clientele, whether served as individuals, as participants in literacy programs, or as members of specific population groups, are representative of the full range of literacy and educational levels. A developmental continuum from the nonliterate to the independently literate and from readiness to literacy exists.

Let us consider the groups in the nation that may be differentiated by certain common characteristics. In the context of national literacy concerns, client groupings include: literacy level groups, groups by age and schooling, rural and urban groups, ethnic and language groups, and the disadvantaged, grouped by particular handicap. This latter group covers a broad representation of different client groups. The participants in the many literacy and lifetime learning programs are students or clients in a wide range of programs, which include early education; secondary/high school; out-of-school youth programs; and adult literacy programs in adult basic, secondary, and higher education, including independent, self-directed learning.

In every community there are four important groups that are or may be involved in developing literacy abilities. These groups may be defined both broadly and specifically. In general, for the purposes of this manual, they include:

1. Those adults and young adults who cannot read or function at a basic survival level of reading, and whose literacy abilities range from what may be described as complete illiteracy to fourth-grade level.

2. Those adults of various ages, stages of growth and development, and ethnic background who are hampered by their limited level of basic literacy; that is, literacy below eighth-grade level.

3. Those students in higher education who have not attained the level of developmental skills necessary to subject matter requirements; that is, literacy at a secondary-school level.

4. Those preschool-aged children whose parents or society cannot provide them with the cultural, educational, and literary stimulation necessary for the achievement of literacy. These children are recognized as a potential source for the other three groups.

Each group has certain cultural characteristics and needs that may be generalized to some extent, but also can be identified in the assessment of the local community. One classifies with caution, as overlapping of characteristics among groups is apparent. Stereotyping must be avoided.

Adults begin to outnumber children and youth as continuing education becomes an established part of the educational system. The 1970 census figures show a total of 54.3 million persons of working age who had not completed high school. This group included men and women, blacks, whites, the Spanish-speaking, American Indians, persons of other races and nationalities, and all ages. The age pattern shows that two among every three persons were 45 years of age or over. Those over 65 years of age account for one in four persons. The trend indicates a movement away from the traditional rigid pattern of going to school ⟶ working ⟶ retiring. More and more people combine school and work, full-time and part-time work and education, and in retirement often enter alternate careers. Such a pattern need not be confined to educated and professional populations.

The libraries of the country can be of particular service to those people who have limited education and low incomes, and who do not have their own resources or the means and knowledge to obtain the learning materials they need. Libraries can create an environment conducive to learning. The indigent as well as the poor, the completely uneducated as well as those with limited education, the various groups who have suffered under discriminatory practices and attitudes, those who have had no access to quality education—all make up a population for whom the library can establish new priorities of service.

Variable clients require variable service. No one service or method of delivery can satisfy the needs of all clients. Different and changing clientele, different age groups, require different services to fit particular needs and interests. Services must be adapted, new services adopted, and changes initiated to meet the changes that constantly occur in a community.

Brenda Dervin and the Appalachian Adult Education Center have found six major barriers to the use of libraries as part of adults' communication system:

1. *Institutional barriers*—The long wait, the putdown, staff hostility, pointing behavior ("It's over there"), and professional neglect ("Look in the catalog") turn clients away.

2. *Social barriers*—Many people, particularly poor and isolated persons, do not know that certain information exists. Most people turn first to other people for information, rather than to libraries.

3. *Physical barriers*—Distance, lack of transportation, lack of easy access and of comfortable furnishings, and many other factors are barriers to library use.

4. *Intellectual barriers*—As Ann Hayes Drennan, on the basis of her experience at the Appalachian Adult Education Center, has said, "One of the consuming concerns in any discussion of library services is whether the materials being offered are comprehensible to the patron." Are there literacy materials available in the language best known? The technical language of library science is useless, and is to be used sparingly and explained.

5. *Psychological barriers*—Libraries may represent strange and frightening, unknown places. (It is important for librarians to get out to the community—to industrial plants, to the apartments, the stores, the homes. Institutional personnel titles should be dropped. Personal and friendly relations should be developed within the professional context.) The image of past learning experiences as failures, and the heavy demands of work and adult responsibilities present further barriers.

6. *Cost barriers*—The cost to client or potential users in money, time, and anxiety discourages use of library services.

Such factors are considerations to be taken account of in planning service. Service location, hours of service, procedures and regulations, and transportation can be adjusted as much as possible to the work hours, schedules, and other demands of the clientele. For more details about service, see *Information Needs of Urban Residents,* by Edward S. Warner, listed in the References.

THE LEARNER AS CLIENT

The learner, whether child or adult, is the central figure in any literacy program. The learner stands in the center and commands respect and attention. The librarian's understanding and knowledge of the individual learner client are crucial factors in the literacy effort.

It is important to consider the individual's attitude toward self and others; values, belief in self, and attitudes toward reading; physical abilities; living conditions and such basic requirements as food, shelter, and safety; the psychological as well as the physiological, economic, and spiritual conditions; and positive as well as negative abilities. The client, in developing and learning, is changing and is becoming more independent and self-directed. What is meaningful to the client will strike the responsive chord based on experience. The client often places major importance on the practical result and immediate return.

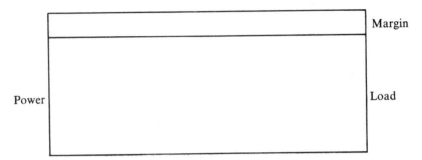

Fig. 4. McClusky's Power Load Concept

Negative factors—fear, discrimination, hostility, illness, family and marital problems, impossible study conditions, poverty, insufficient food and clothing, unemployment, and lack of transportation—are stronger than the desire to learn, and create obstacles to overcome. Scorn, ridicule, and unsympathetic or unresponsive teachers and librarians can do irreparable harm. Success, even limited success, is essential to overcome the discouragement of the other obstacles and failures.

Consider the idea presented by Howard McClusky, an adult educator at the University of Michigan. He points out that each person has a certain amount of power available to draw on for the load each must carry—in a job; in a family; in relation to health, to one another, and to oneself, and to problems of living and citizenship (see figure 4). Each draws on this power, and what is left over is the margin for learning. This is a small margin. When the load equals the power, the energy for learning is destroyed. Literacy skills, ability to solve problems, and money give power.

Information that librarians provide lightens the load. They can help to eliminate obstacles by their attitudes toward the clients; by finding ways to provide food, health care, and transportation; and by securing legal and civil rights through information and referral services to other social agencies. They can encourage and reinforce the learner by the process of providing guidance, counseling, and personal direct service. They can eliminate many procedures and regulations. They must be flexible and ready to support the learner's or reader's own personal goals.

It is important, obviously, to recognize the positive strengths in each individual's personal motivation and will to learn in spite of the great odds. The librarian, like the teacher, builds on the experiences and knowledge, that is, the survival skills, that adults develop. Such skills may be of even greater importance than the basic literacy skills.

A major motivation for library use or nonuse and for reading activity is participation and enrollment in some educational or vocational program. Also important are some measure of familiarity with community resources, and attendance at cultural events. These factors are strong characteristics of both white and black library users. For Latino users, the perception of the library as a friendly and helpful place is more important than any other factor in determining use. An important question, not answerable here, is "How many potential clients for literacy education are there who are part of the community's mainstream?"

Education continues to remain a major correlate to reading activity. It is recognized that everyone's reading efficiency can be improved. Developmental reading programs usually are continued from sixth grade through college and beyond. Individual capabilities and problems are taken into account. Cultural and ethnic differences are major matters of consideration and should be seen as strengths on which to build a realistic assessment of the problems and difficulties posed by each individual and the school or library, the teacher or librarian.

Reading is a developing ability. It is built upon a foundation of language abilities developed and expressed by means of the oral skills of listening and speaking. The use of language begins at an early age. The oral and written language units that are learned from the early childhood years to college age are from six to twelve million words.

Whatever the use of communication media and their importance, literacy remains the foundation on which much of education is based and on which people must depend to get along in daily living. Literacy is learned through many media and many curricula—of which the school's is only one. Literacy should complement what is learned in other ways; it should be seen as an indispensable tool to further communication and intellectual progress. The average reading achievement of children in school is related directly to the home environment and parents' education. Books, magazines, radio, and television, when accessible to children, make a difference in their level of reading achievement. The librarian who is aware of the environmental, economic, and media situation surrounding the child is able to work with the parent, foster parent, or child to provide a growth-fostering environment.

AGE GROUPS

Education, once limited to the young and the first years of life, has been extended to longer and longer periods and now embraces each stage of human development. Social changes, political awareness, and extension of the life span have combined to focus legislation, education, experimentation, and research on both early and lifetime learning. This concept asserts that everyone, regardless of age, has a series of changing demands at different periods in life. The programs of schools and libraries must be shaped to meet the stages of human development, needs, and interests.

Children 1–5 Years of Age
(Preschool and Kindergarten)

This period is crucial to a whole lifetime of learning. In these early years begins the development of readiness—physical, mental, and psychological—to learn basic listening and speaking skills and acquire knowledge of both spoken and written language. Recent studies stress the importance of the environment and of the parent as a model in the child's linguistic development. (See chapter 7, "The Early Childhood Group," page 96.)

In many areas of the country no public preschool programs or kindergartens exist. Mounting evidence indicates that the modern child's facility with oral language as a prerequisite to reading and the child's attitude toward reading are established outside the school, often before kindergarten. Teachers and librarians work with parents to guide reading activities in the home. Equally important are the parents' own use of literacy skills and the atmosphere surrounding the child.

Children 6–12 Years of Age (Grades 1–7)
and Youth 13–15 Years of Age (Grades 8–10)

During these years of life many young people have serious educational and emotional problems. Some have almost no schooling. Others are in poor schools or out of school. Misprized testing handicaps many, particularly among minority groups, and causes children to be underestimated in regard to potential achievement. Some must support themselves. Many are runaways from home, are confused and unhappy, and are cared for by social agencies.

Young Adults 16–17 years of Age (Grades 11–12)

Here the focus may be on the out-of-school youth—out of school either in a mental or physical sense.

Adults 18–34 Years of Age

Included are students in higher education, those who are out-of-school, the unemployed, and those who are moving from place to place; adults upgrading job proficiencies, education credentials, and basic literacy skills. This period is a time of homemaking, child care, and increasing adult responsibilities as well as decisions regarding a career and earning a living.

Adults 35–55 Years of Age

This period of life is the productive time when work and job-training needs, parental and family responsibilities, health needs, and lifetime learning are paramount.

Adults 55–70 Years of Age

Adults continue to be productive, but new roles and interests arise. Preretirement, retirement, health, finances, leisure, continuing education, and residency in hospitals and retirement homes are general concerns.

Adults 70 and Over

The primary concerns during these years are health, leisure, and finances. The elderly, 85 years of age and over, may be most dependent upon others.

The life span of the average American is 69.5 years for men and 75.8 years for women. An ever-increasing part of the population is the group between 55 and 75 years of age. The majority are healthy, educated, and active. One study shows that 20 percent of persons over 65 years of age are in volunteer work, and another 10 percent would be interested in volunteer activities. Here, it should be noted, is a potential source for tutors and for administrators, promoters, and advisers for literacy programs.

RURAL AND URBAN GROUPS

Populations may be identified by geographic areas: the Appalachian area of thirteen states, the Southwest, the reservations and location of American Indian tribes, the migration routes of farm workers, the rural country and small-town population, and the urban inner-city and suburban residents of metropolitan areas.

Americans have been and continue to be on the move. Moving can mean a change of residence within a neighborhood or a city, or relocation thousands of miles away. Movers include everyone making some geographic changes. They cause changes in neighborhoods and community populations that are difficult to keep abreast of and to recognize.

One out of every five persons changes residence each year. Most moves are to find a new or a better job. Although the greatest number of moves is related to persons with higher levels of schooling, professional, technical, managerial, and skilled personnel, many persons who are less fortunate also move. They include: those persons who move constantly for periodic jobs; farm workers who move seasonally; and immigrant groups from other countries. The young out-of-school adult without job training and lacking basic literacy skills and migrant farm workers and their families suffer most in the loss of continuity in learning opportunities.

In some areas of the country, some rural residents are trapped in permanent locations and depressed economic situations. Their farm skills may be obsolete, and they may need to improve their literacy skills. They lack transportation and often are located in isolated, sparsely settled geographic areas of the country. Many are elderly and in the lower income brackets. Forgotten and lonely, they lack factual information and guidance on legal and social rights and benefits, are often unemployed, and have no access to jobs. The drastic change from an agricultural to an urban industrial economy has left many of the areas where these people live nonfunctioning and isolated. This kind of area is quite unlike the economically productive areas of huge wheat farms, cattle ranches, and huge acreages of irrigated land, where a highly educated, affluent population lives.

Many people have no contact with any of the usual agencies that serve rural residents. Where such agencies or organizations exist, libraries may collaborate to advantage. Some possible cooperating groups are: departments of mental health, public safety, education, homemakers clubs, cooperative extension, family life councils, farm bureaus, granges, home demonstration clubs, and church groups.

Residents in urban areas may be confined within the limitations of their immediate location. Many have come from rural backgrounds: Appalachians to northern cities, blacks from the South to the North, Puerto Ricans from the islands to the mainland, Mexican Americans from the Southwest to metropolitan cities. Without funds or education, they face almost insurmountable obstacles. Even with jobs they are confined to a bare existence. Lack of information and means prevents learning and broadening experiences. They fail to know and experience the great resources the city has to offer in its museums, galleries, and libraries. Unlike rural residents, who have few or no such resources, city residents have a multitude of learning opportunities and enrichment resources available if they are able to use them. Outreach and innovative programs among schools, museums, and libraries have helped to meet their needs.

ETHNIC, CULTURAL, AND LANGUAGE GROUPS

Among the pluralistic groups of the United States are a multiplicity of ethnic, cultural, and language groups. A few are noted here. Unique groups can best be identified in the library's local community.

According to the 1970 census, Native Americans, or American Indians, number more than 800,000 persons and are a growing population. Census figures show that from 1960 to 1970 their numbers increased 51 percent. Forty-five percent of all Indians live in urban areas. Thirty-one percent were estimated to speak a Native American tongue as their first language. Of Native American adults, 100,000 have not completed high school. American Indians go back and forth from the reservation to the cities. They are "displaced" persons in a unique way. They are struggling to gain control in directing their lives. Not everyone, of course, is in need; many are educated, successful, and secure.

The Latino population includes Cuban Americans, Mexican Americans or Chicanos, Puerto Rican Americans, Cubans, South Americans, and others. In 1973 one out of every five students in federal/state adult education programs was from one of these groups.

The Latino population is no longer geographically restricted to the Southwest. The 1970 census report documents the increasing flow of Spanish-speaking individuals to the urban centers of the Midwest, particularly Chicago, Milwaukee, and Detroit, in the Great Lakes region. By 1975 there were increasing reports of federal/state adult education programs whose participants were almost wholly Latinos. This phenomenon can be expected to increase in the next decade as both the legal and illegal migration of Latinos throughout the United States increases at a steady rate.

Among the Asian Americans are peoples from the Philippines, Korea, India, Hong Kong, and China. Approximately 130,000 Vietnamese came in 1975. Large numbers of European immigrants also continue to enter the United States, especially from Italy, Great Britain, Portugal, and Greece. In addition, many clusters of people from many countries and places who are in need of literacy education are located in certain areas; for example, Haitians in New York and Cubans in Miami.

Blacks constituted approximately 24 million, or more than 11 percent, of the total population of the United States in 1974. The majority of blacks are metropolitan central-city dwellers; slightly more than half (52 percent) live in the South, about 40 percent in the North, and 10 percent in the West. During the 1960s, blacks made substantial gains in income, employment, education, housing, and health, but today many remain behind whites in most social, economic, and educational areas. A considerable segment is in need of learning skills, professional knowledge, and social and educational experiences that are necessary to advancement in today's society. Young people in particular need basic education; adults need retraining and new vocational skills; older persons need basic skills and educational opportunities that formerly were denied. The black population is a most important clientele for literacy programs. Many are already involved in vocational and adult basic education programs and are acquiring credentials of high school diplomas and higher education degrees.

GROUPS DISADVANTAGED BY A PARTICULAR HANDICAP

The disadvantaged groups in society are potential clientele for adult basic and other educational programs. They include:

The economically disadvantaged—the indigent, the poor, public assistance recipients, and dependent children or adults.

The homebound or physically disabled and the developmentally and learning disabled.

The residents of institutions, such as hospitals or convalescent and retirement homes.

The residents of correctional institutions, either criminal or delinquent, such as prisons, jails, and detention homes. In federal prisons 96 percent of newly committed persons have not finished high school.

The Appalachian Adult Education Center (AAEC) in its 1973 Annual Report, defines disadvantaged adults as those persons over sixteen years of age who are out of school with less than a high school diploma and with a family income below a poverty index. AAEC has identified within this population of fifty-seven million adults four groups with distinct characteristics.

Group I includes those individuals who are more economically and personally secure than those in the other three groups. They have belief in the value of education and of the library and other public services. They also have belief in themselves. They are able to pay for instruction and use various media. They have some skills. Because they can be served in groups and learn more quickly, they are economical to serve.

Group II includes those who have suffered some discomfort from undereducation and are underemployed. They learn quickly and have fewer needs than Groups III and IV. They need learning situations adjusted to their time and work schedules.

Group III includes persons who need to develop basic literacy skills to earn a living wage. Their outstanding service need is for one-to-one services and individual recruitment. They do not interpret problems as information needs.

Group IV is the smallest group, yet has the highest priority on a need index. AAEC describes them as the "stationary poor." They are fatalistic, unemployed, and unemployable. They require various services —transportation, child care, and other supportive services. They are relatively expensive to serve.

All these groups, and particularly Groups III and IV, need to have institutional and social barriers removed. They need special attention and support in using libraries. They also need literacy materials available in the language best known and at appropriate reading levels. They need to know where to obtain accurate information that is useful to them.

Another important group is the economically risen middle- to upper-middle-class housewife who may or may not belong to an ethnic minority. She has a "hidden" literacy need. The importance of these women to the educational well-being of family, community, and nation cannot be overemphasized, yet often they are left behind as their families advance educationally.

LITERACY AND LIFETIME LEARNING PROGRAMS

Libraries serve participants in literacy and lifetime learning programs both indirectly and directly. They reach the client through the service extended to the professional staff of administrators, teachers, volunteers, and tutors. They also reach the client through individual library service and the library's own literacy project. The service, whether organized formally or informally, is supportive of the client and program objectives. The major programs include:

Early Education Programs

Home Start, Head Start, day-care centers, child/parent centers, elementary school education, Reading Is Fundamental (RIF), Boy Scouts and Girl Scouts

High School and Out-of-School Youth Programs

Manpower and job training, apprenticeship programs, business and industrial proprietary schools, military schools

Adult Programs

1. Adult basic education—Adult Basic Education (ABE), public school; Right to Read; Laubach Literacy, Inc.; Literacy Volunteers of America, Inc.; Lutheran Church Women—Volunteer Reading Aides; Church Women United—ABE Program; American Bible Society; Baptist Church Women; English for Internationals; World Education; and other local programs

2. Secondary education—General Educational Development Certificate or Diploma (GED); continuation schools; high school equivalency program; vocational and technical schools; junior colleges; alternative schools; military volunteer education

3. Higher education or college level—College-Level Examination Program (CLEP); Regents External Degree Program; community colleges; university extension courses; open university

Participants in continuing education represent a vast number of people who are enrolled in a lifetime learning program or activity. How great is the actual participation by adults in part-time and continuing education? How great is the potential interest among adults in acquiring more knowledge and developing literacy skills? Although no dependable, agreed-on estimate of participation or potential participation exists, the figures that are available are high and increase annually. According to varying estimates, from 15.7 million to 27 million adults participate in some formally organized program of adult education. Nonparticipants or potential participants are estimated at from 111.5 million, or 80 percent, to as high as 90 percent of the adult population.

Adults are part of a mass movement in postsecondary education. They are the consumers of education. They are part-time participants or students. They outnumber the people enrolled in public and private schools and high schools combined. They are of great significance to the learning resource centers and public libraries of the country. Already they have influenced and brought about new directions in library service.

Adult Basic Education

The Adult Basic Education program is designed to:

1. Assist states in providing necessary instruction in basic educational skills for adults 16 years of age or older.

2. Expand educational opportunity and encourage the establishment of adult public education that will enable adults to continue their education to the level of completion of secondary school.

3. Make available the means to secure training that will enable the ABE learner to become a more employable, productive, and responsive citizen.

Over a decade ago the Adult Basic Education program was established by the Economic Opportunity Act of 1964 and funded in 1965 to combat poverty. The Adult Education Act of 1966 and subsequent amendments, including the Education Amendments of 1974, have broadened and strengthened the program. The Act provides a state grant-in-aid program administered by the Department of Health, Education, and Welfare through the Office of Education. States are required to match funding on a 90 percent federal and 10 percent state basis.

The Adult Basic Education program offers service and opportunities for adults to obtain instruction in basic education and secondary education below the college level. Adults who are not enrolled in school and who do not have a certificate of graduation from secondary school or have not attained an equivalent level of education are eligible. Special projects provide educational programs for elderly people and for those adults whose ability to speak and read the English language is limited or who live in an area where the culture is different from their own.

The ABE program is a mature means of enabling adults to develop literacy skills, cope with daily problems, and achieve vocational training. Although the program has made positive achievements, it successfully reaches only a small fraction of those needing it, particularly among the more educationally deficient. To date only a small percentage of the ABE population has been reached by the federal ABE program or by other groups attempting to help, and the dropout rate is high. Much remains to be done in assessing the needs of the ABE groups as well as the positive qualities they have to offer; in discovering more creative ways of motivating ABE learners and in helping them to progress; and in making the availability of relevant, first-rate materials, programs, and services a top priority. In countless cases where the ABE student was personally motivated and received help and encouragement, the results have been dramatic and extremely heartening. In terms of economic self-sufficiency, personal adjustment and satisfaction, and community enrichment, the value of such efforts has been amply demonstrated.

General Educational Development

The General Educational Development Certificate is known also as the high school equivalency diploma, the GED certificate, and HEP (high school equivalency program). The GED Testing Program (the official name) is sponsored by the Commission on Accreditation of Service Experiences, a unit of the American Council of Education. The Commission was established in 1945 to evaluate achievements of military personnel. It works with state departments of education, business, industry, civil service commissions, and state and local boards of licensing examiners that recognize certificate achievers as meeting the requirements of high school graduation for job eligibility and promotion. Many colleges, universities, and armed services accept the credential.

The GED test is taken at official GED centers. Centers are located in accredited high schools and colleges, at adult schools, boards of education, community colleges, and state departments of education. The GED test is made up of five comprehensive examinations: English, social studies, natural sciences, literature, and mathematics. A standard score of 35 on each of five tests and a standard score of 45 on all five tests are common criteria for awarding the diploma. Tests are available for handicapped students, and Spanish versions are available. The GED test is used widely by the military and administered through the United States Armed Forces Institute. It is a second-chance school system of special appeal to the black community. Many public libraries are providing guidance and materials for GED examinees. In a few libraries, diagnostic and tutorial assistance is being made available.

Right to Read

The Right to Read (R-2-R) program is a federally sponsored reading improvement program authorized under Title VII (PL 83531), National Reading Improvement Program, Education Amendments of 1974. The program is a coordinated national endeavor involving all segments of society—public and private, professional and nonprofessional—to increase functional literacy and to ensure that everyone has an opportunity to possess and use the needed reading competencies. It provides financial support to other programs.

Volunteer Literacy Organizations

Two major organizations in the literacy effort are Laubach Literacy International and Literacy Volunteers of America, Inc. Both organizations train volunteers to tutor adults and teenagers, produce materials for training and guidance, publish materials for students, and assist in the organization of literacy programs.

Reading Is Fundamental

Reading Is Fundamental (RIF) is a national organization designed to motivate children to read through personal ownership of books. The major goals are to create the desire to read among children and to demonstrate that books are essential to a child and should be available to all children. RIF projects serve principally children from preschool through elementary grades. The program is funded by foundations and is sponsored by the Smithsonian Institute. The program stresses the enjoyment of reading and the ownership of books, which are distributed free or at low cost to the children.

College-Level Examination Program

The College-Level Examination Program (CLEP) opens up new possibilities for those who have been unable to participate in full-time postsecondary education. The program provides adults with a flexible means for certifying their knowledge, a way to progress at their own speed toward a postsecondary degree, or to satisfy their own curiosity about the extent and quality of their learning. It saves time and money. Hundreds of colleges grant college credit to people who pass the CLEP examination in college subjects.

The examinations are given at centers around the country. The two kinds of college-level examinations are a general and a subject examination. The five general-level examinations include English composition, mathematics, natural sciences, social sciences, and humanities. The forty-one college-level subject examinations are considered as final course examinations. Fees are paid by students when registering for these examinations.

LIBRARIES AS LEARNING CENTERS

Librarians recognize the needs of adults with a fourth- through eighth-grade education but have found it difficult to provide appropriate materials and adequate staff to interpret the materials. In comparison, it is relatively easy to provide service and materials at the ninth- through twelfth-grade levels, even fourth through eighth grades. As more basic education materials have become available and knowledge of the library's capability for participating in the program has grown, more libraries are providing services and materials to various ABE programs. Although the formal school is the more usual setting for ABE classes, learning resources centers and libraries provide an alternative environment and way of learning that can be beneficial and effective.

A literacy program in a library environment:

Provides an alternative way for learning outside the school setting. It is less formal, has no matriculation, and has no required pre-registration qualifications. It is not a structured adaptation of the educational system; and, frequently, it is less threatening to the participant than a formal school environment.

Provides a choice of places to learn that will help to meet the learners' requirements and desires. Because of previous failure in a school situation, some adults may not want to go back to a school building.

Is more community-oriented, and is sometimes closer to the geographic area or the housing situation where a literacy program is needed.

Is not bound by the limitations of an age group, the pace of others, or the pace of the teacher, and the learners can progress at their own pace.

Is not deterring because of physical facilities, such as small desks and lockers built for children.

References

Appalachian Adult Education Center. *The Interrelating of Library and Adult Education Services for Disadvantaged Adults.* Annual Report 1973, Vol. 1-2. Washington, D.C.: United States Department of Health, Education, and Welfare, Office of Education, 1973.

Greenberg, Bradley S., and Dervin, Brenda. *Use of the Mass Media by the Urban Poor.* New York: Praeger, 1970.

McClusky, Howard Y. "An Approach to a Differential Psychology of the Adult Potential" in Malcolm Knowles. *The Adult Learner: A Neglected Species.* Houston: Gulf Publishing Co., 1973.

Parker, Ronald K., Sibbison, Virginia H., Steiner, Karl W., and others. *A Multisite Evaluation of Reading Is Fundamental: Technical Report.* Report No. Case-16-75. New York: Center for Advanced Study in Education, Graduate School and University Center, City University of New York, 1975.

Warner, Edward S., Murray, Ann D., and Palmour, Vernon E. *Information Needs of Urban Residents.* Prepared for Regional Planning Council, Baltimore, Maryland, and Westat, Inc., Rockville, Maryland. Washington, D.C.: United States Department of Health, Education, and Welfare, Office of Education, 1973.

7
Profiles of
Selected Client Groups

Within the diverse population of the United States, it is possible to differentiate various client groups with similar and distinguishing characteristics and literacy needs and to describe various responses by libraries to the literacy needs of these groups. The following groups selected for review represent large populations that are classified in the context of this manual and are listed as follows:

The independent learner
The ABE learner-client
The early childhood group
The student in higher education
Bilingual and bicultural clients
The imprisoned and incarcerated client.

The profiles present information about the client or client groups in relation to such characteristics as: sex, age, ethnic and cultural background, language, place of residence, moving, leisure, income, health, attitudes and values, experience, schooling, and literacy abilities and needs. Information about the libraries' responses include: collaborative agency arrangements, services, staff, staff development and training, material resources, equipment and facilities, funding, and information references. See "Clientele Assessment ... Checklist" and "Program Profile Outline" in appendix 1.

THE INDEPENDENT LEARNER

More and more people are combining schooling and work, are engaged in part-time and full-time education and training, are preparing for new careers, and are seeking to educate themselves in ways that enhance their lives and result in a desired action. They help one another and turn to teachers and librarians—mentors or facilitators—who can link them to resources and assist in clarification of objectives and problems.

The process of planning and guiding the learner is the same whether the learner is somebody else or oneself. Alan Knox terms this process the "mentor role." This approach to self-directed or assisted independent learning consists of five interrelated components: needs, setting, objectives, activities, and evaluation. (See figure 5.)

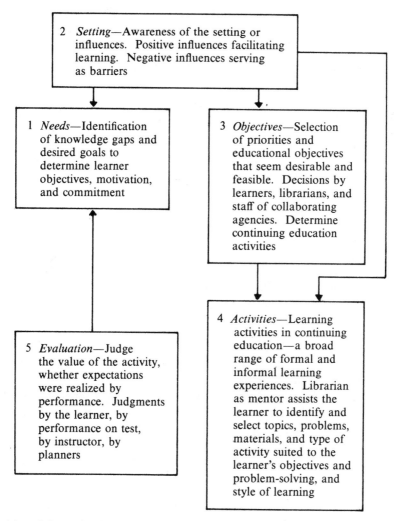

Adapted from Alan B. Knox, "Helping Adults to Learn"—Mimeographed paper, June 1974.

Fig. 5. Components of Self-Directed or Assisted Independent Study

The application of this process can assist librarians in the advisory role, which requires interaction of each component (this is not a step-by-step procedure), and also in planning and administering learning centers. Libraries and librarians can help the adult learner by providing the information and encouragement to learn and by support of existing motivation through the provision of promotion informational leaflets, brochures, radio and television announcements, and personal contacts. They can remove obstacles by providing information about continuing education activities, developing instructional situations, and personal advisory service. They can provide supportive environments with pleasant atmospheres, appropriate physical facilities and few regulations, and opportunities for studying and practicing what is learned. It is important that curriculum designs and methods and learning environments fit the learner's life-style.

An emerging role moves from mentor to educational broker. Such a role places the librarian in the role of middleman or woman acting as an educational consultant.

Credentials are an important part of today's society. Persons without the customary credentials—certificates, diplomas, and degrees—are at a disadvantage vocationally, economically, and socially. Reliance upon formal education for acceptance into the world of work has been unjust to millions of workers who are less educated and to potential workers who have the need, the desire, and the basic competence to perform useful work. The means of acquiring or continuing education from whatever point formal education is interrupted becomes the basis for the concept of continuing education. Alternative opportunities for completing elementary and secondary school, getting the necessary vocational training, and continuing into higher education are appearing. More options are open now to people whatever their needs and capacities, whether they are poor, indigent, or handicapped.

For the many adults of all ages who are studying, wish to study, or would study independently of a formal education plan, libraries can be learning centers—the community intelligence center—where the adults' learning and information needs can be met. The library's services for the independent learner include: an analysis of needs, objectives, and background problems; diagnosis; a study plan; advice and counsel on learning activities; provision of materials from library and community resources; some evaluation feedback; and possibly follow-up activities. The determination of objectives, the study plan, and the selection of materials and activities are arrived at through mutual decisions between learner and librarian. Final responsibility must be with the learner.

The type of library and type of institution involved in developing such services depends on the nature and level of the learning that is taking place. The independent learner may be working for credits in secondary school or college courses, or may be interested in self-improvement or in gaining a practical skill and knowledge in a specific field. At the same time the learner will need or want to acquire or improve the qualifying literacy skills. Several programs have evolved to meet these needs. In some respects they have been formalized, but they are less structured and have fewer rigid procedures than the regular course curricula. Particularly valuable to the independent learner is flexible time. Days, hours, and locations are no longer fixed or dependent on the convenience of others. Major programs are General Educational Development (GED), the College-Level Examination Program (CLEP), and the Open University External Degree Program. Libraries must work closely with the academic agencies. In most situations, agreements that are defined in writing and agreed upon by all involved are essential.

In the Library Project Profile Reports (appendix 3), Jean Brooks, director of the 3D Library Learning Center Project at the Dallas Public Library, on the basis of her experience, concludes that "coordinative action can take place between institutions, but underlying service philosophies are often difficult to mesh into a new kind of service unit, outside the parent agency. Each agency gives some in order to coalesce with the others, but unless all are willing to make changes, coordinative action is not successful." She further states that "the resource pooling is excitedly valid when the educational agency is willing to move out of its traditional institutional roles in creation of a new learning mode."

Characteristics

As individuality is paramount, a profile of the independent or self-directed learner is difficult to draw up. Some general characteristics may be listed:

Adult men and women of all ages engage in independent learning, but the trend may be toward younger and older learners.

They are individuals who are improving their literacy skills to meet the requirements of their learning objectives and of the subjects that are studied.

They are likely to be persons with elementary school (up to eighth grade) education.

They are not enrolled in secondary or high school or college.

Their study project is not designed or controlled by a formal educational situation.

Their financial resources are apt to be limited, and they may need scholarship support.

They are apt to be highly motivated, desirous of finding alternative ways for continuing education, and they will want to work at their own pace.

They may need encouragement and sustained guidance and support because of past failures, disappointments, and fears. Some may be described as "turned off" and "fed up."

The Library's Response

Collaborative Agency Arrangements

Collaborative agency arrangements, formal and nonformal, that link multiple community education resources can be developed. Collaborative agreements make possible the sharing of responsibilities and of the community's education resources. The various agencies to be linked may include local libraries; community schools; high schools, colleges, and universities; the Adult Basic Education program, including General Educational Development (high school diploma credential); the Department of Health, Education, and Welfare; the Commission on Community Relations; state libraries; city, county, and town commissions; business and industry.

Staff

The staff for adult learner programs may include: director of library, director of project, coordinator (of a special service unit), regional and unit heads, learner consultants, coordinator of volunteers, community recruiter, and volunteers.

Staff Responsibilities

The staff has the responsibility to:

Carry out an assessment of the community.

Identify collaborative agencies, such as industry, business, vocational schools, or community schools.

Identify, by contact, points and agencies where self-directed or independent study would be acceptable.

Search out and identify sources for records giving information about learners.

Encourage and possibly support research in the field of adult self-directed learning.

Train staff in interviewing, guidance, advisory, diagnostic, and recruiting techniques.

Identify and provide the kind of facilities and media equipment needed to aid learners.

Recruit volunteers as staff; recruit participants.

Assess resource needs in the library system and in other agencies.

Plan and produce materials when necessary.

Conduct a public relations campaign.

Administer study and learning resource centers with print, audio, and visual, including video, materials.

Staff Development and Training

Librarians will need to know or learn:

Curriculum requirements and content.
Reading guidance techniques.
Roles of the learners' adviser.
Materials appropriate for courses in high schools, colleges, and vocational schools.
How to evaluate readability levels of materials.
How to diagnose the client's abilities and reading level.

Material Resources

The entire collection of the library may be drawn upon to:

Acquire, in quantity, multilevel learning materials.
Develop materials collections of consumable workbooks, tape/print kits, cassettes, flash cards, signs, and other aids at reading levels from elementary through college.
Develop basic bibliographies for study of a particular subject, area, or topic.
Develop study plans for general or individualized use.
Develop and maintain a referral file.
Develop and maintain an inventory of information sources.
Suggest appropriate authors and titles.
Use instruments for diagnosis of client's abilities.

Funding and Budgeting

Funding for independent learner programs may include:

Allocations from the library budget.
Donations and gifts.
Outside sources, such as state and federal programs, ABE and Right to Read, Library Services and Construction Act.
Supportive funds and services shared by collaborative agencies.
Funds from business and industry.

Suggested Reading

Ahrendt, Kenneth. *Community College Reading Programs.* Newark, Del.: International Reading Association, 1975.

Brooks, Jean S., and Reich, David L. *The Public Library in Non-Traditional Education.* Homewood, Ill.: ETC Publications, 1974.

Mavor, Anne S., Toro, José Orlando, and DeProspero, Ernest R. *Final Report. The Role of the Public Libraries in Adult Independent Learning.* 2 vols. New York: College Entrance Examination, 1976.

Monroe, Margaret E., "A Conceptual Framework for the Public Library as a Community Learning Center for Independent Study," *Library Quarterly* 46, no. 1 (1976): 54–61.

Program Summaries of the Participating Project Libraries. New York: Office of Library Independent Study and Guidance Projects, College Entrance Examination Board, 1974.

The Role of Public Libraries in Supporting Adult Independent Learning: An Interim Assessment. New York: Office of Library Independent Study and Guidance Projects, College Entrance Examination Board, 1974.

Trivett, David A. *Academic Credit for Prior Off-Campus Learning.* ERIC/Higher Education Research Report, no. 2. Washington, D.C.: American Association for Higher Education, 1975.

THE ABE LEARNER-CLIENT

This profile is based primarily on the reports of the Adult Basic Education Program (ABE) listed in the References at the end of this chapter.

Characteristics

Sex

More women than men have enrolled in ABE programs. In 1971, 56 percent were women, 44 percent men; that is, there are 11 women to every 9 men, although there are more men in the total potential ABE group.

Age

Learners span all age groups. During the period 1966 to 1971, the 18-24 age group of ABE enrollees gradually increased. By 1971 this group was predominant; one in four was 25 to 34, and one in five 35 to 44 years of age.

Ethnic and Cultural Background

Any ethnic group may be represented, but blacks (32 percent), Latinos, and those newly arrived in the United States are represented more heavily in the total ABE group. Over 50 percent of ABE enrollees have been white.

Language

A primary language other than standard English is one of the most common characteristics of the ABE learner.

Many students speak either a dialect or another native language.

Approximately 9 percent of the ABE students sampled in one
longitudinal study spoke Spanish most often in their homes.
Speakers of other languages among immigrant groups include Asian-
Americans, Europeans, and others.

Geographic Residence/Location

ABE learner-clients are found in all geographic areas but are concentrated particularly in urban areas; in the rural South and West; in
Appalachia; and in institutions, such as correctional institutions and
those for the handicapped.

Migration and Immigration

Migration and immigration into new cultural settings is a common
factor among the groups represented in the ABE population.

Work or Occupation

ABE learner-clients represent a variety of occupations, but usually the
lack of literacy skills restricts them to manual-type jobs, such as those
performed by household workers, farm laborers, service workers, or
factory workers. Some are unemployed, particularly among the undereducated; a few are on public assistance; a majority are urban residents.

Leisure or Free Time

Many have little free time because of work and family responsibilities.
Interests may be keen in a variety of areas—visiting, sports, music,
church involvement, social activities, gardening.

Dependency and Income

In 1970 ABE enrollment indicated that about 12 percent of ABE
students had public welfare assistance and 75 percent had an income of
less than $5,000. Potential ABE groups are found among the indigent,
the temporarily unemployed, the physically disabled, displaced persons,
and others who lack literacy skills to retrain for jobs.

Health

People in the ABE population often have health problems. They are
improperly nourished, have had poor or no dental care, are in need of
proper eye corrections, have a high incidence of job-related accidents,
have frequent illnesses, and often show signs of fatigue.

Attitudes and Values toward Learning and the Library

Many ABE students are skeptical of "book learning" and of those
who are seeking to "help" them. Some try to hide their literacy

inadequacies; some have surmounted the literate world requirements. Some have had distasteful experiences with school, teachers, or other authorities, and with books and classes. Some are highly motivated because of a desire for personal and vocational improvement, while others are extremely eager to learn and seize the opportunity to compensate and to acquire literacy skills of which they have been deprived. Still others are reluctant to be in the position of learner, and are learner-clients only because of outside pressure from family or employers.

Experience
To many ABE students the common-sense knowledge that they have acquired through living is a great source of pride.

Many have backgrounds rich in interesting experiences that can be drawn upon to expand their literacy skills.

Some have an exceptional practical knowledge of various subjects.

Some have developed abilities such as powers of observation, acute memory, and oral skills that are independent of literacy skills, to compensate for their inability to comprehend and react to the written word.

Many rely on the visual and auditory communications of others and on television and radio for information and experience.

Others have had a poverty of experience because of isolation, deprivation, failures, and lack of opportunities.

Some have not traveled beyond their own plot of ground, farm, town, city block, or neighborhood.

Some are handicapped by a short attention span, a multiplicity of life problems, and overwork.

Schooling
Many are out of school as "dropouts" or "pushouts."

Others have had limited schooling because of the immediate necessity of earning a living.

Still others attended poor schools and had no access to quality education.

For some, school attendance lacked continuity, or they were dropping out mentally while still in school.

Others have been "passed along" without attaining the necessary literacy skills because of poor testing, lack of individualized opportunities, irrelevant materials, indifference, discriminatory attitudes and practices, and school systems that offered inadequate education to their students because of lack of funds or other problems.

Literacy Abilities and Needs

In general, ABE students function with difficulty at one of the four levels defined by Kohl (p. 16); or is less proficient at the APL functional performance levels (p. 20); or is below the grade level of schooling; or fails to meet job literacy levels as defined by HumRRO research (p. 21).

ABE learner-clients, in gaining literacy skills:

Develop skills of looking and listening.

Decode words (symbols) and learn word meanings.

Develop the ability to conceptualize and comprehend.

Develop the ability to think, reason, interpret, and assimilate.

Develop a multitude of skills, from basic "survival" needs such as learning letters of the alphabet and digits, learning to sign their names, and reading safety and directional signs, to the skills and subject knowledge needed for employment and for enrichment of personal life.

Demonstrate that literacy is a relevant part of their lives by production of student-tutor materials and selection of interesting, challenging materials in all types of formats.

Clarify their objectives and take part in the choice and adaptation of material in relation to occupational knowledge, consumer economics, government and law, health, and community resources.

Find ways by which the skills of listening, reading, problem-solving computation, and writing can be related and integrated within subject knowledge areas.

Assess and adapt at frequent intervals.

Find a model. The librarian can become a personal model by actively participating in all levels of learning experiences.

The Library's Response

Collaborative Agency Arrangements

The library should make collaborative agency arrangements in relation to:

Sharing evaluation and selection of reading materials.

Acquiring and organizing the materials collection.

Sharing personnel and other resources.

Sharing administrative and training functions.

Providing space, such as meeting or work places.

Recruiting, identifying, and referring potential clients.

Cosponsoring the literacy program.

Promoting and publicizing literacy services.

Literacy programs with which the library may collaborate (dependent on local situation) are ABE, Right to Read, Literacy Volunteers, Laubach, Volunteer Tutoring Centers and World Education.

Other relevant community agencies are social service, public assistance, welfare; adult education and vocational schools; Red Cross, family counseling, churches, clubs and organizations, civic groups, the Junior League, or Ys.

Services

Adults, wherever they may be, regardless of their level of literacy skills, have the right to quality library service. The client's needs, objectives, and abilities are a prime concern.

Libraries and other collaborating agencies and individuals in the community should explore and implement their complementary roles so that the strengths of all may be utilized, resources used to the greatest extent, and unnecessary duplication or fragmentation of those resources eliminated.

All types of library services contribute to the literacy effort. The library can provide the background for literacy by creating an inviting, acceptable place where clients are introduced to a multimedia communication environment to which they can respond in terms of their own interests and needs. Direct services to ABE learners or to the staffs of the literacy program or agency that serve the learner, can:

Provide an atmosphere of warmth and acceptance.

Acquire, organize, and process materials that are appropriate, useful, and enjoyable.

Select a materials collection with ABE interests, needs, and literacy levels, coping skills, subject areas, and ABE and GED courses in mind.

Make these materials visible through displays, bulletin boards, group activities, or personal discussion, either at the library itself or on the sidewalks or at storefronts, churches, or housing sites, via bookmobile, or through visits to the ABE class.

Provide an information directory.

Recruit potential clients and, where necessary, transport them by bus, van, car, or boat.

Invite every ABE learner and other family members to join the library by offering them library cards or obtaining their name and address, as is the practice in some library systems.

Assist learners, whenever possible and appropriate, to clarify and define problems and questions, and have information and resources to aid them. Librarians will use various ways, such as personal conversation, consultation, or interviews, to help the learner identify needs and goals, explore alternative solutions, and search for useful information.

Diagnose reading abilities and assist the client to clarify problem learning areas.

Provide guidance, interpret materials, and outline study plans to provide the learner with choices.

Develop profiles of the learner's characteristics and abilities, needs and interests, goals and objectives to assist in matching materials to needs. (See appendix 1, "Adult Learner Profile," page 145.)

Offer home instruction, individually prescribed instruction study plans, reading programs, bibliographies, and mediaographies as needed.

Provide orientation visits of the ABE class to the library, and periodic follow-up visits.

Collect information about ABE programs in the community so that referral opportunities can be offered.

Act as a resource for information and referral in such areas as health, legal rights, consumer information, family counseling, or recreation possibilities.

Provide space for individuals, classes, and groups.

Provide actual tutoring or class teaching.

Staff

Personnel within the library may be one or all of the following:

Director of the library or the literacy service
Literacy librarians
Coordinators of adult, young adult, and children's services in a library system
Community liaison librarians
Reading specialists.

Personnel from outside the library may be:

Teachers and administrators of literacy programs
Community advisers
Representatives from other agencies, such as social workers, or community advocate worker
Volunteers
Reading specialists.

Staff Responsibilities

Staff responsibilities are various and many. They will:

Establish cooperative and collaborative arrangements with other literacy programs in agencies or organizations.
Advise teachers and administrators of literacy programs.

Bring to the attention of teachers and administrators of literacy programs, as well as to students in those programs, the services of the library.

Demonstrate by active and responsible professional activity the knowledge, resources, and skills librarians can use in service to literacy programs and teachers as well as for the ABE client.

Assess community ABE needs and interests in cooperation with other agencies.

Identify and recruit ABE students.

Plan literacy programs and services with other agencies and literacy organizations.

Develop with other agencies grant proposals for collaboration and support of literacy programs.

Develop literacy collections and identify and promote materials throughout the total collection.

Locate, evaluate, and select instructional and supplementary materials in media other than print.

Obtain approval, support, and commitment for literacy services.

Advise and counsel ABE participants.

Demonstrate the values of reading and how to develop a home library at varying levels of cost.

Work with an entire family unit in assessing needs and providing special materials.

Provide home delivery services in reading instruction and materials.

Conduct group programs and activities, such as reading aloud, discussion, or book talks at class sessions or on radio or television.

Recruit adult men and women who may qualify as volunteers from among older people and ABE graduates for leadership roles, teaching, supervising, and doing office work.

Teach and tutor if necessary and desired.

Staff Development and Training

Staff members will draw on the professional knowledge and experience already acquired. At the same time some specific skills may need to be learned to meet unique or specific demands of the literacy effort. Staff development training programs, library school courses, university courses, and workshops and institutes will be sources of continuing education. Librarians need to know or learn how to:

Assess the community and library resources, as well as other agency resources.

Judge needs and interests of ABE clientele, either as literacy program participants or individually.

Gain specific knowledge of reading development.

Determine the characteristics of ABE learners.

Diagnose and judge a client's reading abilities.

Judge materials for readability and suitable content, and match them to the needs and abilities of clients.

Develop interpersonal skills and relationships.

Develop in-depth knowledge of material resources accessible in the library and available within the interlibrary loan system.

Produce and create materials.

Coordinate library resources with curriculum demands.

Develop their own qualifications through continuing and independent study.

Material Resources

Materials are necessary for reading readiness development and for each developmental stage in ABE learning; tutor-learner materials based on the learner's own experiences are also needed. For example, at the beginning level (grade 0–4), students need to learn basic skills —listening, speaking, and reading recognition of letters, digits, sight words, consonant blends, vowel patterns, structural analysis of endings and prefixes, and distinguishing small from capital letters.

Materials needed for such study include: workbooks, magazines for cutout pictures, flash cards, pamphlets and brochures relating to daily-life skills (coping), newspaper articles, mail-order house catalogs, driving directions, menus, large-type books, books of adult interest at beginning levels, maps, signs, and posters. The best collection begins with simple, everyday "real world" materials. Suitable materials at other levels of ABE study can be identified by reading interest and readability or grade level. (See appendix 1, " 'Real World' Materials," page 146.)

A few publications containing information on selection and acquisition of materials are:

Bayley, Linda, Kearl, Biruta Celmins, and Schexnaydie, Linda. *ABE: Guide to Library Materials.* Austin: University of Texas Division of Extension, 1975.

Gotsick, Priscilla, Moore, Sharon, Cotner, Susan, and Flanery, Jean, comps. *Information for Everyday Survival.* Chicago: American Library Association, 1976.

Lyman, Helen Huguenor. *Library Materials in Service to the Adult New Reader.* Second printing. Chicago: American Library Association, 1974.

———. *MAC Checklist: Evaluation Booklet with Instructions.* 20 to a kit. Elgin, Ill.: Dome Press (in preparation).

Available from Dome Press, 1169 Logan Avenue, Elgin, Illinois 60120.

————. *Reading and the Adult New Reader.* Chicago: American Library Association, 1976.

MacDonald, Barbara J. *Bibliography of Reading Materials for Basic Reading.* Syracuse, N.Y.: Literacy Volunteers of America [1976].

National Multimedia Center for Adult Basic Education. *Abstracts.* Upper Montclair, N.J.: Adult Continuing Education Center, Montclair State College.

A bibliography in the form of abstracts, on 5 × 8 cards. The abstracts contain: title, author, source, date, curricular information, reading level (Fry), format, and comment. Available from the Center, 14 Normal Avenue, Upper Montclair, New Jersey 07043.

Palmer, Julia Reed. *Read for Your Life.* Metuchen, N.J.: Scarecrow Press, 1974.

Pivot. Newsletter of the Reader Development Program, Free Library of Philadelphia.

Available from the Library.

Reader Development Bibliography. Compiled by the Free Library of Philadelphia. Syracuse, N.Y.: New Readers Press [1976].

RIF's Guide to Book Selection, 1973. Washington, D.C.: Smithsonian Institution, 1973.

Usual review sources, such as *Publishers Weekly, Weekly Review, Library Journal, Choice, Previews, School Library Journal.*

Newsletters and publications of national associations, such as those listed below, are helpful.

Adult Education Association, 810 Eighteenth Street, N.W., Washington, D.C. 20006.

American Library Association, 50 East Huron Street, Chicago, Illinois 60611.

International Reading Association, 6 Tyre Avenue, Newark, Delaware 19711.

National Association for Public Continuing and Adult Education (NAPCAE) 1201 Sixteenth Street, N.W., Washington, D.C. 20036.

Teachers of English to Speakers of Other Languages (TESOL), School of Language and Linguistics, Georgetown University, Washington, D.C. 20007.

For names and addresses of literacy and bilingual organizations, see the appendix, pages 151-55.

Other sources of information include:

Agencies and organizations that are part of the collaborative literacy effort in the local community or region

Educational Resources Information Center (ERIC)

The ERIC network encompasses a decentralized group of sixteen Clearinghouses located at universities or with professional educational associations across the country. These Clearinghouses acquire, select, index, and abstract documents and prepare bibliographies and summaries which are announced and disseminated through *Resources in Education (RIE)*, as of January 1975 (formerly *Research in Education)*. Clearinghouses and their addresses are listed in *RIE* and may be obtained from U.S. Department of Health, Education and Welfare/National Institute of Education. Washington, D.C. 20208.

Library and adult basic education bibliographies

A library's entire collection and current acquisitions

Materials at library system media centers, paperback distributors, wholesalers' or jobbers' headquarters

Publishers' catalogs and selected lists (See Linda Bayley's *ABE: Guide to Library Materials* for "Directory of Publishers and Producers" which includes addresses)

Retail outlets where books and magazines are sold.

Equipment and Facilities

Media Equipment

Pads, pencils, pens; reading laboratory; programmed learning cassette study equipment, 16mm filmstrips, Super 8mm projector, video monitors, tape and disc players, cassettes for recording, recording equipment, slides and carousels, Caramate projector, newsprint paper, tachistoscope, Language Master Visualtek or other TV monitor system for magnification of print.

Meeting Facilities

Library meeting rooms and auditorium, study carrels, vans, bookmobiles, homes, schools, churches, community centers, union halls, industrial plants, business meeting rooms, Ys, private and secular clubs, schools and college classrooms, storefronts.

Delivery Facilities

Mail, bookmobiles, vans, video, television, radio, closed-circuit television, rotating depository sites, or personal delivery through the teacher, tutor, volunteer, aide, or librarian.

Funding

Funds may come from:

Allocations from the library budget.

Special grants for literacy programs, which may be solicited from civic groups, business and industry, churches, or private citizens who are interested in supporting the literacy effort. A want list might be developed and made known to the community.

Local and civic groups—sororities and fraternities, small businesses, local industries.

Federal and state funded programs, which are administered through state and local governments. (See appendix 2, "Federal and State Funding," page 150.)

THE EARLY CHILDHOOD GROUP

Characteristics

Age

This group includes preschool and primary-age children aged 0–5 years. These are crucial years, years of discovery. In the first five years of life a child makes greater physical and intellectual progress than during any other five-year period.

Location

Any geographic area and in any ethnic or cultural group.

Schooling

Varies from none to formal, and may also include church school groups or institutional agencies such as hospitals and shelters.

Income

Parents vary from the unemployed to the more affluent income groups. Economic dependency may be great.

Ethnic and Cultural Backgrounds

These children have various ethnic and cultural backgrounds. Many know only a language other than English or have little language facility. The attitudes and values, language, and life-style in the family or community group are paramount factors in a child's experience and future learning. Primary factors influencing the preschool child's literacy development are the home environment, work and leisure time in the family, and moving or migration of the family.

There are at least five million children in the United States who are unable to speak English fluently when they enter school. Most of these children are Mexican American, Puerto Rican American, American Indian, or belong to other well-established ethnic groups; many are native-born Americans who come from homes where English is not the dominant language. Their ability to communicate fluently in a language other than English becomes a severe handicap to their opportunity to learn when school policies and even state laws prevent them from speaking, listening to, or seeking explanations in, the medium of communication they understand best.

America's educationally neglected children frequently are described as deprived, with special education needs, and living in low-income areas. Many are from families with incomes at poverty level or with no income. Their parents have had little schooling. Many children are undernourished and without health care. They live in the poorest of housing units. A disproportionate number are said to be members of minority groups. Dr. Tony Carvajal, a professor of special education, said:

> The crux of the concern is the manner in which educators have
> very neatly categorized minorities as culturally deprived,
> disadvantaged, slow learners, mentally retarded and heaven
> knows what else, without evaluating with sufficient precision and
> accuracy the quality of the individuals doing the teaching. . . .
> In short, we would be far safer to consider the above-mentioned
> population educationally neglected. Yes, it has been through
> sheer negligence, irresponsibility, and lack of genuine concern (on
> the part of the educators) that so many minorities are without the
> power to be.*

The migrant child is almost invisible, ignored and neglected. (These characteristics, descriptive of migrant life, are unfortunately applicable to other groups.) The National Advisory Council on the Education of Disadvantaged Children accurately describes the profile of the migrant child.

> The migrant child is constantly moving; he has no continuity in
> his education, or his life in general. . . . He is out of the main-
> stream of any stable society and has few bases for security.
> His parents are in the fields all day, and in the formative years
> and after, he is either there, working with them, or at
> home babysitting with younger children. . . . There is certainly
> little opportunity for intellectual development in the fields,
> working, or waiting while the mother and father work.
> Most of the migrants are Spanish-speaking, and they are in
> desperate need of teachers who are able to communicate and

* Dr. Tony Carvajal, "The Mulberry Bush," presented before the American Association for Mental Deficiency at Billings, Montana, February 1973, in United States National Advisory Council on the Education of Disadvantaged Children, *America's Educationally Neglected: A Program Report on Compensatory Education* . . . (Washington, D.C.: The Council, 1973), p. 7.

relate to them in Spanish as well as in English. They need day care. . . . [They need] transportation to [education] facilities . . . at other hours than . . . those between 8 a.m. and 3 p.m. The learning needs of a migrant child are dependent on a whole host of supportive services. . . .

Migrant labor is used in 47 of the 50 States, and most of these children will live for various periods of each school year in two or more States. . . . If educational continuity in the migrant child's program is to be achieved, there must be regional and interstate cooperation and planning.

Many other children need service, whether migrant or otherwise; for them many barriers to learning exist. Negative attitudes and prejudices, lack of child care, lack of transportation, cultural constraints, unhappy experiences, lack of parental support and understanding, and fear are major obstacles. *A primary need of many such children is a parent who has become literate.* In many instances, their whole world will change when the parent attains literacy, particularly in Native American, Mexican American, and Puerto Rican families where family members are so close to one another.

Literacy Needs

In these early years when curiosity and interest are intense, the child responds to stimulating, imaginative ideas. Cultural, educational, and literary stimulation is crucial. The child needs:

The stimuli of visual and audible materials as well as verbal human communications

Opportunities to experience print medium and thus to counteract or supplement the pervasive influence of television

An environment of books, pictures, magazines, and toys

Beneficial catch-up programs to overcome deprivation and negative experiences

To learn to relate spoken words to print symbols

Beginning literacy skills and competency level that are essential in developing the will to read, attitudes toward reading, and the various aspects of reading readiness before formal education begins

The involvement and assistance of the parent in the role of guide and model and the creation of a home environment conducive to the child's literacy development

Exposure, if appropriate, to bilingual-bicultural education in which the vernacular is not standard English.

When schools discourage the use of languages other than English and use culturally biased testing and evaluation devices, the result is the improper classification of non-English-speaking children and often of children of the black population. They are improperly classified as retarded. They often suffer irreparable damage to self. Such attitudes by teachers and librarians are destructive. Today a new concern and greater understanding of the effects of such policies is strengthening the effort toward constructive, life-giving philosophy and more precise, fair tests.

The Library's Response
Philosophy of Service
The library must:

Provide service to all preschool and primary-age children.

Assist in providing appropriate experiences and reading environment for developing skills, knowledge, and attitudes necessary for success in schools or in the use of libraries.

Have concern for the social and intellectual growth of the child.

Take the library to the child, and where possible to the parents and then to the child.

Create a media center library that is an innovative, free place.

Seek collaborative efforts between children's librarians in school or instructional media centers and those in public libraries to serve the child and family.

The early childhood group of preschool and primary-school age children needs the unique services both the public library and the public school media center can contribute. The development of collaborative services is an opportunity to establish a pattern of communication and cooperate at the administrative and practicing levels. The services that can and should be developed cooperatively could be identified and planned by librarians in leadership positions, by reading specialists, by parents, by other agency representatives, and by teachers. In this way a specific program for each community would emerge. Programs would be built on specific strengths within each institution and with mutual supportive assistance where weaknesses occur. It is an opportunity for librarians in the same community, and for librarians and teachers, to become acquainted professionally and personally. In such a way they can serve the child more effectively.

There is impressive evidence that learning is crucial between the formative years of one and twelve. It is at these ages that reading initially is taught. Reading readiness is essential for the preschooler and, if at this time successful programs are provided, it is conceivable that children will not later reach their frustration level in school and become dropouts or adult illiterates.

Equally important is the concept of parenting that sees the parent and home environment as a most important force in getting the child prepared for reading readiness. It is a function shared by all individuals and organizations concerned with the nurturing of the child's development. Unfortunately, many children do not have interested families or parents. As ALA Literary Manual Project Resource Board member Kathryn Wright, of the District of Columbia public library system, pointed out:

> In this ghetto area branch, we see very few parents.
> Small children, age six months to three years, are brought to
> the library by siblings or cousins, usually only a year or two
> older. The parents we see are either advantaged educationally
> or economically, or very highly motivated. The library is far
> too often regarded as a "babysitter." Though there are many
> helpful suggestions for reaching the parent, the library is one not
> terribly attractive agency competing for the free time of the
> over-burdened parent.

Head Start, church-related, public, and private day care centers are proliferating all over the country. These are centers that the library should reach. There are other children not in Head Start and not in the library—the children of the alienated poor. They are quiet. They respond slowly. They need to be taught to speak and to react. They live in old houses, in crowded rooms, on narrow streets; they move around the corner, and may not know their own addresses. Many do not know their family names or their own names. Their brothers and sisters are gang members and school dropouts; some are in Youth Corps, working for a high school diploma. Some of their parents are alcoholics, drug addicts, or retarded, but most are only very poor. They may not know how to help themselves, find jobs, feed their families, and fight disease. They are often afraid. Others are learning how to take care of the sick, feed their families, raise their children, and work.

Collaborative Agency Arrangements
A few of the agencies and organizations with which the library should work are:

Home Start, Head Start, day care, cradle centers, child/parent centers, Reading Is Fundamental (RIF), Right to Read (R-2-R), nursery schools, and church centers
Public assistance and social services, such as Aid to Dependent Children (ADC)

Elementary schools, including community school programs and alternative schools

Recreational groups, such as Boy Scouts/Girl Scouts, 4-H clubs, departments of parks and recreation, museums, YMCA/YWCA, YWHA/YMHA, Parents without Partners, Northwest Rural Opportunity (NRO), Community Action Committee (CAC). State-supported programs exist for assisting minorities, handicapped citizens, parents, and others who are not enrolled in or reached by such organizations.

Collaboration may mean, according to the local situation, a variety of possibilities, such as joint planning, sharing funds for purchasing materials, and administration of the programs outside the library, by the library, or through a shared responsibility.

Types of Library Services

It is possible, with careful planning, to develop:

A media library to meet the changing interests of this youngest age group

A collection of picture books with and without words

A collection of nonprint materials

Field trips, visits to the park and the zoo, and bus trips to learn about the community and stimulate expression

Programs that provide opportunities for a variety of language, social, and creative experiences, such as storytelling, reading aloud, wall bulletin boards, window displays, exhibits, photography, radio and television programs, dramatics, music, dance, action stories, puppetry, and art.

Other services that the librarians may provide are:

Special attention and materials for children who are developing literacy abilities under severe handicaps

Development of advisory and counseling services for parents in relation to literacy matters and the child's developmental reading

Collaboration with other agencies whose services reach the parent, the child, or both

Assistance to parents and siblings to acquire skills for teaching and reading at home

Organization of parent/child workshops and concurrent programs for each

Provision of training programs for parents or others who work or live with children through videotaped story hours for parent viewing; courses in children's literature and how to choose and purchase materials for children; story hour workshops; films and demonstration programs; social hours

Administration of a home study program for the family with face-to-face assistance by volunteers and tutors

Provision of service to children without parents who are in broken homes and institutions.

Workshops conducted or cooperatively sponsored by librarians can be offered to parents, teachers, and group workers on principles for introducing picture books to children, on choosing books that will teach children concepts and that they will enjoy. One library held workshops where parents learned to make puzzles, reading games, puppets, and comic strips, which they then took home.

Libraries and other agencies can make cooperative efforts to serve Head Start groups, government-sponsored child development centers, and homebound children through collections of materials sent to them. Programs of stories, films, or puppet shows, taken to the centers, held in the library, or delivered over cable, radio, or video tape are not only entertainment but also mind expanders. Before one learns to read, one must have an oral or speaking vocabulary and a listening vocabulary. These types of programs can provide these skills so necessary to reading and writing.

Imaginative programs such as storytelling can strengthen auditory reception and give children a taste for folklore. Folklore and myth, tales from other cultures, are valuable both for ethnic appeal and cultural appreciation.

Film programs introduce appreciation for visual arts and creative activities as well as presenting pleasurable learning experiences.

Games and crafts and educational toys can aid in coordination and prepare for reading readiness.

Supplementary collections of materials for teachers and parents will assist educators in serving children and will provide the opportunity for librarians to interpret materials and advise in their use.

Staff Personnel

A team effort among staff and individuals in the community who are concerned with early childhood education is usually helpful. The team may include:

Public or media center school librarians
Parents, teachers, and administrators
City officials and welfare agency staffs
Volunteer aides—Youth Corps, older citizens, parents
Director who shares in all programs
Professional librarians

Clerical staff

Student teachers in early childhood education and students in library science.

Staff Responsibilities

Staff may have the responsibility to:

Assess community needs and interests.

Plan and carry out programs and activities; analyze data and match community need with the library's ability to respond; obtain approval, support, and commitment from relevant library administrators and representatives of such agencies, such as public assistance agencies, Home Start, Head Start, churches, and parent organizations.

Evaluate and select materials.

Develop children's collections.

Demonstrate ways parents may use books and library media resources.

Build a creative environment.

Establish a clear value system in which learning has an affective objective.

Staff Development and Training

Major characteristics needed are openness, friendliness, patience, compassion, love of children, an understanding of child development, and awareness and spontaneity to create interaction with children and parents. A range of knowledge and skills need to be acquired by children's librarians and others who work with the children, such as:

Knowledge of the psychology of each year of age

Knowledge of reading readiness competencies—talking, listening, identifying symbols, colors, and digits

Understanding of the developmental aspects of early childhood

Knowledge of aspects of childhood deprivation and developmental losses

Empathy with children as victims of fear, joblessness of parents, wretched overcrowded housing or rural isolated shacks, hunger, lack of clothing, parental desertion, child abuse, broken homes

Knowledge of substandard health and possible hearing and visual defects

Recognition of social discrimination due to negative attitudes toward the poor, ethnic group, and differences in language and life-style

Knowledge of specific materials for use in library stimulation, cultural enrichment, and learning experiences

Knowledge of library and community literacy programs related to the child and the parent

Knowledge of federal, state, and local laws affecting the child's welfare and development.

Material Resources

Resources to assist in the development of motor and perceptual skills and in language learning, as well as materials that cultivate the pleasure and enjoyment of learning and are used for enjoyment, are acquired in various subject areas and different formats. These resources may include:

Books of all kinds—poetry, fairy tales, science, stories about history, biographies

Paperbacks, pictures, large-print materials, activity records, music stories, songs

Toys, games, puzzles, animals

Puppets, tutorgrams, show'n'tell

Films

Dial a two-minute story

Art reproductions, slides, realia, paints, magic markers, crayons, easels, clay, homemade or homefound odds and ends, empty cartons.

Equipment and Facilities

Record players, projectors, scissors and paste, cameras, video porta-paks, blocks, autoharp, TV center for Sesame Street, Mr. Rogers cooking equipment, terrarium, aquarium, garden plot, pillows and hassocks, small chairs and tables, scraps of material; a media van and a bus for transportation; a space where cleanup is easy, movie screen, plain white wall, large display area for creative child-size cozy nooks, puppet stage, tape recorders, filmmaking equipment—all these may be used. It should be noted that a transportation facility adds major responsibilities for library boards and management in relation to liability, permission, and insurance.

Funding Sources

See appendix 2, "Federal and State Funding," page 150. Local gifts and foundation grants can also be sources.

Information References

Bell, Thelma, "Community Action—Action for Children," *Top of the News* 24, no. 2 (January 1968):190–97.

Cawthorne, Edythe O., "Toys and Games: The First Reading SJL Interviews," *School Library Journal* 21, no. 8 (April 1975):24–27.

Corrier, Mary Ann, "Early Childhood: Agencies, Organizations, and Periodicals," *Top of the News* 31, no. 1 (November 1974):60–62.

Fasick, Adele M., "Helping Children to Help Themselves Learn; Relevant Research," *Top of the News* 31, no. 1 (November 1974):73–79.

The Good Seed; Library Planning for Urban Disadvantaged Children Ages Three to Seven. Kalamazoo: Western Michigan University, 1970.

Granstrom, Jane, and Morris, Jacqueline. "Capsule Comments on Current Programs for Preschoolers," *Top of the News* 31, no. 1 (November 1974):55–59.

Greene, Ellin, "The Preschool Story Hour Today," *Top of the News* 31, no. 1 (November 1974):80–85.

Heins, Ethel, and Johnson, Ferne. "Start Early for an Early Start," *Top of the News* 31, no. 1 (November 1974):39–40.

Johnson, Ferne, "Planning a Parent/Child Workshop," *Top of the News* 31, no. 1 (November 1974):68–72.

———, ed. *Start Early for an Early Start.* Chicago: American Library Association, 1976.

Pierson, Donald E., and Yurchak, Mary Jane H., "Brookline Early Education Project: One Model for an Early Start," *Top of the News* 31, no. 1 (November 1974):41–48.

Sivulich, Kenneth G., and Sivulich, Sandra Stroner "Media Library for Preschoolers: A Service of the Erie Metropolitan Library," *Top of the News* 31, no. 1 (November 1974):49–54.

Thorndike, Robert L. *Reading Comprehension Education in Fifteen Countries: An Empirical Study.* New York: John Wiley & Sons, 1973.

Ward, Martha Coonfield. *Them Children: A Study in Language Learning.* New York: Holt, Rinehart & Winston, 1971.

A short, readable book filled with observations that illuminate the life-styles of preschool children from different social backgrounds. This study is of children in rural Louisiana who lack encouragement from adults when they start talking.

THE STUDENT IN HIGHER EDUCATION

The basic literacy skills are thought by many to be the mark of an educated person. They are prerequisites to achieving the purpose of a university education. However, national assessment reading studies and colleges and universities throughout the country find that the basic skills of entering freshmen have declined sharply since the early 1960s. Recent and widespread publicity in the national communication media about these declines and the judgments of many individual faculty members support this fact.

Recent reports by the Educational Testing Service and the American College Testing Program indicate declines in the verbal skills of prospective college students across the nation.   Studies by the National Assessment of Educational Progress reveal that the ability of 17-year-olds to write, as demonstrated by actual writing samples, has deteriorated over the last five years.   At the University of Wisconsin-Madison, as at other universities, clear-cut evidence shows that students' verbal skills are inadequate.   The student body now represents the entire population more broadly than it once did.   As a consequence, some students come with inadequate preparation and need to improve their literacy skills.   Their work indicates that their language skills are not adequate.   Students are sometimes aware of this need and seek outside assistance.   Reading, writing, and speaking skills are all in need of improvement.

A concerted effort within the colleges and universities has begun to make certain that every graduate has attained competency in language. Higher entrance requirements, new courses in composition, writing, and speaking, reading and writing laboratories, and other efforts are being considered or developed.

How much attention is given to the place of the library resources and the role of the library in this effort is unclear.   The literature contains almost nothing.   But it seems clear that the college and university libraries have an important supportive and developmental role to take. The librarian who knows what the library can do must initiate and volunteer services.   Undergraduate collections need to contain some basic adult education materials. Bibliographies, guides, and guidance in the use of materials can be provided by librarians who know subject content, readability levels, and interests.   The academic library is in a position to provide the same services and conduct literacy programs in collaboration with faculty in the same way as the media centers in secondary schools and public libraries in the community serve clients.

The educationally disadvantaged students in general are individuals who are lacking in the educational background and communication and study skills necessary for successful college work.   More often than not, they are members of various minority groups.   The needs of the educationally disadvantaged student have received little attention. Colleges and universities are only beginning to confront the problem. Academic libraries have not responded to the needs of their respective institutions' educationally disadvantaged students.

E. J. Josey, a New York State consultant to academic libraries and a leader among black librarians, defines the role of the academic library in serving the disadvantaged student.   He identifies four characteristics of an effective service program: staff members who demonstrate true empathy with the special needs of the students; the organization of a wide range of library resources; the implementation of innovative, action-oriented programs; and close and regular contact with the faculty who teach disadvantaged students. This contact with the faculty seems essential, but rarely is achieved.

Academic libraries, like public libaries, have a potential role that administrators, faculty, students, and librarians should be aware of and try to develop. If librarians are to meet their responsibilities to disadvantaged students, they must establish new priorities, aquire a sense of mission, and institute fresh and innovative services.

Such services require highly individualized and personal relationships among Educational Opportunity Program (EOP) students, faculty, and library staff. Librarians must be responsive to the intellectual needs of the students and able to cross not only departmental barriers but also racial and ethnic gaps. Special collections, guidance, and interpretation of reading and audiovisual materials must be developed. A regular, full-time librarian is needed. Collection development is improved by collaboration of faculty and librarians in selection and evaluation. The content of the materials should range from ethnic and cultural subjects to books that deal with study and literacy skills. Workbooks and textbooks may be necessary at the first stages of learning. Instruction in the use of the library and reference aids is required.

Even greater demands are indicated by the emerging radical change in student body from full-time to part-time. According to statistics cited in "Part-Time Students," part-time students are essentially different from full-time students. They are employed (three-fourths in the labor force), older, and with adult responsibilities. The part-time students have completed secondary education or are beyond the compulsory school attendance age. Recent reports on the part-time student indicate different types of motivations and behavioral patterns among this most recent majority. They continue their education for personal and family reasons, for occupational and professional goals, and for participation in public problem-solving programs.

In 1972 approximately half the students in collegiate institutions of higher education were part-time students. In two-year institutions and in graduate programs, the enrollments are increasing rapidly; in 1972 63.1 percent attended on a part-time basis. External degree programs, open university plans, the College - Level Examination Program, and non-residential degree programs recognize the right of persons of all ages to work toward self-fulfillment and credentials. They recognize the lack of access to traditional forms of higher education and the need to adapt to the learner. Programs and services must be adapted to include all ages, be flexible in length of time and course of study, and be available wherever the students are located. Funding support must be offered to needy students. The mobility of the population requires flexibility and opportunities for those who move and for those persons who are isolated from the general population and from institutions of higher education. Federal aid to students supports such programs.

Educational arrangements for the resources of learning become uppermost in the study and preparation necessary to quality in this nontraditional study method.

The implications for libraries are tremendous. Existing institutions, labor unions, vocational/technical schools, two-year colleges, four-year colleges, and universities will be involved. The library should be the center of such an educational system. Resources and materials for instruction and study may be even more necessary than in the traditional, more rigid system with full-time students. The part-time student clientele will need and use all library delivery systems and services.

Among the less advantaged part-time student group there is a need to learn how to learn, a need to have access to knowledge about learning opportunities and financial support, and to know how to use the opportunities for learning. Many mobile groups are in need of literacy instruction. They are potential clientele who must learn to read, to study, and to take advantage of the learning opportunities.

What better source for the general knowledge resources and specific course and curriculum topics is there than the library? Libraries must prepare for such service through collaborative programs among academic, school, and public libraries. Reading guidance, maximum use of resources, relevant and up-to-date subject collections, new policies and selection principles, and informed staff are necessary to meet these new needs and new student clientele.

BILINGUAL AND BICULTURAL CLIENTS

The United States has moved through three general phases in regard to the provision of non-English-language programs and collections.

From 1839 to 1880, non-English-language programs were available in both public and private schools. German-language schools flourished in the eastern United States, French-language schools in the Louisiana region, and Spanish-language schools in New Mexico after 1848. There were also many Scandinavian and some Dutch schools in the Midwest.

The development of bilingual schools occurred from about 1880 to 1917. During this period the first true bilingual schools developed in the United States. There were German-English bilingual schools in Cincinnati, Indianapolis, and Baltimore, as well as in many rural places. French-English schools developed in the New England area and continued in the Louisiana region. Numerous schools also developed for Eastern and Southern Europeans, such as Poles, Lithuanians, and Slovaks.

Between the two wars the first bilingual schools and programs for the Chinese and Japanese developed in Hawaii and on the West Coast. At the same time the massive migration of the Spanish-speaking people from Mexico and Latin America, coupled with the large indigenous Latino population of the Southwest, threatened to turn the formal school system by necessity into a bilingual system.

The third phase saw the gradual acculturation and the decrease of the European immigrant wave, which gradually eroded the position of bilingual and bicultural schools in the East and Midwest. The position of the large Spanish-speaking population in the Southwest and increasingly in the Midwest, however, did not improve in relation to the advance of bilingual schools and bilingual-bicultural materials provision through libraries and other institutions. The increasing isolation of the Spanish-speaking child in the public schools of the Southwest sparked a resurgence of concern by governmental agencies, as witnessed by the series of reports issued by the United States Commission on Civil Rights. The isolation of Spanish-speaking adults from the larger Anglo mainstream became a critical concern of adult educators and other professionals. A parallel situation developed with the recent influx of Vietnamese and other Southeast Asians.

By 1975 the United States Office of Education estimated that at least 5 million children currently in school needed special language programs. The number of adults in need of bilingual education programs can be conservatively estimated at twice that figure. Whether the individual be a child in a school or an adult participating in a basic adult education program, the need for current and relevant bilingual-bicultural materials must be met by schools and libraries.

In 1963 the Dade County School Board in Miami, Florida, began the rebirth of bilingual education with the opening of a completely bilingual program in grades one through three. This first program was directed at the large Cuban population. It was noted that the English-speaking pupils were learning a second language and the Spanish-speaking pupils were learning to read and write their native language. The need for both classroom and supplementary materials became immediately evident, and the libraries in the Miami region began searching for language and cultural materials that would reflect the historical and cultural backgrounds of the new Americans.

In 1965 Congress passed the Elementary and Secondary Education Act (ESEA), and in 1967 the Bilingual Education Act became Title VII, which was to open the door to full participation in society for millions of American schoolchildren from non-English-speaking homes. Title VII was conceived primarily to meet the needs of "children who come from environments where the dominant language is other than English." The beginning of Title VII adds an important and long-needed chapter to the story of educational opportunities for this nation of immigrants. By 1969 there were fifty-six bilingual education programs, and Spanish and English were the two languages used in about 90 percent of the projects funded. Other bilingual education programs have focused on Asian-Americans and a few isolated European-language groups in the United States.

Since the introduction of Title VII and the revitalization of bilingual education in the Southwest, libraries have sought to provide materials to the bilingual-bicultural individual. A permanent commitment to bilingual programs and collections is difficult for libraries, however, considering the lack of trained bilingual librarians available to help plan such programs. In 1976 there were fewer than 300 Spanish-speaking librarians throughout the United States and Puerto Rico, and even fewer Asian librarians with foreign-language abilities. A large number of trial and demonstration programs directed at non-English-speaking people, particularly Latinos, have been funded by outside sources, such as Library Services and Construction Act (LSCA) funds. To ensure that such efforts are incorporated into permanent ongoing programs, funds must be budgeted through local and library allocations.

Bilingual collections are an absolute necessity if the library plans to serve both the individual client and educational programs such as ABE and English-as-a-Second-Language (ESL). The adult student in these programs is often directed to the library for additional materials to supplement the often meager offerings of the classroom. It is necessary, therefore, to have bilingual materials in the library and to develop a staff with a bilingual background and, if possible, a bicultural background.

Bilingual collections and bilingual-bicultural librarians enrich the total community. Broadened understanding among various cultural and linguistic groups occurs when there are increasing opportunities for better communication.

Increased opportunities for many Americans to travel outside the United States and an increased awareness of the variety of linguistic groups that are a part of America's own heritage have brought about a new appreciation of the importance of verbal communication and the value of being bilingual or multilingual. The proximity of Puerto Rico, Mexico, and South and Central American countries to the United States and the area occupied by United States Latinos and Latinos from other countries has allowed the Spanish and English languages to move across national borders. The monolingual United States is discovering that the bilingual child or adult is a gifted person and is recognizing the rich cultural resources that other people and nations contribute.

Recent immigration movements to and within the United States represents one of the most massive language shifts in world history. In Illinois alone 141 different languages have been identified. The Spanish-surnamed population of Illinois has increased from 9 to 21 percent of various northern Illinois communities alone in the last two decades. In 1975 nearly 16 percent of the population spoke a native language other than English, especially Spanish, German, and Italian. By 1975 there were entire areas of Chicago where upwards of 75 percent of the neighborhood people spoke Spanish as their native tongue.

Federal and state governments have recognized the needs of non-English-speaking people, and libraries have tried to respond to those needs, but much is still to be done. In the case of Chicago alone, the existing programs that attempt to meet the need of the Spanish-speaking children are currently serving only 20,000 of the 48,000 Latino students. As bilingual and bicultural programs are developed and expanded for both children and adults, there is a parallel need for the expansion of library programs and services for bilingual-bicultural individuals. As the students in child and adult classes reach a higher level of fluency in both their native languages and English, the libraries must increase and improve the quality of resources and services to these new patrons.

An example of a response to an immediate and urgent need was the assistance given to the education and acculturation of thousands of Vietnamese into both urban and rural communities throughout the United States. Some of the problems encountered were that:

Many were fishermen or farmers without the skills necessary for jobs available here.

Theirs was a language unfamiliar to most in the United States, and the lack of available resources of materials or personnel made communication particularly difficult.

Culturally the new immigrants were family-centered units and needed total-family and multifaceted assistance.

In response to the problem, many organizations and individuals across the country developed programs to assist the Vietnamese immigrants. Among the first of these groups were wives of servicemen and the American Red Cross. School programs for the children and tutorial programs for adults were begun through churches, clubs, schools and colleges, international houses, commercial organizations, and existing literacy programs.

Special funding came from the Department of Health, Education, and Welfare for schools with large numbers of Vietnamese students. The National Education Association also supported the funding of programs to provide education for Vietnamese refugees, and the National Institute of Education sent out brochures to the nation's 18,000 school districts telling them of resources it could provide to interested districts:

A Vietnamese-English phrase book to help teachers and students
A handbook for teachers on Vietnamese culture and background

A bibliography on textbooks for teaching English to Vietnamese speakers

A resource book listing local Vietnamese or English educators who could act as school consultants.

The library organization and administration will need to include within its structure bilingual and bicultural programs if it is to become a viable and important part of the bilingual individual's life.   Staff development, materials, and program objectives must consider differing languages and historical backgrounds.   Libraries will provide human and material resources and opportunities for the student and independent learner to continue their own education and develop their awareness of their own cultural richness through their close relationship with the library and its resources.   A future generation of educated bilingual-bicultural adults will have much to contribute to the advancement of American society.

Suggested Readings for Evaluation of Bilingual Materials

Allen H. B., and Campbell, R. N., eds. *Teaching English as a Second Language: A Book of Readings.* New York: McGraw-Hill, 1972.

Duran, Daniel, Pulles, Patricia, and Varela, Frank, comps. *Latino Resource Series.* Madison, Wisconsin: Department of Public Instruction, Equal Opportunities Office, 1977.

Series of four bilingual-bicultural annotated lists of print and multimedia resources for Mexican Americans and Puerto Ricans, from the Latino Communications Project, Library School, University of Wisconsin—Madison. Free. Order from the Department of Public Instruction, Room 108, 126 Langdon Street, Madison, Wisconsin 53702.

El Paso Public Schools. *Bilingual Bicultural Materials: A Listing for Library Resource Centers.* El Paso: El Paso Public Schools, 1975.

This is an excellent annotated 108-page guide to identifying and evaluating materials for library resource centers. It is divided into sections covering print and nonprint materials and does an excellent job of covering English, Spanish, and bilingual materials for school-age children. Recommendations are given and grade level indicated. Free.

Grebler, Leo, Moore, Joan W., and Guzman, Ralph C. *The Mexican American People, the Nation's Second Largest Minority.* New York: Free Press, 1970.

Information Clearinghouse.

Available from Department of Public Instruction, Equal Educational Opportunities Office, Room 108, 126 Langdon Street, Madison, Wisconsin 53702.

Latin American Family Education Program, Inc. *Survival Guide.* Gary, Indiana: Latin American Family Education Program, 1976.

Free. Distributed by John A. Hurst, 1169 Logan Avenue, Elgin, Illinois 60120.

Michigan Education Association. Division of Minority Affairs. *A Selected Annotated Bibliography of Material Relating to Racism, Blacks, Chicanos, Native Americans and Multi-Ethnicity.* East Lansing: The Association, 1975.

Beginning in 1971 the Michigan Education Association (MEA) began publishing this wide-ranging and useful list of "recently discovered" materials. It reflects only these materials which MEA considers most representative and relevant in terms of the involvement and contribution of Third World people in the United States. This is a valuable document for teachers and librarians although it occasionally contains subjective biases.

Pialorsi, Frank, comp. *Teaching the Bilingual: New Methods and Old Traditions.* Tucson: University of Arizona Press, 1974.

Proyecto Leer Bulletin.

Evaluates and recommends books and other reading and instructional materials in Spanish, or in complete bilingual editions, for children and adults. Appropriate for schools and public librarians. Order from Proyecto Leer Offices, 1736 Columbia Road, N.W., Suite 107, Washington, D.C. 20009.

Ulibarri, Horacio. *Bilingual Education: A Handbook for Educators: Interpretative Studies on Bilingual Education.*

Available through Educational Research Information Center, ED 028 428, 1970.

Vivo, Paquita, ed. *The Puerto Ricans: An Annotated Bibliography.* New York: R. R. Bowker, 1973.

This book is an excellent compendium of materials dealing with Puerto Rican culture and history. There are more than 2,300 entries of books, pamphlets, dissertations, articles, government documents, periodicals, and audiovisual materials dealing with Boricua's past and present. It is fully indexed and should prove an invaluable reference tool for individuals interested in Puerto Rican studies.

THE IMPRISONED AND INCARCERATED CLIENTELE

The imprisoned and incarcerated clientele poses a problem and a challenge to libraries and librarians greater than that of any other group. In most instances these people are ignored, neglected, or unknown. For this reason, it is accurate to name them "potential clients." Within the last decade more attention has been directed to library service for inmates or residents of jails and prisons. In the immediate past attention to illiteracy among these residents has revealed the extent and gravity of the problem.

In 1964 illiteracy among residents of prisons was reported to be three times greater than among the general population. In 1973 in federal prisons, 96 percent of the newly committed had not finished high school. It is estimated that 20 percent of imprisoned are functionally illiterate; some estimates state 50 percent.

Among the group of incarcerated children who are classed as delinquents or victims of outdated laws, mistreatment, and misplaced IQ systems is to be found the highest illiteracy of any group. Behind the walls of juvenile and adult penal institutions are thousands of young people. Kenneth Wooden in his recent research, *Weeping in the Playtime of Others,* states:

> Here more than 80 percent of them are locked within
> yet another prison whose walls are more formidable, whose
> confinement is more restrictive and whose sentence is harsh and
> unjust. The walls are the printed word, the confinement is the
> inability to read and the life sentence is that imposed by an
> arbitrary judge—American Education. . . . After assessing the
> reading levels of juvenile inmates in twenty-four states, I found that
> clearly these youngsters are crippled in the most basic skill—
> reading. Their average age is fourteen, but their reading ability
> is approximately fourth-grade level. . . .

Because of this inability to read, the children are labeled retarded, and little or nothing is done to provide the all-important literacy. Wooden finds a direct correlation between the inability to read and future delinquency.

Prisons and jails place residents in a constrictive, regimented environment. Routines and movements are restricted. Privacy is invaded. Identity is submerged in threatening and unfamiliar situations. The prison and jail population is primarily from minority groups and from both urban and rural areas.

The first goal in working within a correctional institution is to establish a relationship of trust with the authorities and staff of the institution as well as with the prisoners. The library staff and volunteer assistants must pass all tests. They must be patient, persistent, consistent, and diplomatic. They must never attempt to break any of the rules established by the institution.

Realistic service goals are essential so that residents will not be disappointed. The materials and the services that can be provided and the time and frequency of service hours must be practical and meaningful. Proof of sincerity of purpose and interest in the imprisoned client is shown by keeping promises, by being consistent in both negative and positive responses, and by stating how and when requests will be filled.

The basis of library service to this population has been varied. Libraries are provided because of humanitarian, religious, or educational reasons, legal necessity, and for rehabilitation. Rehabilitation looks to academic and vocational education. Bibliotherapy aims at substituting new interests for undesirable attitudes. No program has much chance that does not assist the jail or prison resident to achieve a literacy level adequate for functioning with competency in present-day society.

Correctional institutions are multiple. They operate from sheriffs' offices, police departments, delinquency projects, and federal minimum- and maximum-security prisons. They include county jails, houses of detention for men, community residential facilities, county hospital prison wards, county holding facilities, county penitentiaries, forestry camps, correctional and treatment centers, schools for girls, schools for boys, youth camps, adolescent and adult remand shelters, and residential correctional institutions. They are little known or recognized by the detached community.

The clientele will have the same interest in and demands for materials as the outside community. They will have individual interests that are determined by the restricted environment and the nature or cause of their incarceration. Materials will need to be matched to reading levels, language, and cultural and curriculum-oriented requirements. The range may vary from adult basic education to college-level study.

Collaborative agencies with which the library will be able to work, in addition to the correctional institution, include: state departments of correction and of education, Right to Read, Literacy Volunteers of America, Inc., Project R.E.A.D., and the American Bar Association Clearinghouse for Offender Literacy Program.

Library services may include: tutorial programs, mail-order or books and other materials by mail, book trucks rolled from cell to cell, a library and staff within the prison, and bibliotherapy.

Staff members must have a wide and deep concern for this unserved, alienated population. They must be dedicated and honest in every particular. Patience, persistence, and responsiveness are characteristics of the successful staff member. The public library is well equipped to staff and provide the literacy materials needed. The philosophy of service for all, freedom to read, and right to intellectual materials is most appropriate in otherwise restrictive settings.

Qualifications for staff include concern for people, maturity, emotional stability, communication skills, and endurance or "guts." They must develop survival techniques and political knowledge. They must know the power structure, life-style, and rules.

Inmates, the residents of the correctional institutions, are most valuable staff members. They can serve as tutors, librarians, library assistants, and aides. Training programs are necessary, either individually or in groups. The Literacy Volunteers of America is engaged in active program training of tutors among inmates, who in turn teach literacy skills to others.

Ross Laursen, Folsom Prison, California, writes:

> I'd heard of men over the years who had actually learned
> to read by coming to the library every day, which is open
> on a seven day a week basis, and laboriously working their way
> through thinly plotted western or mystery novels. Some of
> these men, it is said, became such devotees to the printed page
> that they not only read their way through the hundreds of fiction
> and nonfiction books available but eventually graduated
> to becoming knowledgeable classics scholars. Others, devoting
> their time and energies to the law library section, developed
> into highly competent and case winning convict lawyers.

Library literature includes many articles on library service to prisons and jails. Little is found concerning literacy programs, however. The following items are useful:

Brown, Eleanor F. *Bibliotherapy and Its Widening Applications.* Metuchen, N.J.: Scarecrow Press, 1975.

Gulker, Virgil. *Books Behind Bars.* Metuchen, N.J.: Scarecrow Press, 1973.

Inside/Outside. Newsletter on library service to youths and adults in prisons, jails and detention centers. Available from P.O. Box 9083, Berkeley, Calif. 94709.

New Jersey Library Association Outreach Services Committee. *Prison Papers: A Checklist on Prison Materials.* Trenton: New Jersey State Prison, 1975.

Reading—Where It's At—In Prison. Washington, D.C.: American Bar Association, Clearinghouse for Offender Literacy Programs.

Social, Educational Research and Development, Inc. *Institutional Library Services. A Plan for the State of Illinois.* Chicago: American Library Association, 1970.

Waite, Marion, "Adult Basic Education in a County Jail: A Library Response," *Texas Library Journal* 50 (December 1974): 227–29, 258–59.

Wooden, Kenneth. *Weeping in the Playtime of Others: America's Incarcerated Children.* New York: McGraw-Hill, 1976.

References

"Adult Learning: It Can Happen in the Library, Too." Slide-tape presentation. Austin: The University of Texas at Austin, Division of Extension, Industrial and Business Training Bureau, 1974.

American Council on Education. *Financing Part-Time Students: The New Majority in Postsecondary Education.* Washington, D.C.: The Council, 1974.

Bequette, Neva, "Outreach: Another Direction. Migrant Farm Workers Learn English in Library Project," *Library News Bulletin* 40, no. 1 (January-March 1973): 1–5.

Carvajal, Tony. "The Mulberry Bush." In United States National Advisory Council on the Education of Disadvantaged Children. *America's Educationally Neglected: A Program Report on Compensatory Education. . . .*Washington, D.C.: The Council, 1973.

Establishing Library Centers for Adult Basic Education. Austin: The University of Texas at Austin, in cooperation with the Texas Education Agency and the Texas State Library, 1975.

Groark, James J., "Utilization of Library Resources by Students in Nonresidential Degree Programs," *The Bookmark* 34, no. 1 (September-October 1974): 14–19.

Johnson, Laura S., "Bilingual Cultural Education: A Two-Way Street," *The Reading Teacher* 29, no. 3 (December 1975): 231–39.

Josey, E. J., "The Role of the Academic Library in Serving the Disadvantaged Student," *Library Trends* 20, no. 2 (October 1971): 443–44.

Knox, Alan B. "Helping Adults to Learn." Mimeographed paper, June 1974.

————. "Life-Long Self-Directed Learning." In *Fostering the Growing Need to Learn.* Project Continuing Education for Health Power. Syracuse, N.Y.: Syracuse University, 1973.

Laursen, Ross, "The Importance of a Good Library in Prison as Seen through the Eyes of One of Its Thankful Users," *Illinois Libraries* 56, no. 7 (September, 1974): 542–43.

Mounce, Marvin W., "The Open University and External Degree Programs," *Pennsylvania Library Association Bulletin* 28, no. 1 (January 1973): 31–35.

National Commission on the Financing of Postsecondary Education. *Financing Postsecondary Education in the United States.* Washington, D.C.: U.S. Government Printing Office, 1974.

"Part-Time Students: The New Majority in Postsecondary Education," *Wisconsin Library Bulletin* 70, no. 6 (November-December 1974): 301–3.

The Role of Public Libraries in Supporting Adult Independent Learning: An Interim Assessment. A report of the Office of Library Independent

Study and Guidance Projects. New York: College Entrance Examination Board, 1974.

Shaughnessy, Thomas W., "Library Services to Educationally Disadvantaged Students," *College and Research Libraries* 6, no. 36 (November 1975): 443–48.

Szczypkowski, Ronald B. *A Guide to Understanding the Adult Learner.* The Office of Library Independent Study and Guidance Projects. New York: College Entrance Examination Board, 1974.

U.S. Department of Health, Education, and Welfare, Office of Education. *Tutor Trainers' Resource Handbook.* DHEW Publication no. (OE) 74-00102. Washington, D.C.: U.S. Government Printing Office, 1975.

————. *Tutoring Resource Handbook for Teachers: A Guide for Teachers Who Are Working with Volunteer Reading Tutors.* DHEW Publication no. (OE) 74-00103. Washington, D.C.: U.S. Government Printing Office, 1974.

————. *Tutors' Resource Handbook: Assessment Items and Sample Lessons.* DHEW Publication no. (OE) 74-00101. Washington, D.C.: U.S. Government Printing Office, 1974.

United States National Advisory Council on Adult Education. *A Target Population in Adult Education.* Washington, D.C.: U.S. Government Printing Office, 1974.

United States National Advisory Council on the Education of Disadvantaged Children. *America's Educationally Neglected.* Annual Report to the President and the Congress. Washington, D.C.: The Council, 1973.

8
The Nature of Reading and Reading Instruction

READING SKILLS

What is "reading"? When someone cannot read, what does that mean? Look at the word below.

library

You can pronounce the word "library," and you know what the word means, so we agree that you can "read" it.

Now look at the word below. Can you read it?

carne

You may be able to, or you may not. It would be helpful in reading this word if you knew a little Spanish. Without that, you might have difficulty reading "carne" because (1) you would probably mispronounce it and (2) you would not understand its meaning.

Reading Readiness

What does a person have to learn to become an effective mature reader? First, he or she must develop physical and mental readiness to learn to read. Readiness to learn to read involves both the *desire* and the *ability* of an individual to learn. It is virtually impossible to teach anyone to read who does not have the desire to learn. And this desire has to be more than a passive willingness. It has to be a *motivating* desire, a *dedication* that will lead the learner to do what is necessary *right now* to learn. While it is true that no one can supply the motivation for another person to learn to read, a great deal can be accomplished through

This chapter was written by Don A. Brown, Professor, Reading Center, University of Northern Colorado, Greeley.

encouragement and support. A learner may start out with high hopes but become discouraged. A teacher's or tutor's kind words combined with good instruction can often help dispel the discouragement and rekindle enthusiasm and hope.

Ability to learn to read is also necessary. The average two-year-old will not be able to learn to read, no matter how great the desire. Most two-year-olds simply have not developed the necessary physical and mental abilities. Adults also may lack readiness. Some are severely mentally retarded. Some have other handicaps that make them unready to learn to read. It is easy to dismiss people as *unable* to learn to read because they lack the mental or physical *readiness.* Almost everyone can develop readiness.

Four basic factors are of highest importance in becoming ready to learn. The first factor is the ability to distinguish quickly the differences between various letters and words, that is, to have visual discrimination.

Some differences are distinguished easily. Virtually no one confuses the letters *o* and *x,* for example. But other letters, such as *n* and *m,* are much more nearly alike and cause greater difficulty. The greatest problems rise from those letters that are different only because of their positions in space. The letters *d, b, p,* and *q* have the same general configuration. Their difference lies in the direction they face, or, in other words, their positions in space.

Until a person starts learning to read, he or she seldom encounters any situation in which the identity of an article depends on its position in space. A dog is a dog, no matter which direction it may face. But the person who is first learning to read quickly discovers that differences in position make *big* become *dig* or even *pig.*

It is common for people who have not learned to discriminate visually to be misdiagnosed as being "perceptually impaired," "neurologically dysfunctioning," or "dyslexic." But almost everyone can learn to discriminate visually if given the time and opportunity to do so. It is a disservice to the learner to assume that one who cannot discriminate between certain words or letters must suffer from some sort of "short circuit in perceptual wiring." Not only is it a disservice—it is usually incorrect.

The second factor in readiness to read is auditory discrimination, that is, being able to hear and differentiate between the sounds in words. Auditory discrimination may be especially difficult for a person trying to learn to read in a language that is not the native one. Several sounds in English are not used at all in Spanish; for example, if the words "pin" and "pen" sound the same to a person who is not able to distinguish the difference between the short *i* and the short *e* in those words, it can be expected that that person will have a lot of trouble learning to read those words correctly.

Factors necessary to success in learning to read	1. Desire and motivation
	2. Mental and physical ability
	   Visual discrimination
	   Auditory discrimination
	   Attention or "focus"
	   Language base

Fig 6. Reading Readiness

A third factor in readiness is the ability to give full attention to what is being taught. It is necessary to be attentive to what is being taught long enough to learn what is being presented. A child may lack this focus of attention because of not being able to sit still long enough. An adult who is too tired or worried to bring full attention to the task may also have difficulty.

A fourth factor in readiness to learn to read is the student's language base. The reader must be able to understand the language in which the material is written. First-grade reading instruction usually is based on the assumption that the student has had five or six years of familiarity with the language to be read. When either a child or an adult has an inadequate language base, it will be more difficult to learn to read in that language.

Readiness is the foundation on which effective reading instruction is built. It is sometimes surprising that adults who are trying to learn to read may not as yet have developed reading readiness. But many adults come with minds and bodies poorly equipped to handle the task of learning to read; they frequently become discouraged and quit. Whether in a learning center or library, the instructor or tutor must be willing to meet them at their own reading level, and this occasionally may mean helping them develop readiness for reading instruction.

Sight Vocabulary

An individual beginning to learn to read usually starts to recognize words by their form. The learner recognizes the word *stop* not by sounding it out but by simply remembering the way it looks, in much the same way as we recognize a pencil as a pencil—because it *looks* like a pencil, not because we analyze it and find it has a rubber eraser, wood, graphite, and paint. When we say a person recognizes a word quickly by recognizing its form, it can be said that that word is in the reader's "sight vocabulary."

How does a word become a part of a person's sight vocabulary? It usually takes twenty-five to forty-five meaningful repetitions before a word becomes immediately recognizable.   That is why a beginning reader will seem to know a word today, but tomorrow will not remember it.   An adult who has learned a number of word confusions must have them straightened out by consistent help. This may take longer than the twenty-five to forty-five meaningful repetitions a child usually needs.

A person who becomes able to read rapidly and effectively must be able to call the words almost as rapidly as they are seen. Think how many meaningful repetitions one needs to build a sight vocabulary that is large enough to allow smooth reading. How does a person get those repetitions? Certainly the reader cannot ask someone else to identify every word that is not recognized. The learner has to be able to develop word-analysis skills, or "break the code," as some reading specialists say. This means that the learner needs to learn the sounds the various letters and letter combinations represent in words. Sometimes that is very difficult. According to Webster's Dictionary, no less than fourteen sounds can be represented by the letter *e*, not including the times it may be silent. The other letters are easier, of course, and some letters represent only one sound. But a good reader has to be able to associate the letters with the appropriate sounds and blend the word parts together to recognize words that are not part of the immediate sight vocabulary.

Another way of recognizing an unknown word is to use the setting or context in which the word appears to help recognize it.   If you heard someone read, "He put the rifle to his shoulder and pulled the *tiger*," you would know which word had been misread, and what the correct word should have been.   The context tells you the word should have been "trigger" and not "tiger."

The ability to use context clues is important to good reading.   Paul McKee conducted a study several years ago showing that children in the middle grades used context clues effectively only one third of the time when it was possible to use them to identify a word.   The context will not always tell a word or its meaning, but when this tool can be used, it is most effective.

Comprehension

It goes almost without saying that comprehension is the most important reading skill. A person who does not understand what is read might as well not have spent the time.

There are four different kinds of reading comprehension; each contains different subsets into which it can be divided.   First is vocabulary—understanding the meaning of the words in a sentence. Second is understanding of details.   Third is understanding of the main idea or general significance of a passage. And the fourth is understanding the inferences or implications of a passage.

Understanding the main idea involves the ability to extract and generalize. Such understanding is somewhat more difficult than understanding vocabulary and noting details. Understanding implied or inferred meanings sometimes can also be difficult. A person may not understand what is peculiar about the statement, "I walked downhill all the way from my house to the store, and downhill all the way back to my house," because the implications of the statement are not grasped. A student may read the paragraph, "George crumpled the paper, threw it in the fire, glared at the secretary, then turned and stalked out, slamming the door behind him," but cannot answer the question, "How did George feel about losing his job?" because the text does not say in so many words, "George was upset." Such a reader has trouble making inferences.

A good reader also reads with fluency and efficiency. Fluency in reading is the ability to make reading "sound like talk written down," as we say. The fluent reader makes reading communicate. What is read makes more sense. In addition, because fluent reading comes closer to the way we talk, a text can be read faster, that is, more efficiently, in this way. When we talk to someone, we do not give equal emphasis to each word. Instead, we barely touch some words, and emphasize others to get our meaning across. When we read with fluency, we do much the same thing. We group our words in thought units; this allows us to read faster. A fluent reader may not always be a fast, efficient reader, but has the foundation to become one. The person who reads in a jerky, word-by-word fashion has much more trouble becoming a rapid reader.

Locational and study skills are helpful to the good reader who applies other reading skills in special ways to help find information needed or to get the most out of the time spent studying. One has to learn how to use a dictionary, an encyclopedia, a road map, a telephone book, a cookbook, and dozens of other sources of information. One also has to be able to study effectively, do a good job of taking tests, and generally make reading serve in the most efficient way possible.

The last reading skill is one the late William S. Gray, University of Chicago reading specialist, called the most important: the ability to react to the reading material. There is more to reading than just understanding what the writer has to say. The good reader reacts as well, and evaluates. Is what the author said true? Is the author qualified to say it? Is the author biased?

The good reader also reacts to the writer's style of writing, appreciates good writing, and knows the difference between good writing and bad. And finally, the good reader enjoys reading. Reading tells the reader things he or she is interested in.

<table>
<tr><td>Sight vocabulary</td><td>Fluency and rate</td></tr>
<tr><td>Word analysis</td><td>Locational and study skills</td></tr>
<tr><td>Context clues</td><td>Reaction</td></tr>
<tr><td>Comprehension</td><td>Evaluation</td></tr>
<tr><td>Vocabulary</td><td>Appreciation of style</td></tr>
<tr><td>Details</td><td>Enjoyment</td></tr>
<tr><td>Main idea</td><td></td></tr>
<tr><td>Inference</td><td></td></tr>
</table>

Fig. 7. Reading Skills

These three: evaluation, appreciation, and enjoyment, are all part of the reader's reaction to reading, and part of good reading ability (see figure 7).

ADULT PROGRAMS

Are there differences in reading instruction for adults and children? The major goals are the same for both groups: to understand what is read; to gain needed information; to evaluate, appreciate, and enjoy reading.

But there are differences, too. The adult wants to learn to read for his or her own personal and family improvement. The child more frequently wants to read for enjoyment. The adult beginning reader has less confidence in his or her ability than a child at the same level, even though the adult brings more experience and a broader vocabulary to reading. Adults have more ability to reason than first-grade children, although children have a greater tolerance for repetition and seem more willing to engage in rote learning.

Adults differ from children in that they must usually maintain serious responsibilities at the same time they are trying to learn. As Goldberg reports in his *Army Training of Illiterates in World War II,* he found that there was an advantage to the program in that the army assumed all responsibility for survival and maintenance while the soldier-student was being taught to read. This is seldom the case with adults. They usually must take care of themselves and their families (if they have them) at the same time they are learning to read. This divides their attentions, siphons off much of their energies, and decreases the amount of time they are able to devote to learning.

Literacy programs for adults should be available when they need and can use them. This usually means that instruction must be offered in the evenings, and at places where students can attend either before or after work.

A library or any other institution hoping to work with adults should remember that adult literacy instruction is best offered in a relaxed adult environment. Students should be free to move about the learning center and talk with others. They prefer to assume their own responsibility for learning. Regular attendance is often impossible, and there must be some means of keeping track of what each student is doing so that the student who returns will be able to pick up where he or she left off.

Adult students' reading performance usually differs, too. An adult who is able to read at, say, fourth-grade level, will generally read more slowly than a child able to read at the same level. The adult will tend to have greater comprehension, however, probably due to a broader background of experience and larger vocabulary. Even the beginning adult reader usually has a greater grasp of our sound-symbol system than a child at the same stage.

With these advantages, it may come as a surprise that it is generally more difficult to teach an adult to read than to teach a child. This may be partially accounted for by the fact that most adults who cannot read have a poor self-image. They often feel they are "dumb" and probably will not be able to learn very well. Adults have often learned things that are incorrect and now must "unlearn" them. In addition, many adults have been "turned off" by school, and when they do go back to learn to read, they take their memories of failure back with them. Contrast that with the attitude of enthusiasm that most children have for going to school and learning to read!

Data gathered by the New York State Department of Education in 1966 found that adults in the first four levels learn better in an individualized program working with a teacher or tutor. An individualized program may work with students in small groups or singly, but the necessary ingredient is direct teacher contact. Students did not do well when they were expected to work without teacher help or when they were taught by a machine-centered approach. Adults reading at fifth-grade level and above were found to be more capable of working independently and with machines.

Identifying the Reading Level

The first key to good instruction is identifying the instructional reading level for each student. There are several ways to do this. If the teacher or tutor has time and knowledge to make one, an informal reading inventory will give a good indication of a student's appropriate reading level. There are a number of sources that describe how to make an informal reading inventory, but one of the best was written by Marjorie Seddon Johnson and Roy A. Kress and published by the International Reading Association in Newark, Delaware. (See references.) The administration of the informal reading inventory, or IRI, as it is called, takes from fifteen to thirty minutes. It is sometimes frightening to a new student, who may be uncomfortable answering an examiner's questions orally so soon after coming into a library or learning center program.

Another measure used by many learning centers is the Science Research Associates Reading for Understanding placement test. It takes less than fifty minutes and does not ask for oral responses to questions. It seems to be an effective indicator, but resembles a standardized test, which again scares some students.

A new measure, as yet less well known, is the *T-NAT* (the *T*est that's *Not A T*est), published by the Basic Education Trade House in Greeley, Colorado. It gives a quick indication of the grade level for starting reading instruction. It does not use questions, but is based on mechanical reading ability and may be given in about five minutes. It is only intended for initial reading placement.

In addition to knowing the student's reading level, the teacher should be aware of the readability of the materials that are available in the center. Sometimes this information is accurately supplied by the publishers, but not generally so. It is helpful to have a simple tool such as the Fry Readability Formula with which to make a quick estimate of reading difficulty. A copy of the Fry graph as adapted by Maginnis and with direction for its application has been included for the reader's use (see figure 8).

After a learner begins the program, it is important for the tutor or teacher to be observant, noticing the areas where the student has difficulty. After identifying these skill deficits, the teacher must be sufficiently familiar with the available skill development materials to guide the student to the appropriate resource material for skill improvement. Because of the individual differences and needs presented by students, it is a good idea to have a number of different materials rather than trying to use only one system. Adults, more than children, often become bored unless there is a good deal of variety in their instructional materials.

Patterns of Organization

Three patterns of instructional organization for adults who need basic education are home study, learning center, and traditional classroom. Five audio filmstrip packages showing various adaptations of these have been published by the International Reading Association in Newark, Delaware, in a series entitled *Model Adult Basic Education Programs.* (See references.) Each package describes one center's program. The

Average number of SYLLABLES per 100 words

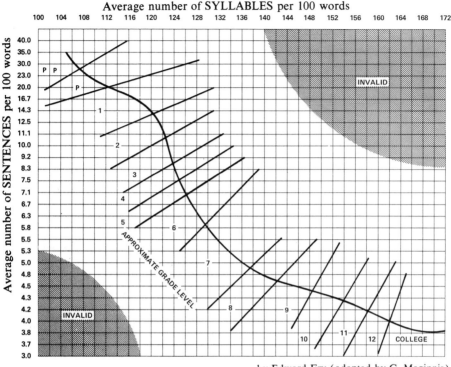

by Edward Fry (adapted by G. Maginnis)

Purpose: The major purpose of this graph is to indicate the estimated technical reading level for a given piece of reading material.

Directions: Randomly select three (or more) one hundred-word passages from the reading material. Avoid the beginning of chapters, however, and skip all proper nouns. Count hyphenated words as one word. Count the number of syllables for each passage and find the average number of syllables. Count numbers (274, 1975) as one syllable. Count the number of sentences for each passage and find the average number of syllables. If the one hundredth word falls in the first half of the last sentence, do not count the sentence; if the one hundredth word falls in the last half of the last sentence, count the sentence. Plot the average on the chart above to determine the general area of reading difficulty. Add one year to your finding if the material was translated from another language and if the material was written before 1900. Choose more passages per book or chapter if great variability is observed.

Reprinted with permission of George H. Maginnis and the International Reading Association, from *The Reading Teacher,* March 1969.

**Fig. 8. Fry's Readability Graph
         Extended Through Pre-Primer Level**

programs were all chosen for their excellence. They are often available through the adult education offices in state departments of education on a loan basis.

One commonly used pattern is the learning center, housed in a library, community college, or other agency. Learning is usually wholly or mostly individualized, with instructional assistance available whenever the student feels the need for help. A variation of the learning center is the use of one major center with a number of satellites that serve other areas. These may be housed in mobile units, homes, schools, recreation centers, etc. A center in Longmont, Colorado has even opened a satellite in Clyde's Barber Shop, probably the only emporium of tonsorial splendor where you can get a high school equivalency diploma!

Another organizational pattern is the home study program, in which tutors usually work out of a learning center or library, going to the homes of the students.   Sometimes the program is based on one-to-one instruction, and at other times and in other places the tutor may go into a home in which several people have gathered for instruction.

Still another pattern is the somewhat more traditional classroom setting. It is commonly used, and under certain circumstances, it can be effective. Much of the basic education offered on military bases or in Job Corps centers and United Auto Workers Halls is conducted using this pattern of organization.

Approaches

What are some of the instructional approaches used with adults to teach them to read? There are a number of them. Programmed, machine-centered, linguistic, individualized, management systems, language-experience, eclectic approaches—the names sound familiar to many because they are largely the same approaches by *title* that are used with beginning readers in elementary school. But there are major differences between the way these approaches are used with adults and the way they are used with children.

No mention has been made of the most frequently used children's approach—the basal reader. There is no "basal" that can be used with adults, although there are systems approaches that attempt to do some of the same things.

In looking at the various approaches, it becomes apparent that no approach is perfect. But there is an opposite, very positive aspect to this. What may not work for one person may be exactly what another student likes, and may learn very well with. Also, one teacher may not do very well with an approach that another uses very well.

This does not mean that all approaches are equally sound. Even though an energetic, vivacious teacher may be successful using a poorly constructed approach, that does not mean the approach suddenly becomes a good one. It simply means that the teacher has been able to teach people to read despite the limitations of the approach.

Let us take a look at some of the more frequently used approaches.

The *linguistic-phonemic approach* is relatively common. It is based on an attempt to regularize the learning of the written language. This approach seems important in learning to read English because there are so many different possible letter-sound combinations in the language. Letter-sound relationships are taught in a carefully programmed fashion with only one or two "phonemes" or sounds taught at a time. At the beginning levels this approach tends to produce a somewhat peculiar style of materials with sentences similar to "The man in the van had a tan fan" or "The cad who was sad hit the lad with a pad." The aim of the program is to familiarize the beginning reader with each sound-letter relationship so that the student learns it completely before going on to the next.

Perhaps the people who object most vehemently to the linguistic-phonemic approach are structural linguists, who maintain that the sense of the sentence is the greatest aid to the reader in being able to read. They argue that the necessarily low concept load to be found in the phonemic approach is actually detrimental to learning to read. They point out that adults are even less willing to tolerate nonsensical content than children.

Two other considerations are: (1) materials used to teach reading by the linguistic-phonemic approach often delay the introduction of useful reading, or introduce it without the opportunity for the student to have mastered the necessary sound-letter associations; and (2) this approach is difficult for a person untrained in linguistics to use in informal instruction in a learning center or library.

Nevertheless, many use the linguistic-phonemic approach successfully. Some have found it to be particularly effective in working with students who think they cannot learn. Because there are only a very limited number of choices for sounds, the student usually has a greater degree of success at the beginning.

Another common approach is *programmed reading*. Most of the published materials identified as "programmed" are based on a linguistic-phonemic approach. In fact, one of the publishers of programmed materials has succeeded in producing materials that are more linguistically consistent than any of the popular linguistic-phonemic materials. Like the linguistic approach, programmed reading is often useful in working with the discouraged beginning reader because the authors have tried to arrange the steps to mastery in the materials so that there is a high likelihood of success.

Programmed instruction allows students to proceed at their own rates, but unfortunately most of the published programmed reading materials have each student go through the same steps as every other student. The *rate* of progress is up to the student, however.

A third approach is *machine-presented instruction.* There is a tendency for some people to be motivated by this approach, especially as they begin. While they are motivated, their learning is good. Some difficulties arise with the use of machines, however. Most of them are somewhat expensive, and there is little indication that long-range gains with any of the programs developed to date are any better—or as good as—gains made by using other less expensive materials. Also, as was indicated earlier, adults at the lower levels generally dislike the impersonality of such an approach.

A fourth approach is *individualized reading.* Individualized reading for both children and adults is based on self-seeking, self-selection, and self-pacing, with the student being his or her own best teacher. The student will, if given the opportunity, reach out for, select, and pace himself or herself through appropriate reading materials. In an elementary school this means one thing, but in an adult learning center, it means something else. Both situations need a great number of materials, but these are more easily come by in the elementary school. For adults, teachers are forced to use a great number of kits and paperbacks, carefully selected to be at appropriate levels of difficulty. Unlike the elementary school, there is generally greater homogeneity of reading ability in the learning center. A person seldom is placed at the second or third level only to find he can really read seventh- or eighth-grade level materials, although this happens frequently in the elementary school because children are placed in their grade levels mostly by chronological age rather than by achievement levels, as is the case with adults.

At any rate, the first requirement for using an individualized reading approach with adults is to gather a number of adult-oriented, interesting, readable, utilitarian materials. Each student must be started in material appropriate to ability, and followed in progress by regularly scheduled conferences.

Skill work depends on the tutor or teacher. Progress charts or contracts are often helpful means of following the student and checking to see what sort of skill work may be needed next. Skill work consists of exercises, worksheets, class cards, and any activity outside applied reading aimed at developing reading skills.

Fifth is the *language-experience approach.* It is probably the hardest, but certainly one of the most interesting, approaches to be used with adults. Essentially it is an approach that teaches reading by having students write their own stories and then read them. To do this the students develop word banks or files of the words they are using. Later they share their writings with other students, and eventually they are introduced to the writings of other people in a manner that blends into an individualized reading approach.

This approach demands the active direction of a tutor or teacher who is completely involved with the students. It is not possible to use the language-experience approach without being immediately available to the students. For this reason some have said this is a poor approach to use in a learning center. However, it *is* used in many learning centers, sometimes through the use of a specific area within the center for reading and writing help. As in the individualized reading approach, the teacher is responsible for reading skill development. This necessitates a knowledge of the scope and sequence of reading skills.

What is the answer? If there is something wrong with each of the approaches we have mentioned, which one is the "right" way to teach reading to adults? There are two answers: none of them, and all of them. There is no single way to teach reading to every person who may walk into a library or learning center. People are different. They learn differently, they are interested in different things, and they come knowing different things. No one approach will be equally effective with everyone.

And teachers are different, too. One approach may "fit" one teacher's personality, while another approach may fit another teacher much better.

The best approach, then, is the one that involves several methods. Evaluate what you are doing. If a student does not seem to be doing very well in one method, have something else to try. The teacher who does this has a good start on effective reading instruction.

References

Brown, Don A. *Model Adult Basic Education Programs.* Newark, Del.: International Reading Association, 1975.

————. *T-NAT, the Test that's Not A Test.* Greeley, Colo.: Basic Education Trade House, 1974.

Goldberg, Samuel. *Army Training of Illiterates in World War II.* New York: Columbia University Teachers College, 1951.

Johnson, Marjorie S., and Kress, Roy A. *Informal Reading Inventories.* Newark, Del.: International Reading Association, 1965.

Maginnis, George H., "The Readability Graph and Informal Reading Inventories," *The Reading Teacher* 22, no. 6 (March 1969):518.

McKee, Paul. *The Teaching of Reading.* Cambridge, Mass.: Houghton Mifflin Co., 1948, p. 73.

Thurstone, Thelma Gwinn. *Reading for Understanding Placement Test.* Chicago: Science Research Associates, Inc., 1963.

9
Questions
and Answers

This chapter deals with questions asked by librarians. Answers to those questions are suggested. The chapter takes note of some issues and controversies in the field. In the interest of brevity these questions were not discussed in the previous chapters. Answers are of necessity concise; some are even superficial in view of the complexity of the problem. It is thought that librarians will be able to search out other answers in the literature and among specialists and colleagues.

How do you find publishers and producers of adult basic education materials?

Various sources are noted in chapter 7. The University of Texas at Austin's *ABE: Guide to Library Materials* has a "Directory of Publishers and Producers." The New Readers Press; the New Readers Press bibliography; and the bibliography in *Pivot,* the newsletter of the Free Library of Philadelphia, are other sources. The American Library Association publication *Information for Everyday Survival,* by Priscilla Gotsick and others, has an annotated list of free and inexpensive materials compiled at the Appalachian Adult Education Center.

What sources can one depend on?

The sources noted above are dependable. The ABE, GED, Manpower Training, and other programs in a library's local community should have suggestions about specific materials. Such reliable sources are useful. A word of caution: select with great care in relation to the local clientele's and the community's needs and interests and the type of library program. It is wise not to rely on any one list as a sole selection tool and to guard against the use of outdated and nonevaluative lists. Of course, the publishers' own catalogs are valuable.

Do libraries buy workbooks for adults who are in literacy programs?

Yes, if the library is committed to the support of adult learning and various levels of literacy study. Workbooks help to meet the need for single-concept materials and materials written at a beginning level. First- to fourth-grade materials must have an instructional emphasis and are used in tutoring and small class situations. Self-instruction is difficult, yet many people, after basic instruction with a tutor and instruction on how to use the workbook, can use workbooks alone.

Are literacy materials considered basic materials for a library collection?

Literacy materials are basic not only in their use but in a library collection.

Are children's books useful?

Although, in general, children's books are not considered for adults because many are too simple, moralistic, and with child-oriented content, some excellent material is available in the fields of biography, history, and how-to-make-things. Some bilingual materials are of this nature. In some instances, great literature is equally useful and interesting to adults and children. Because one has few books to choose from at the beginning levels, the well-written material for a juvenile audience that exists can be used; for example, *Black Is Beautiful* and *Malcolm X* by Arnold Adoff. Such material can be of help in such specialized areas as astronomy, geography, biography, crafts, myths, folklore, and poetry.

Why are children's books not generally suitable?

They are not designed to take into account adult experiences and judgments. The subject matter of children's books seldom provides the practical information that adults need to cope with everyday problems.

What is a readability formula?

A readability formula uses counts of language variables and word and sentence counts in a section of writing to provide an index of probable difficulty for readers. It is a means of rating the writing after it is written. It has limitations and is controversial.

Should librarians check readability levels?

Yes. It is important to assess readability of materials to match them with adult reading achievement levels and to evaluate published statements. It is important to select one formula and use it consistently. In that way, it comes to have meaning. Such formulas as the Gunning Fog Index, Fry's Readability Graph, and the Flesch Pattern of Reading Ease are easy to compute. The Fry graph is included in chapter 8 of this manual. The others are found in the literature. All three are included in Helen Lyman's *Reading and the Adult New Reader* (Chicago: American Library Association, 1976); see especially chapter 8, "Evaluation of Reading Materials."

How can a library get literacy materials without any budget?

Many free materials are available, such as "real world" materials (see appendix 1, page 146), government publications, and agency and organization publications. Foundation grants and organization and individual contributions may be obtained. Collaborative arrangements with literacy programs and agencies may make it possible to obtain funds for materials or the materials themselves by sharing resources.

What three titles should I buy?

It depends on the clientele and the program. Although three titles do not make much of a collection, it is a start. If purchase of three titles is made regularly, a collection will grow quickly. See the sources and lists noted throughout this manual.

Generally, do the criteria of selection for literacy materials differ from those used in traditional library practice?

In some instances, popular appeal may be more important in selecting literacy materials than in selecting other materials. Greater use of "real world" materials, more paperbound books, and more pamphlet material is required. In another way, selection criteria are stricter, broader, and applied more specifically, so that the content, the readability, the adult appeal, and the student's goals are considered in relation to each item.

Selection of literacy materials may mean a change in priorities. Ideally materials should be readable, provide accurate and current information, and be suited to the ethnic background of the clientele, but reality demonstrates that the information is of primary importance. Some materials will be purchased because they are the only ones available with the concrete information wanted, such as materials on opening a bank account or selecting groceries; they will have some difficult words, and all the illustrations will be of white middle-class families, while the clients are blacks or Latinos. More and more appropriate materials are becoming available, however, so it is essential to keep up with the lesser-known sources.

Is quality an important criterion?

Yes. It is one criterion, but for first-, second-, third-, and fourth-grade materials, the question of quality may be pointless. It may be necessary to create the materials needed, as well as to purchase them.

Why is the tutorial method of learning important?

This one-to-one teaching method permits support of and individual attention to the learner's needs and interests. It may result in attention to the entire family and direct knowledge of problems, not only in relation to study but also in relation to the family, and may become a source for referral to other agencies. The tutor also serves as an intermediary to the library.

Are separate learning centers and personal outreach service advisable?

They are increasingly important. They can ensure confidentiality, interested and qualified staff, and suitable materials. They are useful as first contacts, in preparing the reader to use a library, and in helping clients to feel more comfortable in a regular library setting. The library may be the learning center.

Who might be asked to refer clients to the library literacy programs?

The collaborating agencies' staff, the administrators and teachers in literacy programs, social workers, judges, lawyers, probation officers, doctors, clinics, speech therapists, clergymen, friends, relatives. Particularly important are the self-referrals and word-of-mouth referrals by satisfied clients.

Do libraries need special funds for literacy programs?

Funds may be helpful, but much can be done at relatively little cost. Even more can be accomplished by setting the literacy objectives as priorities. It may be a question of allocating funds more justly to represent more fairly the requirements of the literacy clientele groups.

What reading methods are best?

Perhaps each has a place. Librarians may find that rivalry and vested interests create various opinions and result in disagreements. Don Brown discusses this problem in chapter 8 of this manual.

What is poor planning?

A plan that does not have a rational sequence or, in a word, is disorganized; an overly ambitious program that fails to meet the expectations raised; failure to plan at all; a program that fails to anticipate and acquire appropriate materials; a lack of imagination.

What are basic vocabulary lists?

Basic vocabulary lists are compilations of what the compilers have identified as the most frequently used words. They may be arranged alphabetically or in rank order of frequent use.

Where are basic vocabulary lists available?

Henry Kucera and W. Nelson Francis, "Three Hundred Most Frequently Used Words in Rank Order," in *Computational Analysis of Present-Day American English* (Providence, R.I.: Brown University Press, 1967); M. Adele Mitzel, "The Functional Reading List for Adults," in *Adult Education* 16, no. 2 (Winter 1966):67–69, published by the Adult Education Association of the U.S.A. The Kucera and Francis and the Mitzel lists are reproduced in Ruth J. Colvin and Jane H. Root, *Tutor* (Syracuse, N.Y.: Literacy Volunteers of America, Inc., 1976). Another source is *The Living Word Vocabulary: The Words We Know,* by Edgar Dale and Joseph O'Rourke (Elgin, Ill.: Dome Press, 1976). Write to 1169 Logan Avenue, Elgin, Illinois 60120 for this national vocabulary inventory.

Should librarians diagnose the reading abilities of the learner-client?

Some librarians feel that this is not their role because they are not teachers, or that diagnosis is acceptable only where the library staff member is also a reading teacher. However, to assist the learner-client effectively, diagnosis is necessary before advisory or tutorial referrals can be made. The client level of entry for learning must be established to build on what the client's store of knowledge is, to clarify what the client wishes to learn, and for placement purposes. Diagnosis has been used successfully by librarians in such public libraries as Brooklyn, Chicago, and Dallas, and in the R.E.A.D. Project in Mountain View Public Library, California. Study and training are necessary to qualify for this responsibility.

Is there a standard English? A black English?

The question of language, particularly in written materials, is an issue familiar to librarians. It is a new issue that has arisen because of an increasing awareness and attention to the spoken language of children and adults and its relation to teaching and learning to read, write, and speak. A significant increase in research and writing on dialects and reading reveals conflicting theories and points of view. It is not possible to discuss the problem here except in a very brief way. Decisions must be made by librarians in relation to the situation and their own study.

Many persons are bidialectal, that is, are proficient in understanding and using two dialects of a language. "Standard language" may mean merely that members of a group use features that are identified as characteristic of one dialect or another. Standard English may be defined as a prestige dialect or the language generally spoken by educated Americans in the conduct of professional and government business and used in most writing.

A considerable number of people believe that there is a particular form of the English language that is more clearly understood and more habitually used by black Americans than is standard English. Disagreements arise on what use should be made of this spoken language in teaching and in writing materials for learning and reading. Certain distinctive features may be identified. An overlap exists between black English and standard English. Many blacks do not speak black English. Blacks who do speak a dialect are frequently bidialectal, that is, they use forms from both standard and black English and may be able to speak consistently in either way.

What is the Kentucky Television high school program?

The Kentucky Educational Television Network (KETV) has TV high school programs to assist adults in obtaining a high school diploma. The Kentucky Department of Libraries, the state library agency, is part of the cooperative program. The agency has made educational study kits and television sets available through local public libraries where patrons can participate. Copies of the GED High School Equivalency Diploma Test are purchased and circulated. Regional librarians conduct regular classroom sessions after participants view KETV lessons. Textbooks and other materials are provided, as well as follow-up class sessions.

In what ways may potential participants be reached?

Only a brief answer to this important problem is possible here. The obvious methods in making use of all communication media include newspapers; radio; television; talks to clubs and organizations; notices in churches, schools, plants, union halls, other libraries, or general meeting places; leaflets; brochures; and bibliographies. A library newsletter and bibliography published at regular intervals is valuable. Cooperative work with an educational counselor who meets with adults in homes, schools, and libraries, at work, restaurants, and community centers, is helpful.

Does the military have any educational programs?

Prior to entry into the military services, candidates are given a series of vocational aptitude examinations; that is, the Armed Services Vocational Aptitude Battery (ASVAB). Candidates are scored on a ratio of one (high) to five (low) for the "mental category" within this battery. Those persons who achieve only category five or low four are not accepted into the services. Those persons who achieve a rating of between 15 and 30 in category four (high four) may enlist. Anyone who has not completed high school may voluntarily enroll in training for GED. This is a service contracted for with the high school in a locale near the army base. The training may be given on or off the base.

The PREP program, training for GED and postsecondary education, is administered by:

Office of Defense Education
Manpower & Reserve Affairs
Assistant Secretary of Defense
The Pentagon
Washington, D.C. 20301 (202) 545-6700

What is community education?

Community education is the process through which all educational institutions in a community function together in the education of the members of that community. Through the involvement in the community process the needs and interests of individuals are identified and met regardless of the area of concern or the organization that provides the program.

What is collaboration?

Collaboration denotes independence and equality in decisionmaking. In our context it means cooperative and interagency programs. It may include other libraries or library units in a system or region, as well as other social agencies such as public assistance, social welfare, churches, neighborhood centers, educational agencies, schools, and other literacy programs.

What are the benefits of a literacy program?

The achievements of a literacy program have mutual and multiple benefits for individuals, families, and the total community. A person who has attained literacy can become more productive, independent, active in community affairs, and make use of more channels of communication than can the less literate or functional illiterate. Adults testify to a feeling of greater confidence, easier communication with others, and both practical and pleasurable uses of their new-found literacy skills. The community benefits may come through deeper and broader understanding among various groups and individuals in the community. Libraries can be seen as learning centers, information exchanges, and a major resource for information and materials. Any library actively engaged in a literacy program and activities will discover not only these evident benefits but many others. The concept of service that is based on community needs and interests, initiated by the library, supportive of learning activities, providing guidance and counseling and planned learning experiences, requires a setting of service priorities and a plan for reaching into the community.

How-to Suggestions

Community Analysis Checklist

The Community Analysis Checklist has been developed for this manual to be used as a guide by librarians. It is suggested for use in planning and assessment. It may be adapted or changed to fit the local situation and the library's need.

Information on each of these items is needed for analysis of the community in relation to literacy needs and resources and the community's historic cultural attitudes.

Information obtained from

	Official documents	Reports, newspapers, organizations, etc.	Formal interviews	Questionnaires	Conversation	Observation
Population						
Size of population	____	____	____	____	____	____
Rate of growth or decline	____	____	____	____	____	____
Age range	____	____	____	____	____	____
Ethnic origins	____	____	____	____	____	____
Languages spoken	____	____	____	____	____	____
Schooling	____	____	____	____	____	____
Continuing education (potential)	____	____	____	____	____	____
Employment categories (actual or potential)	____	____	____	____	____	____
Income levels	____	____	____	____	____	____
Geography and transportation						
Location and nature of neighborhoods or units	____	____	____	____	____	____
Distribution of population by neighborhoods or units	____	____	____	____	____	____
Location of barriers— natural and man-made	____	____	____	____	____	____
Public transportation	____	____	____	____	____	____
Main thoroughfares—for cars and for pedestrians	____	____	____	____	____	____

(Continued)

Information obtained from

	Official docu- ments	Reports, newspapers, organizations, etc.	Formal inter- views	Ques- tion- naires	Conver- sation	Obser- vation
Historical-cultural climate						
History of community settlement	___	___	___	___	___	___
Ethnic, linguistic	___	___	___	___	___	___
Educational	___	___	___	___	___	___
Labor-management	___	___	___	___	___	___
Governmental	___	___	___	___	___	___
Rural-urban	___	___	___	___	___	___
Major cultural holidays, festivals, events	___	___	___	___	___	___
Resources						
Educational institutions and units	___	___	___	___	___	___
Formal agency literacy programs	___	___	___	___	___	___
Community centers	___	___	___	___	___	___
Health centers	___	___	___	___	___	___
Social welfare centers— private and public	___	___	___	___	___	___
Government agencies and services	___	___	___	___	___	___
Churches, religious centers and representatives	___	___	___	___	___	___
Organizations						
Educational, civic, special- interest, etc.	___	___	___	___	___	___
Volunteer and other special literacy programs	___	___	___	___	___	___
Private and public funding agencies	___	___	___	___	___	___
Political implications						
Control of available funds	___	___	___	___	___	___
Competing programs	___	___	___	___	___	___
Majority-minority conflicts	___	___	___	___	___	___
Conflicting jurisdictions	___	___	___	___	___	___
Limitations on use of funds or other resources	___	___	___	___	___	___
Restraining administrative structures	___	___	___	___	___	___

**Preplanning Information for Expanding Services
for Disadvantaged Adults**

This form was developed by the Appalachian Adult Education
Center, Morehead State University, Morehead, Kentucky, as a practical
guide.

State_____ Town_____ Date_____

Instructions: Please describe your community by answering the following
questions as completely as possible.

Area of information	*Information to include*	*Source of information*	*Fill in here*
A. Population Statistics	How many people in your service area?	1970 U.S. Census State Departments of Education School Boards	_____
	Age of population No. of children 0-18 years No. of adults 18-64 No. of adults 65+		_____ _____ _____
B. Educational Levels of Population	Percent and number of out-of-school adults over 25 who have less than 8 years of schooling	1970 U.S. Census, or Area Supervisor of Adult Basic Education	% _____ No. _____
	Percent and number who have not completed high school		% _____ No. _____
	Median school years completed		_____
C. Economic Levels of Population	Percent of families whose income is $3000 or below	1970 U.S. Census Employment Security	% _____
	Median Income Family per Capita	Welfare agencies Community Action Programs	_____ _____
	Percent of unemployment of adults over 16		% _____

(Continued)

Area of information	Information to include	Source of information	Fill in here
	What are the chief employers for your service area?	Employment Security Mayor's Office Local planning Commission Community Action Programs	NAME KIND OF WORK PRESENTLY _____ _____ _____ NEW _____ _____ _____
D. National and racial background of population	Give percent of racial and national groups which make up the population of your service area.	1970 U.S. Census City, County, or Area Supervisor of Adult Basic Education NAACP	*City County* White __ __ Black __ __ Non-English-Speaking __ __ Indian __ __ Oriental __ __ Other __ __
E. Geographic area you serve	Square miles		_____
F. Annual Income of the Library	Total cash	Head Librarian	_____
G. Library card holders		Head Librarian	_____
H. Educational offerings in community for disadvantaged	List of adult basic education and other educational activities available to your service area	City or County Supervisor of Adult Education Community Action Program Public Schools Private Schools Area Vocational Schools Bureau of Rehabilitation Services MDTA (Manpower Development Training Act) WIN (Work Incentive)	KIND/SITE/NO. ENROLLED _____ _____ _____ _____ _____ _____ _____ _____

Area of information	Information to include	Source of information	Fill in here
		NYC (Neighborhood Youth Corps)	_____
		CEP (Concentrated Employment Programs)	_____
		New Careers Program	_____
		Voluntary Groups	_____
I. Other Community Services available to disadvantaged adults	List of community services available to disadvantaged adults	Health Department	SERVICE/ AGENCY
		Welfare Department	
		Social Security	_____
		Community Action Programs	_____
		Comprehensive Care	_____
		Food and Nutrition Services	_____
		Child Care Programs	_____
		Housing Authorities	_____
		Voluntary Groups	_____
		Planning Commission	_____
		Mental Health	_____
		Family Planning Clinic	_____
		Radio Stations	_____
		Newspapers	_____
		Senior Citizens	_____
		Home Demonstration Agent	_____
		Agricultural Extension Agent	_____
J. Information and referral services available	Is there a central source of community agency and organization in your community?	United Fund	_____
		Public Library	_____
		Planning Commission	_____
		Comprehensive Health Care	_____

Additional information

_____	_____	_____	_____
_____	_____	_____	_____
_____	_____	_____	_____
_____	_____	_____	_____
_____	_____	_____	_____
_____	_____	_____	_____

Appalachian Adult Education Center
Revised October, 1974

Clientele Assessment and the Libraries' Responses Checklist

This checklist has been developed for this manual to be used in developing a profile of a client group or individual. It may be adapted or changed to fit the special needs of the client group profile characteristics and the local library situation.

1. The client as learner or client group (general)
2. Client profile assessment:
    Sex
    Age
    Place of origin
    Language
    Ethnic and cultural background
    Place of residence or geographic location
    Moving and migration
    Work or occupation
    Leisure or free time
    Dependency
    Income
    Health (for example, visual, auditory, physical, developmental, and nutritional disabilities)
    Attitudes and values toward learning and the library
    Experience
    Schooling
    Literacy abilities
3. Literacy needs of client group
4. Collaborating agencies and literacy programs
5. Library programs and services:
    Philosophy
    Types of services and activities
    Organization and administration
    Collaborative arrangements with others
6. Library staff responsibilities
7. Staff development and training
8. Material resources
9. Equipment and facilities
10. Funding sources
11. Information references

Program Profile Outline

This outline has been developed for this manual to be used by librarians who wish to develop an information file of programs in the library's community. It has been used very successfully in the collection of information about current literacy activities in various libraries of the country. The outline may be adapted or changed to fit the local situation.

      Program—a general description
      Program—(title)
      Location—Name of library:
              Address:
              Telephone:
  Contact person—Name:
              Address:
              Telephone:
      Clientele—Primary
              Secondary
Program purposes and objectives
Staff
Staff development and training activities
  Beginnings of program   Program facts
  and sources of funding   Results
Program Content Areas
  (For example, training for other than librarians, bibliographies, special collections, classes, production of materials)
Materials collections
  Types   Content and subject areas
  Reading levels   Languages
Collaborative agencies and literacy programs
Results: follow-up; evaluation
Your opinions about the program

Adult Learner Profile (Individual Assessment)

The Adult Learner Profile has been developed for this manual. It is suggested for use in recording an individual assessment of the adult learner. It may be adapted or changed to meet the local situation and the library's need.

Name: _____
Resident address: _____
Work address: _____
Occupation: _____
Approximate age:_____ Language:_____
Ethnic and cultural background: _____
_____
Special interests:_____
Last year of schooling completed: _____
Literacy programs enrolled in:_____

Goals: To learn to read_____ write_____ compute_____
  To solve daily problems_____ personal relations_____
  To get through elementary school requirements_____
  To get high school diploma equivalency GED_____
  To get college course credit_____
  To improve or advance on job_____
  To get into another line of work_____ What kind?_____
  Other _____
Need: To learn the following:
                              Referral: _____
What are requirements? _____
What is learner's knowledge? _____
What level does learner need to begin at? _____
What courses are wanted?_____
Where may courses be taken? _____
What subjects should be studied?
What materials are needed?   Where are they?
Does learner wish to study by self_____, in class_____, with tutor_____,
  with librarian adviser_____; other_____.

"Real World" Materials

  "Real world" materials include actual objects, free materials, forms,
and reading matter of all types that are used in the everyday affairs of
life. These materials may range from newspaper items, signs, grocery
labels, packages, and prices to complicated credit forms. The following
items are suggestions that are based on what the practical experience of
teachers, librarians, and learners has found useful. What is collected will
be what is relevant to local needs and what the alert search and
imaginative vision of the librarian suggests. Real world materials are
available from other agencies and organizations in the community. They
may be organized into a collection for consultation purposes or loan.

Community Resources
Library materials and library skills
  Applications for library cards
  Card or book catalog
  Checking out books from library/due date
  Dictionary
  Encyclopedia
  Index
  Table of contents
Maps
  Municipal   State   World

Medicare forms
Social Security forms
Telephone directory
Transportation
Bus schedules
Stop signs
Maps
  Road
  Highway
  State maps and state names
Directions for safety
Driver's license
  Driving manual
License plates
Parking area signs
Road signs
  Directions: exit signs; north; south, etc.; road curves
  Left lane, right lane
  Road signs: Construction Ahead; Stop, etc.
  Street, avenue, drive, road
Service-station signs and trademarks
Tickets for bus; train; airplane
Traffic tickets
Warning signs
Consumer Economics
Bank checks
  Deposit slips
  Withdrawal slips
Canned goods labels
Clothing labels
Credit contracts
Directions
  In a cafeteria
  Labels on food
  On product uses
  In a plant
Food stamps
Insurance-policy statements
Menus, restaurant bills, fortune cookies
Newspaper ads for groceries
Products and packages
Sales catalogs
Sears' and Ward's catalogs
Store/supermarket signs

Want ads: job; purchasing
Warning signs
Forms/Schedules, etc.
  Application forms (for example, jobs, courses)
  Driver's license forms
  Income tax forms
  Medicaid/Social Security
  Racing forms
  Baseball schedules
  Calendars
  Church programs
  Railroad schedules
  Brochures   .
  Handbooks (union)
  Manuals (scouting)
  Regulations: hunting/fishing
  Instructions: (variety)
    Hiking and skiing, games
    Cleaning and washing clothes
    Plant raising, gardening
  Job specifications: for work contracts
  Tickets (variety): bus; sports; entertainment; lottery; racetrack
  Want ads
Miscellaneous
  Collection of learner-written stories
  Collection of poems
  Collection of slides (illustrating local points of interest), signs,
    storefronts
  Comics
  Crossword-puzzle magazines
  Current song texts
  Horoscopes
  Human rights:
    Civil rights
    Legal rights
    Women's rights
  Motion pictures—notices, advertising, announcements
  Modern plays—announcements, advertising
  Paintings—exhibition announcements
  Political speeches in newspapers and magazines
  Scrapbooks of news or magazine pictures
  Tape recordings of books being read that can be used as the reader
    "follows" the book

Television programs
TV guides
Word recognition:
  Anagrams
  Flash cards
  Greeting cards
  Plastic letters
  Word games, shopping games

Resources

Federal and State Funding

Office of Education

ABE legislation (see The Adult Education Act, P.L. 91-120 and P.L. 93-380)

Library Services and Construction Act (LSCA)

Bilingual Education Act (1967–68, 1974) Elementary and Secondary Education Act, Title VII (OMB Cat. no. 13.403)

Elementary and Secondary Education Act, Title I

Indian Education Act, P.L. 92-318, Title IV, Parts A and B

Older Americans Act, Title VII

Ethnic Heritage Act, Title IX

Bilingual Education Act

  Elementary and Secondary Education Act (OMB Cat. no. 13.403)

Indian Education Act (P.L. 92-318), Title IV, Part B, Indian Education (OMB Cat. no. 13.535)

Higher Education Act, Title II B, Research and Demonstration

Right to Read

Federal Funding—Children

Elementary and Secondary Education Act, Title I

Programs for Children in State Institutions (OMB Cat. no. 13.431)

Programs for Disadvantaged Children (OMB Cat. no. 13.428)

Programs for Indian Children (OMB Cat. no. 13.428)

Programs for Migratory Children (OMB Cat. no. 13.429)

Special Grants to Urban and Rural School Districts with High Concentration of Poor Children, Title I, Part C (OMB Cat. no. 13.511)

Programs for Children in State Institutions for the Neglected and Delinquent (OMB Cat. no. 13.431)

Community Services Act (P.L. 93-644), Title V. Follow-through Act (OMB Cat. no. 13.512)

Elementary and Secondary Education Act, Title IV-B School Library Resources and Equipment (OMB Cat. no. 13.480)

Reading Improvement, Title VII

Cooperative Research Act
Right to Read (P.L. 83-531) (OMB Cat. no. 13.533)
Library Services and Construction Act Title I Library Services (OMB
    Cat. no. 13.464)
Adult Education Act of 1966, as amended (OMB Cat. no. 13.400)
Education Amendments of 1974, Special Projects Act Career Educa-
    tion (OMB Cat. no. 13.544)
Reading Improvement, Title VII

Literacy Programs and Organizations
Sources for bilingual-bicultural materials and information:

English as a Second Language Program
Center for Applied Linguistics
1611 North Kent Street
Arlington, Virginia 22209

Teachers of English to Speakers of Other Languages (TESOL)
James Alatis, Executive Secretary
School of Languages and Linguistics
Georgetown University
Washington, D.C. 20007

Proyecto LEER
1736 Columbia Road, N.W.
Suite 107
Washington, D.C. 20009
Phone: (202) 265-3275

Bilingual Education Service Center
500 South Dwyer Avenue
Arlington Heights, Illinois 60005
Phone: (312) 255-9820

Executive Secretary
National Council of Teachers of English
1111 Kenyon Road
Urbana, Illinois 61801

National Association for Bilingual Education
Dr. Alvar A. Peña, President
The University of Texas at San Antonio
4242 Piedras Drive East
San Antonio, Texas 78285

Dissemination Center for Bilingual Bicultural Education
6504 Tracor Lane
Austin, Texas 78721

National Farmworker Information Clearinghouse
3001 South Congress
Austin, Texas 78704
Phone: (512) 444-1863

Cross-Cultural Southwest Ethnic Study Center
University of Texas at El Paso
Box 13
El Paso, Texas 79968

Library Services Technical Assistance Center
3036 University Avenue S.E.
Minneapolis, Minnesota 54414

Bilingual Materials Development Center
6000 Cany Bowie Boulevard
Fort Worth, Texas 76116

Literacy program components:

Armed services
   PREP (training for GED)
   Office of Defense Education
   Manpower and Reserve Affairs
   The Pentagon
   Washington, D.C. 20301

Job Corps program
   U.S. Department of Labor
   Manpower Administration
   Washington, D.C. 20210

PACE
   Program Activities for Correctional Education
   Cook County Department of Correctional Education
   220 South State
   Chicago, Illinois 60608
   Mr. Joseph R. Russo, Director

Women in Community Service (WICS)
   Department of Labor
   1730 Rhode Island Avenue, N.W.
   Suite 400
   Washington, D.C. 20036

Media programs:

The Electric Company
Children's TV Workshop
One Lincoln Plaza
New York, New York 10023

Kentucky Education Television Network and
The Cambridge Book Company
Mr. William H. Wilson, Asst. G.E.D. Specialist
KETV
600 Cooper Drive
Lexington, Kentucky 40502

National programs:

Adult Basic Education Program
Division of Adult Education
Department of Health, Education, and Welfare
Office of Education
F.O.B. 6
400 Maryland Avenue, S.W.
Washington, D.C. 20202

Manpower Development and Training Program
Adult Vocational, Technical and Manpower Education
Bureau of Occupational and Adult Education
Department of Health, Education, and Welfare
Office of Education
F.O.B. 6
400 Maryland Avenue, S.W.
Washington, D.C. 20202

Project READ
American Correctional Association
4321 Hartwick Road
Suite 306
College Park, Maryland 20740

Reading Is Fundamental, Inc. (RIF)
c/o Smithsonian Institution
Washington, D.C. 20560

Right-to-Read Program
United States Office of Education
Room 2131
400 Maryland Avenue, S.W.
Washington, D.C. 20202

Organizations and associations:

Clearinghouse for Offender Literacy Programs
Janet F. Carsetti, Director
1705 De Sales Street, N.W.
Washington, D.C. 20036

Education Commission of the States
822 Lincoln Tower
1860 Lincoln Street
Denver, Colorado 80203

National Advisory Council on Adult Education (NACAE)
(President's Advisory Council on Adult Education)
425 Thirteenth Street, N.W.
Room 323
Washington, D.C. 20004

National Association for Bilingual Education
Dr. Alvar A. Peña, President
The University of Texas at San Antonio
4242 Piedras Drive East
San Antonio, Texas 78285

National Association for Public Continuing
   and Adult Education (NAPCAE)
1201 Sixteenth Street, N.W.
Washington, D.C. 20036

National Council of Teachers of English
Executive Secretary
1111 Kenyon Road
Urbana, Illinois 61801

National Education Association Adult Education Clearinghouse
Dr. Richard Cortright, Director
1201 Sixteenth Street, N.W.
Washington, D.C. 20036

National Home Study Council
1601 Eighteenth Street, N.W.
Washington, D.C. 20009

Teachers of English to Speakers of Other
   Languages (TESOL)
James Alatis, Executive Secretary
School of Languages and Linguistics
Georgetown University
Washington, D.C. 20007

Volunteer groups:

American Bible Society
1865 Broadway
New York, New York 10023

Church Women United
Mrs. Alice Leppert, Program Specialist in ABE
Room 812
475 Riverside Drive
New York, New York 10027

Laubach Literacy, Inc.
Box 131
Syracuse, New York 13210

Literacy Volunteers of America, Inc.
3001 James Street
Syracuse, New York 13206

Lutheran Church Women—Volunteer
 Reading Aides
Mrs. Martha A. Lane, Coordinator
2900 Queen Lane
Philadelphia, Pennsylvania 19129

Sorority Literacy Programs
Mrs. M. B. Grays, National President
Alpha Kappa Alpha, Inc.
5211 South Greenwood Avenue
Chicago, Illinois 60615

World Education
1414 Sixth Avenue
New York, New York 10019

Handbooks for Tutor Training

Tutoring others to read requires basic skills as well as willingness. The librarian who wants to be a tutor or who wants to train others to tutor can obtain how-to ideas and information from some of the published handbooks available on the topic.

Although there are other tutoring handbooks available from a variety of agencies involved with reading, this brief list includes only those that have become available to ALA's literacy project. No attempt is made to evaluate the guides, since their usefulness depends a great deal on the background of the potential tutor.

The handbooks are listed by the address of the resource agency.

1. National Commission on Resources for Youth, Inc.
36 West 44th Street, New York, New York 10036
(212) 682-3339

   The Commission has produced a series of manuals for the tutor of youth in after-school settings. The series is paperbound. Practical, unsophisticated, easy-to-follow ideas on relating to and practicing reading with "tutees." Copyright 1970.

   For the Tutor. $3.00.
   Learning and Growing Through Tutoring. $3.00.
   Manual for Trainers: Youth Tutoring Youth. $3.00.
   Supervisor's Manual: Youth Tutoring Youth. $2.50.
   Tutoring Tricks and Tips. $2.50
   You're the Tutor. $1.75.

2. RALSU—Regional Adult Literacy Service Unit
309 Aderhold Building, University of Georgia
Athens, Georgia 30602

   Twelve "instruction concept guides" developed as a project of a R-2-R community-based grant. The guides are designed for volunteer or paraprofessional tutor training in adult literacy. Copyright 1975. $3.00 each.

   The Directed Reading Approach: A Lesson Organization Procedure Adapted for Use with Adults
   Getting Together: Establishing a Working Tutorial Relationship
   Help: Inside and Outside the Tutoring Agency
   The Language Experience Approach: Application for Tutoring Adults in Reading
   The Newspaper: A Source of High-Interest Instructional Material for Adults
   Process and Product: A Guide for Assessment of Community Tutoring Programs
   Resources: A Guide for Using Published Materials in Adult Literacy Programs
   Splitting Up: Terminating a Tutoring Relationship
   Student-Centered Tutoring: Using Initial Lesson Results to Set Future Goals
   Teaching One-to-One: A Diagnostic Approach to Beginning Tutoring
   The Teaching of Sight Words: Ways and Means
   Word Concepts: An Adult Approach to Decoding Skills

3. Literacy Volunteers of America, Inc.
   3001 James Street, Syracuse, New York 13206

   Easy-to-follow guides that lead the tutor from diagnosing the prospective learner's level of entry to methods of teaching reading.

   Colvin, Ruth J., and Root, Jane H., *READ: Reading Evaluation—Adult Diagnosis*. 1976. $2.75.
   ————*Tutor: Techniques Used in Teaching of Reading*. 1976. $4.00.

   Note: LVA, Inc. and Laubach Literacy, Inc. (Box 131, Syracuse, New York 13210) will provide training sessions for volunteers. Check for cost and schedules of training sessions.

4. Right to Read (R-2-R) has developed many materials for national dissemination among educators, parents, and the general public. The following three handbooks are aimed mainly at teachers who are interested in training volunteer reading tutors. They may be ordered from the U.S. Government Printing Office (give title, number of copies desired, stock numbers, and enclose payment), Washington, D.C. 20402.

   Tutor Resource Handbook for Teachers. $.75; GPO stock no. 1780-01332.
   For effective utilization of tutors by classroom teachers.
   Tutors' Resource Handbook. $2.15; GPO stock no. 1780-01333.
   For tutors to develop their roles both inside and outside classroom.
   Tutor-Trainers' Resource Handbook. $1.90; GPO stock no. 1780-01334.
   For planning, development and administration of a volunteer tutor program.

5. Book-Lab, Inc.
   1449 Thirty-seventh Street
   Brooklyn, New York 11218

   Pope, Lillie. *Guidelines to Teaching Remedial Reading to the Disadvantaged*. 1975. $3.85
   Provides do's and don'ts on tutoring adults reading on levels from grades three through nine. Includes charts, lists, and bibliographies.
   ————*Tutor: A Handbook for Tutorial Programs*. 1976. $3.60.
   Not examined.

6. International Reading Association
   800 Barksdale Road, Newark, Delaware 19711

Rauch, Sidney J., comp. *Handbook for the Volunteer Tutor.* 1969. $2.50.
    Not seen, although referred to by many sources.

Resources for School Libraries

The following is a brief list of materials that provide basic information and ideas to assist the school librarians in enlarging their activities in developing literacy skills in youth.   Although there are many more materials available, this list includes those available to ALA's literacy project.   In most cases, no attempt has been made to evaluate the materials listed since their usefulness depends a great deal on the varieties of application adopted by the school librarian.

Articles

Strader, Helen B. "An Audiovisual Approach to Literacy," *Booklist* 73, no. 3 (October 1, 1976):258–63.
Toys, Games and Realia Committee, Children's Services Division (ALA). "Realia in the Library," *Booklist* 73, no. 9 (January 1, 1977):671–74.

Books

Beach, Don M. *Reaching Teenagers: Learning Centers for the Secondary Classroom.* Santa Monica, Calif.: Goodyear Publishing Company, Inc., 1977. 167p. $8.95 paper.
Wehmeyer, Lillian Biermann.   *The School Librarian as Educator.* Littleton, Colo.: Libraries Unlimited, 1976. 266p. $11.50.

Brochures/Pamphlets

American Association of School Librarians (AASL)
American Library Association
50 East Huron Street
Chicago, Illinois 60611

Essentials for a Literacy Campaign, 1972	single copy–free
Literacy: A Goal of Right to Read, 1972	single copy–free
The Reading Management Team: The Right-to-Read, 1972	single copy–free
The Role of the Media Specialist in the Right-to-Read Program, 1972	single copy–free
Aids in Selecting Books for the Reluctant Reader, 1970	single copy–25¢
School Media Services and the Right-to-Read Program, 1972	single copy–25¢

Children's Services Division
American Library Association
50 East Huron Street
Chicago, Illinois 60611

Resources for Underachievers in Reading single copy –free

Office of Young Adult Services
New York Public Library
8 East 40th Street
New York, New York 10016

Easy-to-Read Books for Teenagers: 1976

Santa Clara Public Library
2635 Homestead Road
Santa Clara, California 95051

Gray, Brenda, and others. *Literacy Programs and Public Libraries.* $2.00.

Mentioned here for the excellent ideas it provides on making and using games for literacy.

Film

Audiovisual Services Branch
Division of the State Library
State of North Carolina
Raleigh, North Carolina 27611

Reading Is the Family. 1974. 10m. Color.

Demonstrates ways young children can be encouraged to read. Emphasizes child-parent relationship in helping young children develop reading skills.

Comic Books and Magazines

Children's Television Workshop
1 Lincoln Plaza
New York, New York 10023

Electric Company Magazine
Sesame Street (text in English and Spanish)

Marvel Comics Groups
575 Madison Avenue
New York, New York 10022

"Spidey Super Stories"

Johnson Publishing Company
820 South Michigan Avenue
Chicago, Illinois 60605

Ebony Junior (magazine)

Saturday Evening Post Company
1100 Waterway Boulevard
P.O.B. 567B
Indianapolis, Indiana 46206
Jack and Jill Magazine

Games

Milton Bradley Company
Learn the Alphabet (alphabet picture flash cards)
Sequence Cards (visual literacy)

Kenworthy Educational Service
Phonic Rummy

Suggestions (see also chapter 5—The Public School/Media Center Library)

1. Make the library/media center a world of words.
2. Provide bulletin boards in which students can participate, e.g., boards on which they can add words, pictures, ideas, names, etc.
3. Many materials that support reading skills can be made. For example:
   picture/word dictionaries
   student-made books, word games, etc.
   word "tic-tac-toe"
   word "bingo"
   word "wheels"
   "traffic sign bingo"
   matching word/picture games
4. Learn how to pre-teach "hard to read" words before read-aloud sessions.
5. Use popular records as a means of learning new words to discuss and to read.
6. Follow the reading of books as often as possible with a project related to the book or to the book's theme.
7. Provide reading skills kits that can be made by duplicating specific work sheets from Spirit Duplicator Masters (buy at a school supply store). Make the kits accessible for the students to use by themselves.

Library Project Profile Reports

These project reports are from project directors who are conducting literacy or learning programs in various libraries.

Bay County Public Library Service to Adult Basic Education Centers and Students

Program Title:
Service to Adult Basic Education (ABE) Centers and Students

Location:
Northwest Regional Library System
Headquarters: Bay County Public Library
25 West Government Street
Panama City, Florida 32401

Contact Person:
Sandra O'Bryan
Bay County Public Library
25 West Government Street
Panama City, Florida 32401
Phone: (904) 785-3458

Clientele: Economically disadvantaged
  A. Primary—The new adult (16 years or older) reader
  B. Secondary—The student working toward diploma or studying for GED

Program Purposes and Objectives:

To reach the new adult learner through the recognition of the public library's responsibility as a change agent

To select, organize, provide, and stimulate the use of materials for communication and learning for the new adult reader

To increase library service to adult basic education centers

To encourage ABE students to utilize library resources by gaining their confidence in the personnel, services, and materials

To encourage ABE students to involve family and friends in ongoing library use

Staff:

A specialist, part-time help of other librarians, library assistant, and clerk, plus part-time supportive help of other staff members in branches and the main (resource) library and on bookmobiles

Staff Development and Training Activities:

In-service training workshops for library personnel, which introduced them to specialized ABE materials, their use, and determination of readability levels, have been conducted.

Several of the branch people have spent a full day in the ABE department and on the outreach bookmobile.

A slide program was produced for staff and others interested in the program.

Beginnings of Program and Sources of Funding:

The program began in 1972 as a disadvantaged program.

Federal funding is $57,000, and local funding is $28,500 (estimated budget for 1976–77).

Program Content Areas:

This Service to Adult Basic Education (ABE) Program serves the six-county, 3,946-mile area of the Northwest Regional Library System. Nine libraries and three bookmobiles serve this part of the rural panhandle of Florida. The total population served by the system is 118,555, with 45.1% of these being rural. There is an average of 30 people per square mile in the six-county area. Bay County has 75,283 population. This is the largest county populationwise.

The program depends upon cooperation between the public library system and the Adult Education Department in each county. We are now serving 40 classes with 1,000 students. Because of the rural nature of the area, a lot of time is spent driving to provide library service to these classes.

Personal car, bookmobile, mail, and telephone service are the main ways of transmitting the materials and information.

Weekly bookmobile stops are made at the main adult education centers in Bay and Calhoun Counties. Night centers in the Bay County area are also visited by bookmobile. Night centers in the other counties are visited once a month and have book deposits, which are rotated at the end of each visit. In addition, each center can request materials to support its curriculum.

Library personnel provide personal reading guidance on an individual basis when needed and work with the teachers to coordinate materials and develop programs.

Films and other educational programs are provided through local agencies when interest is shown at the center.

A nucleus of materials is being ordered, processed, and placed in branch libraries. Workshops on the ABE materials will be held in the branch libraries for students and teachers. One of these was held in Bay County in the fall.

The ABE services have been extended to the local boys' club, girls' club, juvenile detention home, Oak Grove School for the Mentally Retarded, Council on Aging, federal housing projects, and the Cerebral Palsy Center.

Visits to and use of all library outlets are promoted.

Those directing the program make every effort to respond to the adult learner's needs as defined by health, welfare, and educational agencies. Subject matter, reading level, interest level, and format are considered.

Training (for Other than Librarians):

A workshop was held in Bay County to introduce adult education teachers and students to specialized reading materials.

Bibliographies:

Adult Basic Education Bibliography materials are available through the Northwest Regional Library System. Level eight and below (divided by coping skills).

Special Collections/Demonstration Collections:

There is a core collection of ABE and EASL materials, which is divided by series or title. This material is for demonstration and does not circulate.

There is also a special collection of materials divided by coping skills, which is used with the outreach program. Material for the new reader is also available in the main library and in all branches.

Materials Collections:

The collection is made up of books (paperback and hardcover), pamphlets, newspapers, cassette tapes, and filmstrip-print kits.

The material is divided by coping skills and subjects: language arts, consumer skills, family and health, personality and self-awareness, career, black literature and minorities, leisure reading, mathematics, United States government, and English as a second language.

Most of the specialized collection is level eight and below.

The English-as-a-second-language collection includes some general materials and some specialized tapes on Chinese, Japanese, Korean, Thai, and Vietnamese. We are trying to collect more Vietnamese materials for the three classes we serve.

Some materials are being produced by the library.

Collaborative Agencies and Literacy Programs:

County and state health departments
Bay County School Media Center
Division of Youth Services
Council on Aging
Panhandle Alcohol Council

Washington-Holmes Area Vocational-Technical School
Tom F. Haney Vocational-Technical School
Shaw Adult School
Boys' club
Oak Grove School for the Mentally Retarded
Federal housing projects
Calhoun County Adult Education Department
Gulf County Adult Education Department
Gulf County Jail
Gulf Coast Community College
Bay County Day Care Center
St. John Baptist Church Group
Redemption Lutheran Church
Cancer Society
Welfare Department
USDA and Food Stamp Office
Social Security Administration
American Heart Association
Insurance broker
Ministerial Association
Calhoun County Extension Office
Bay County Extension Office
Public Employment Agency
Cerebral Palsy Center
Girls' club

Results; Follow-up; Evaluation:

Teachers and students have found that their programs of study are more interesting because of the variety of materials the library provides. Lack of time and money restrict teachers and students from seeking materials on their own.

Some students who had never been in the library before came as a result of this program. New readers who have walked in off the street have found support from the branch, bookmobile, and main library service.

The library has helped the Vietnamese refugees in their study of English as a second language and in introducing them to the American culture.

Up to this time evaluation has developed through the positive/negative comments of both teachers and students about the ABE program. Some teachers and students have been quite good with feedback. The library personnel have been able to determine some success through their monthly visits to the centers.

To collect more information beyond the traditional library statistics such as circulation and library cards issued, we are doing some very flexible questionnaires. We are evaluating the library service to each adult class. This evaluation is being conducted as the school year ends for the classes. Questions relate to library service to the classes and to new reader students coming to the library.

As of January 1976, a subject circulation count of materials at ABE centers has been kept, based on coping skills areas.

More statistics are going to be kept on a regular basis on ABE students actually coming into the library or using the bookmobile. Several names of students will be requested with their permission so that a follow-up letter can be sent to them. This letter will be sent after six months or a year to see if the student is using any library service.

Our (My) Opinions about the Program:

Teachers and students have expressed their appreciation for the program. This program is providing a very necessary service, as practically none of the ABE classes were receiving library service before. While some of the students have used other library services besides ABE services, it has been a small percentage. Hopefully, time will show more students using these services. Personal contact with the students is very important, but difficult with only an average of one visit a month per class. It is hoped and expected that more work can be done through the teachers as time goes on.

Dallas Public Library Learning Center Project

Program (General Description):

The cooperative Library Learning Center Project in four Dallas Public Library System branch libraries pooling the resources of Dallas Public Library, Dallas Independent School District, Dallas County Community College District (the 3 Ds) and KERA-TV/Channel 13 in serving undereducated adults from ABE through college level

Program Title:

3D (Library Learning Center Project)

Location:

Audelia Road Branch Library
10045 Audelia Road
Dallas, Texas 75238
Phone: (214) 348-6160

Hampton-Illinois Branch Library
2210 West Illinois
Dallas, Texas 75224
Phone: (214) 337-4796

Dallas West Branch Library
2332 Singleton Boulevard
Dallas, Texas 75212
Phone: (214) 637-1204

Martin Luther King Jr. Library/Learning Center
2922 Forest Avenue
Dallas, Texas 75215
Phone: (214) 421-4171
Contact Person:
Jean Brooks, Project Director
1954 Commerce Street
Dallas, Texas 75201
Phone: (214) 748-5256
Clientele:
Primary: Undereducated adult
Secondary: Enrichment-oriented adult
Program Purposes and Objectives:

To create a nonthreatening adult learning environment in a public library where special equipment, materials, and personnel are available to guide undereducated adults to self-direct their own learning. Students enter learning at an entry level suited to their capabilities and move on up the learning ladder at their chosen pace, freed from group pressure and time limitations.

To provide a minimally structured approach to learning at all levels, encouraging the learner to move independently into library resources with the concept of the total library as a learning center.

To incorporate guidance and information on career and other community learning opportunities into the general learning process.
Staff:
One guidance associate
Four facilitator/teachers
Five work study/student guidance assistants
Staff Development and Training Activities:

The ABE/GED facilitator/teachers are pretrained by the Dallas Independent School District in the basic ABE/GED program.

A guidance associate is pretrained by the Dallas County Community College District in general information and career guidance.

Orientation is given by the Dallas Public Library staff to the library system for ABE/GED facilitator/teachers and the guidance associate. Training sessions are held with the Dallas Independent School District and the Dallas County Community College district coordinators and librarian director. Continuing training is provided by the 3D librarian director in the library philosophy of learning facilitation vs. individualized instruction and guidance to open community options vs. limited source direction.
Beginnings of Program and Sources of Funding:

1973–75: Local foundation funding to Dallas Public Library for joint learning center proposal with Dallas County Community College

District, providing guidance personnel, audio-visual hardware/ software, and other materials for two learning centers.

1974–76: ABE/GED LSCA funding for library learning centers for materials only from Texas State Library. Dallas Independent School District funding from Texas Education Agency for three teachers and minimal audio-visual hardware/software.

Program Content Areas:

Training (for other than librarians)

Bibliographies/study guides

Special collections

Production of materials, i.e., informational brochures

Materials Collections:

Types: Consumable workbooks, tape/print kits, video cassettes, programmed tape/filmstrips, slide/tapes, flash cards, signs, etc.

Reading Levels: 1st through college

Languages: English, Spanish, Russian, Vietnamese

Collaborative Agencies and Literacy Programs:

Dallas County Community College District

Dallas Independent School District—ABE/GED

KERA-TV/Channel 13

Referral Agencies:

Dallas County Community Colleges

Dallas Volunteer Action Center

Jewish Family Services

Mental health/mental retardation

Operation LIFT (reading and writing for adults)

Probation officers

Southern Methodist University

Texas Employment Commission

Texas Rehabilitation Commission

Texas State Welfare Department

Veterans Administration

WIN (Work Incentive Program)

Results; Follow-up; Evaluation:

Students at all levels have used the library learning centers. The project has reached over 1,643 learners, many of whom are new library users. Many GED test takers move on into CLEP test preparation or into a college. Community agencies and learners attest to job achievements and continuing learning. Learners have successfully passed over 1,600 GED and CLEP tests.

The concept of the 3D Library Learning Center is valid. The librarian, facilitator, guidance associate, user, and referring agencies all testify to 3D's validity. However, at the lowest ABE levels 3D has limited capability, and at the special education and foreign-language level its capabilities are even lower. These very low-level learners, learners with learning disabilities, and foreign-language students require services from a learning laboratory fully equipped and staffed where audible response and kinaesthetic responses may be practiced, and where psychiatric and other special diagnostic aid is available. Attempts of a library learning center to meet *all* low-level learning needs are not only presumptuous but may have a potential for learning impairment.

When the 3D Library Learning Center operates in bringing together its services for the individual who can function with a minimum of personal help, the results are highly successful. The Library Learning Center cannot encompass all levels of learning. The area where it is least successful, due to lack of suitable library space and staff/volunteer limitations, is at the illiterate to very low literacy level, including those illiterates learning English as a new language. Experiments during 3D have indicated that added staff/volunteers is not an answer where suitable library space is not available to house sufficient staff and equipment to meet the numbers to be served.

Coordinative action can take place between institutions, but underlying service philosophies are often difficult to mesh into a new kind of service unit outside of the parent agency. Each agency gives some to coalesce with the others, but unless all are willing to make changes, coordinative action is not successful. The 3D program does not wish to duplicate programs available elsewhere but has presented a new learning package in a new way within the city of Dallas. It has offered an alternative, independent learning experience for adults who find they like to self-direct their learning experiences. The support to help them guide their learning comes from the resource pool. Independent study/learning is the core of 3D, and within the 3D Library Learning Centers it has taken place this past year. The student likes it, and 3D Library Learning Center personnel recognize its validity in handling large numbers of students to reach their goals.

If a learning center is used heavily for one-to-one tutoring, other learners will drop off. The percentage of learners who can be aided to attain goals in a limited space drops with the learning level.

Independent learning can and does function at the lowest learning levels. Until all coordinating agencies understand and recognize this concept, 3D is divided and cannot achieve its highest potential.

Your Opinions about the Program:

The concept of library learning centers with educational agency resource pooling is excitingly valid when the educational agency is willing to move out of its traditional institutional roles in creation of a new learning mode. Unless the "teacher" is library-paid or library-directed, however, the learning center can become merely an outside agency implant in the library setting with no assimilation into the library as a learning resource and could operate as well at any other site. The basic needs at all levels are development of reading comprehension and mathematics skills.

Denver Public Library Right to Read
Adult Reading Academy
Program:
 Provides individual instruction to illiterate and non-English-speaking adults through volunteer tutors in reading skills and English as a Second Language
Program Title:
 Denver Public Library Right to Read Adult Reading Academy
Location:
 Denver Public Library
 1357 Broadway
 Denver, Colorado 80203
Contact Persons:
 Graham Sadler, Director
 Denver Public Library
 1357 Broadway
 Denver, Colorado 80203
 Phone: (303) 573-5152, ext. 256

 Diane Davalos, Coordinator
 Byers Library
 675 Santa Fe Drive
 Denver, Colorado 80204
 Phone: (303) 572-1149
Clientele:
 Functionally illiterate adults, 16 years and over (served approximately 500 in fiscal year 1976) and Spanish-speaking adults (approximately 400 in fiscal year 1976)
Program Purposes and Objectives:
 Bring literacy and survival skills (jobs, driver's licenses, consumer education, etc.) to as many as possible of Denver's 30,000 potential target student population
 Bring awareness of skills necessary for living well in this society as well as appreciation for students' own cultural heritage
Staff:
 Director—Graham H. Sadler
 Coordinator—Diane Davalos
 Recruitment Coordinator—George Gallegos
 English As a Second Language Coordinator—Gladys Pensado

Reading Specialist—Bill Knuth

Secretary—Chris Arrieta

Staff Development and Training Activities:

Volunteer tutors receive initial interview and orientation (1.5 hours) and bimonthly training workshops on methods, materials, troubleshooting, and sensitivity to the unique problems of adult nonreaders.

Beginnings of Program and Sources of Funding:

A HEW Right to Read grant (since 1972)—approximately $72,000 annually

Program Content Areas:

Training of tutors

Individual tutorial sessions in reading

Small classes (3–15) for ESL students

Production of tutor-made materials (shared with all staff)

Production of tutor manual for introduction to program and training purposes

Materials Collection:

Types—books, magazines, workbooks, low-level (fourth-grade) newspapers

Content—how-to-use information, culturally relevant materials, high-interest low-vocabulary literature

Reading levels—0–6

Languages—English, Spanish

Collaborative Agencies and Literacy Programs:

Three branch libraries serve as satellite centers—sessions held there

Adult Education Resource Center (State Department of Education)

National Right to Read Effort, Washington, D.C.—dissemination of materials, procedures, training modules

Community Agencies—human services who refer clients

Results; Follow-up; Evaluation:

Have accomplished what was proposed in federal grant application

Serve approximately 1000 students

Bring 75 percent to a second-grade level achievement

Assist in obtaining jobs, filling out necessary forms, awareness of rights and responsibilities as United States citizens

Plans are to increase numbers served for next fiscal year

Opinion:

This program is serving an important need in Denver, particularly to minorities and disadvantaged. It is also increasing awareness in the community of the problem and is striving to develop a city-wide literacy campaign, involve greater numbers of people, and eventually eliminate illiteracy in the city.

Brooklyn Public Library Reading Improvement Program

Program Title:

Brooklyn Public Library Reading Improvement Program

Location:

Brooklyn Heights Branch Library

280 Cadman Plaza West

Brooklyn, New York 11201

Phone: (212) 636-3289 Branch phone

(212) 636-3297 RIP phone

Contact Person:

Richard L. Keller, Chief

Reading Improvement Program

280 Cadman Plaza West

Brooklyn, New York 11201

Phone: (212) 636-3297

Clientele:

Adults 18 years of age and over

Program Purposes and Objectives:

To enhance reading skills on all levels and to increase understanding and appreciation of the written word

Staff:

Richard L. Keller—head of program, instructor of developmental classes, and tutor of 18 remedial readers per week

1 Clerk/Receptionist—Mrs. Ethel Garrison

Staff Development and Training Activities:

When city finances were better, I had an assistant who also taught classes and tutored remedial readers. When assistants began, they had a month's orientation and observation before beginning their own classes and working with individual readers under my guidance. I am now alone and have been since October 8, 1975.

Beginnings of Program and Sources of Funding:

This program started in September 1955 as a joint experimental research program between the Brooklyn Public Library and Brooklyn College. It was financed by a grant from the Carnegie Corporation of New York. It was to last five years. The purpose was to examine methods and procedures to find the best ways to help adults learn to read better and to determine what machines, if any, are necessary in such courses, whether libraries are a feasible place to have such courses, and whether or not a library can have such a program without the aid of a neighboring college.

The program was designed as an action-research project in two parts. The Brooklyn College staff organized the format of the program, the testing procedures, the organization and teaching of classes, and the methods to be used in the evaluation of results.

During the first three years Brooklyn College staff assumed complete control of the administration of the program, including training and supervision of all staff. During the two years after the withdrawal of the Brooklyn College staff, it was planned that the program would be continued under the direct supervision of a library staff member (Richard L. Keller) who had been trained by the college staff during the first three years and who, during those first three years, was also the reader's adviser, giving guidance in book choices to all students in the program.

Research results at the end of the five-year project showed that librarians could teach such courses effectively, and this program has been part of the Brooklyn Public Library since that time.

Program Content Areas:

We only give classes, tutoring, and reader's advisory service. We do not have special collections, outside of a few titles we can hand to remedial readers. We use the library downstairs for reading material. We have, for classroom work, some workbooks and materials, such as SRA, which are only used here and in classes. We do not produce materials.

Literacy and improvement of reading skills course work includes help in increasing such reading skills as vocabulary, speed, comprehension, and general reading efficiency, as well as remediation and individual guidance for readers below a fourth-grade level. Advice is also given in building reading programs to meet individual needs and interests. Our classes for developmental readers meet twice a week for two hours; the courses last for six weeks. Remedial readers (below fourth grade) are tutored individually for one hour per week. This is also true of foreign-born students who come to learn English as well as reading. We see the remedial students for as long as two years. This program is free to adults 18 years of age and over. We also give a visual screening test with the Keystone Telebinocular and refer to clinics those who have a lack of fusion. Reader's advisory service is offered to all students.

Materials Collections:

Some workbooks and texts dealing with vocabulary, speed, comprehension skills, paragraph structure, précis writing, concentration, retention, study methods, etc. These are used in class. Some other workbooks and materials are used with remedial readers, and two workbooks are used with those learning English. The people we work with range from nonreaders up through various levels to college graduate reading. Our classes are arranged on a homogeneous basis to facilitate the teaching and learning.

Collaborative Agencies and Literacy Programs:

There are no specific ones with whom we collaborate. We have become a referral source for doctors, hospitals, clinics, schools, universities, guidance counselors, unemployment agencies, etc. We take everyone, but they have to wait to be grouped or seen individually.

Results; Follow-up; Evaluation:

Although we need periodic publicity, we get a good percentage of our students by word of mouth from those who took our course and profited. Not everyone improves on the end tests. Some have tensions that get in their way at test taking; some haven't practiced reading and remain where they were in their reading; some have low IQ and poor reasoning skills, low vocabulary, little or no background (experiential) and/or frame of reference for understanding. However, most seem to feel that they have made progress, no matter what the end test may show. Six to eight weeks after the end of the course a follow-up questionnaire is sent each graduate. The returns in general are very favorable, some ecstatic.

My Opinions about the Program:

Doing this work for twenty years has caused mixed reactions in my mind from time to time. In general, I feel it is a worthwhile venture. However, the ones we cannot help, the ones who drop out, the ones who do not show gains bother me. There has been a general decline in the abilities of our applicants in the past ten years, and also a general decline in the number of applicants. We now get mostly students reading below seventh-grade level, and also many reading on seventh-, eighth-, ninth-, tenth-grade levels who have actually finished high school and even some college, and some are college graduates. Those from a seventh- to tenth-grade level have more problems and give us more problems than any other category. They are disorganized, poorly motivated, and have greater absenteeism and more dropouts than other levels. They practice less, seem to expect miracles without effort on their part, etc. This work is difficult, often frustrating, but when working with the more advanced readers with high IQs, good motivation, eagerness to learn and comply with instructions, including a volume of outside class practice, then the rewards are great. It all depends on the individual, not so much the teaching. Two people in the same class can have very different end scores because of attitude, motivation, and practice, even though they are in a homogeneous grouping.

Mountain View Public Library Federal R.E.A.D. Project

Program:

R.E.A.D. is a literacy project aimed at helping people with reading and/or language problems.

Program Title:

Federal R.E.A.D. Project—Reading for Everyone—To Achieve and Develop

Location:
  Mountain View Public Library
  585 Franklin Street
  Mountain View, California 94040
  Phone: (415) 968-6595
Contact Person:
  Brenda Gray, Project Director
  Mountain View Public Library
Clientele:
  For tutoring, anyone aged 9 or older with a reading problem. Presently over 70 students are being tutored every week. More than half the students are adults (18 or older). In addition, through reading readiness classes offered by R.E.A.D., approximately 40 preschoolers are served each week, and 25 children aged 7–12 are offered reading enrichment in the weekly READrunner Club.
Program Purposes and Objectives:
  To provide individual tutoring, based on individual needs, to a limited number of people in a specific target area, using materials and equipment in a library reading laboratory
  To make the public more aware of reading disabilities through community contacts and publicity
  To provide parent workshops, special displays of materials and equipment, and booklists for parents and professionals
  To provide in-service training workshops and reading lab demonstrations, booklists, and recommendations for purchase of books for each member library, about or for the disabled learner
  To cooperate with teachers and reading specialists in student referrals and student problems, and to encourage the pooling of resources and information for better coordination of services to the disabled reader
  To motivate the nonuser through programs, reading enrichment, and appropriate instructional materials made available through the R.E.A.D. Project
  To set up a master community resource and referral file at R.E.A.D. headquarters for use by the R.E.A.D. staff and member librarians; to maintain a special collection of materials on learning disabilities
  To further develop a volunteer program, using graduate library and education students, giving them an opportunity for field training and expanding the tutoring schedule
  To provide a plan of continued reading improvement and library instruction to those adults who have completed beginning English classes through readers' advisory service, library tours, and personal guidance by the R.E.A.D. staff

Staff:
  Project director (Librarian II)
  Librarian I—Supervises and trains volunteers
  Typist/clerk/tutor
  Tutor (half-time CETA [Comprehensive Employment and Training Act])
  Tutor (part-time CETA)
  Volunteers: At the present time volunteers number 11, and most of them were assigned to R.E.A.D. by the San Jose State University Librarianship Department, where they are enrolled as graduate students. The graduate students receive class credit for assisting R.E.A.D. on a semester basis. Other volunteers include a woman interested in making remedial reading her career, a senior citizen who assists with our clipping file, and two young people who tutor and help with children's activities.
Staff Development and Training Activities:
  During the first year of the program, the Librarian II and original clerk/typist received six months of formal training in an adult education reading lab at the San Jose Public Library; they enrolled in education courses at San Jose State University, attended workshops, and joined professional organizations like International Reading Association, Santa Clara County Reading Teachers Association, and California Association for the Neurologically Handicapped.
  Staff development is an ongoing process. Weekly staff meetings are held to discuss tutoring techniques and the progress of students. Volunteers are asked to read a number of suggested books and pamphlets on tutoring and then observe tutoring sessions before they tutor. Volunteers are observed and supervised by a librarian. A manual-directory has been compiled to make tutor training more comprehensive.
Beginnings of Program and Sources of Funding:
  The Federal R.E.A.D. Project has been funded for the past four years under Title I LSCA money. The first two years of the program were centered in the target area of east San Jose at two branch libraries: the Hillview Branch of the San Jose Public Library and the Alum Rock Branch of the Santa Clara County Library. Reading labs were set up at each library. Other services included bringing paperbacks to local community centers, compiling a referral file, establishing a reference collection of books, pamphlets, and clippings, and offering special programs and workshops. During the third year, R.E.A.D. was continued at Hillview Library but was moved from Alum Rock Branch Library to Mountain View Public Library. For the final year R.E.A.D. has been limited to the Mountain View Public Library and serves residents of Mountain View and the neighboring community of Sunnyvale.

Program Content Areas:

Classes:

The project director teaches two reading readiness classes to preschoolers every week. These classes stress the development of fine and gross motor skills and teach children basic concepts like colors, shapes, sizes, numbers, and letters. The classes follow the regular preschool story hour offered by the Mountain View Public Library.

READrunner Club:

This is a reading enrichment activity for reluctant readers aged 7–12. At their weekly meetings READrunners give oral reports, share hobbies and collections, participate in art and craft projects, watch films, and celebrate holidays.

Bibliographies:

A number of these have been prepared to assist librarians wishing suggestions on materials for the new adult reader and the reluctant young reader. Lists have been compiled for parents and teachers attending R.E.A.D. workshops on the under-achieving child and on learning disabilities. The project director has compiled bibliographies for parents of preschoolers.

Special collections:

Parents and teachers are welcome to make use of R.E.A.D.'s reference collections of books, magazines, pamphlets and clippings on early childhood education, remedial reading techniques, and learning disabilities. Preschoolers use a special collection of educational games, toys, and puzzles during reading readiness classes.

Demonstration Collection:

The program uses reading lab equipment, including EDL [Educational Development Laboratories] reading machines and programmed learning materials for adults and children. Staff-developed materials include a variety of inexpensive and attractive games and puzzles.

Community Referral File and Agency Notebook:

These emphasize services for the educationally handicapped and include special schools, testing and diagnostic services, and sources of tutoring, vocational training and counseling.

Programs and Workshops:

These have included an open house, numerous workshops for in-service training and for the public, and recreational programs aimed at enticing the nonreader to the library: game tournaments, decorating contests, multimedia presentations on Mexican history and culture, The Great Overalls Cover-up (decorating overalls), stained-glass techniques, Tarot poetry and card reading, and a lecture and film on hang-gliding.

Materials Collections:

Besides the materials listed in "Special Collections," the program has tutoring materials that include tapes, workbooks, educational games and puzzles, records, and a variety of visual aids like flash cards, word wheels, and tests for visual discrimination. The reading level of materials ranges from preschool to college level.

Collaborative Agencies and Literacy Programs:

The Federal R.E.A.D. Project cooperates with such agencies as Operation SER (job training program), Mountain View-Los Altos Union High School District Adult Education, Santa Clara County Social Services Department, and Mountain View Community Services for student referrals. San Jose State University and Voluntary Action Bureau have supplied volunteers.

Evaluative Methods:

The project director submits a monthly report to the Council of Librarians of the South Bay Cooperative Library System and a quarterly report to the California State Library. Students in the tutoring program are given initial tutoring after being tested with the Wide Range Achievement Test and the Spache Reading Test and are retested at regular intervals. Librarians attending in-service workshops are asked to evaluate the effectiveness of the presentations. In two weeks mothers of preschoolers enrolled in the reading readiness classes will be asked to evaluate the classes and volunteers will fill out evaluative questionnaires.

Personal Evaluation of R.E.A.D.:

This project has given me the opportunity to become involved with people on a one-to-one basis. I have a greater appreciation and compassion for those with reading and learning handicaps. I am convinced that it is possible for every library to become involved in some type of literacy program and for library staff and qualified volunteers to do tutoring, and that the tutoring can be successful—*if* it is done where the student has some privacy (this can be one screened-off table). Every library can serve as a forum and provide programs and information on the learning disabled. Every library should offer cassette and nonbook materials for the dyslexic or nonvisual learner.

Santa Fe Regional Library Adult Education Support Programs

Program Title:

Adult Education Support Programs, formerly titled Living and Learning Project

Program Location:
  Santa Fe Regional Library
  Headquarters, Gainesville Public Library
  222 E. University Ave.
  Gainesville, Florida 32601
  Phone: (904) 377-7540
Contact Persons:
  Thomas E. O'Malley—Library Director
  Memree O. Stuart—Supervisor, Extension Services
Clientele:
  The primary clientele are adults enrolled in the Laubach Literacy
  programs in the community and the high school equivalency and
  adult basic education students who are receiving remedial reading
  instruction. Participation in the Laubach training programs averages
  30 each year, with a constant waiting list of 60 or more applicants for
  enrollment when tutors are available. The enrollment in the various
  remedial reading programs at the Alachua County Adult Education
  Center averages about 500 every school year.
Program Purposes and Objectives:
  To provide materials in print that are especially designed to
  stimulate reading interest in adults who have serious reading disabilities
  To make these materials readily accessible at points where their
  utility to learning in general, to problem solving, to acquiring life
  coping skills can be identified, i.e., places where the person in need of
  such help has come voluntarily to learn the requisite skills
  To aid and encourage use of these materials by professional
  guidance of personnel in the cooperating agencies, by individual
  reader assistance in the library, and by group orientation in lectures
  and tours of the library
Staff:
  This program was designed to be supportive of agencies directly
  concerned with literacy training. Consequently, there has been a
  limited commitment of library staff time to the program except for the
  continuing liaison activities with those agencies. The library director,
  supervisor of extension services, and outreach services librarian
  devoted considerable time to the conception, planning, and initial
  execution of the program. Thereafter, library staff activities in
  connection with literacy training programs comprised no more than 5
  percent of the man-hours of the staff members involved—fluctuating
  with the needs of the cooperating agencies.
Staff Development and Training:
  The two library staff members most involved spent about 40 hours
  on in-service training by familiarizing themselves with the profes-

sional literature on the subject, with the bibliographies of special materials compiled for literacy training and adult basic education functions, and with the agencies and programs to be supported with materials and advice from the library. The director and supervisor of extension services each attended conferences devoted to outreach services. The outreach librarian was assigned to a three-day workshop on library outreach services with emphasis on support of literacy training programs.

Program Origins and Funding:

This program concept originated with the library director as he was developing a multiphased outreach services program for the library system during the years 1971–72. In this process, he became acquainted with the community agencies dedicated to literacy training and their need for and receptivity to support from the library. Federal LSCA Title I grant applications submitted for this purpose were not funded in these years. However, in October 1973, the Santa Fe Regional Library was awarded an unanticipated $36,000 grant for general library services to the disadvantaged in Alachua County. About $3,000 of this windfall grant was allocated to a budget to initiate support of adult basic education and literacy training. The project got under way during the library's fiscal year of October 1, 1973–September 30, 1974 and was continued with increased funds in the amount of $9,500 in fiscal year 1974–75—$6,000 in LSCA Title I federal funds and $3,500 in local appropriations. The program is currently funded entirely with local appropriations, but allocations for this purpose from the operating budget are becoming very difficult with shrinking budgets.

Program Content:

Support of literacy training programs has two areas of concentration: the tutorial training performed by the Gainesville Literacy Advance Council, the local Laubach Foundation group, and the remedial reading instruction conducted in the reading laboratory of the Alachua County Adult Education Center in Gainesville.

Direct materials support, including both instructional kits and supplementary reading, were provided to three Gainesville Literacy Advance Council tutor training workshops (one of which was housed in the library conference room in March 1974). About 1200 volumes are on permanent deposit at the Council's headquarters in a local church for this purpose. The library also provides space in its administrative mezzanine for tutorial sessions, and four Laubach tutors and pupils are currently utilizing this space. The library director has worked in close liaison with all of the officials of this literacy training effort to orient them in the use of the supplementary materials and services supplied by the library.

The original intent of this program as it related to Adult Basic Education activities at the Center and outlying locations was to reinforce the Adult Education Center library with materials selected and purchased by the public library and to stimulate their use by the staff and students. This direction proved to be unproductive and impracticable. The library's effort then concentrated on the Center reading laboratory, where the reading specialist was most responsive to the objectives of our program and demonstrated her capacity to put our support to work to help her clients. As a result, several paperback book racks and about 500 titles and 3500 volumes were installed by the library in the laboratory. These materials were intended to supplement the instructional materials provided in the laboratory and to encourage the habit of reading at rising levels based on a profile of the clientele of the remedial reading classes provided by the reading specialist and on the special bibliographies available for this purpose.

The support described exhibited marked success in both the Laubach literacy programs and the Adult Education Center activities. Cooperating personnel from both agencies expressed their appreciation in written commendations to the library and in their affirmative response to our assistance. The library has now installed its own special adult education collection of about 300 titles and 2500 volumes in response to the requests generated by these two literacy training programs.

The selection and acquisition of the materials in these ABE collections relied mainly on three major annotated bibliographies: those produced by the Reader Development Program of the Free Library of Philadelphia; the Helen H. Lyman project—Library Materials in Service to the Adult New Reader; and the RFD Library of the University of Wisconsin-Extension Rural Family Development ABE project (of which the library director was the original organizer and compiler). The materials are on graded readability levels from third- to eighth-grade level, are intended to supplement instructional reading by appeal to the needs and interests of the handicapped reader, and are heavily inclined toward life-coping skills, such as consumer education, health information, citizenship training, and job-finding and job-holding techniques.

Collaborative Agencies:

Gainesville Literacy Advance Council

Mrs. J. Wayne Connor, Chairman

Mrs. Linda Kunz, Tutor Coordinator

Rev. and Mrs. Waldo Wood, Coordinators

Alachua County Board of Public Instruction
Division of Adult and Veterans Education
Adult Education Center
James A. Talbot, Coordinator
Ellen West, Reading Specialist
Program Evaluation:

The library support effort seems to have been vindicated by the ringing endorsement and enthusiastic reception of the cooperating agencies, as well as the perceptible demand for expansion of these services. Better methods of measurement of results must be devised, but the principal hazard appears to be the cloudy future of local financial support.

Appendix 4

National Literacy Studies

Reading Objectives—National Assessment of Educational Progress*

The National Assessment of Educational Progress defined reading objectives in this second assessment for use in the measurement of abilities of young people. The objectives were identified as important by a national committee of educators, professionals, scholars in the field, and concerned lay persons. They relate to knowledge, skills, and attitudes conducive to reading and reading development. They provide for librarians a guide that will aid in the acquisition of materials supportive to achievements and measurement of such reading objectives.

I. Demonstrate behavior conducive to reading

This section examines reader self-awareness and sensitivity to factors affecting reading. These factors include motivations, attitudes and knowledge of reading skills, as well as ability to judge complexity of reading materials.

A. Demonstrate values related to reading

1. Express an interest in reading

Examples:

Include reading among leisure-time activities

Express preferences for certain kinds of reading matter

Purchase reading material; obtain reading material from a library or friends

2. Indicate an awareness of the value of reading

Examples:

Name ways in which reading is helpful in everyday life

Recognize value of reading as a means of gaining information

Identify problems encountered by those who cannot read

3. Express a commitment to reading

Examples:

Recommend books or magazines to friends

Describe books read

Discuss with friends books and magazines they have read

Read newspapers and magazines with some regularity

* Source: *Reading Objectives: Second Assessment* (Denver, Colo.: National Assessment of Educational Progress, 1974).

182

4. Read to fulfill personal needs
Example:
Describe occasions when reading has been done for enjoyment, escape, information, prestige or aesthetic satisfaction
B. Assess the readability of materials
1. Determine readability of a particular selection
Examples:
Identify the easiest or most difficult of several reading passages
Assess the readability of a passage for their own age group
2. Identify factors which affect readability:
Examples:
Recognize that word complexity affects readability
Recognize that sentence length and complexity affect readability
Recognize that the nature of the subject matter affects readability
C. Demonstrate knowledge of their own reading ability
1. Identify material they can read and understand with ease
Examples:
Distinguish from a variety of passages those which they can read with understanding
Verify their selection of reading materials by demonstrating comprehension
2. Know the adequacy of their reading performance
Example:
Determine whether or not they have performed adequately on tasks requiring various reading skills or knowledge
3. Know their own reading strengths and weaknesses
Example:
Identify factors which affect their ability to comprehend what they read
II. Demonstrate word identification skills
A variety of abilities aid readers in decoding unfamiliar words. This section contains some of those important skills.
A. Know the letters of the alphabet
Examples:
Name upper and lower case and cursive letters
Identify letters upon hearing them pronounced
Match upper and lower case and cursive letters
B. Apply knowledge of sound/symbol relationships
Examples:
Pronounce words containing consonants, vowels, blends, digraphs and diphthongs

Identify words having the same beginning or ending sounds

Utilize letter position in a word to determine the sound/symbol relationship

C. Apply structural analysis techniques

   1. Use syllabication as an aid to pronunciation

      Examples:

      Pronounce polysyllabic words by breaking them into syllables

      Determine the number of syllables in words

   2. Identify the components of words

      Examples:

      Identify the prefixes, roots and suffixes of words

      Identify parts of a compound word

D. Possess basic sight vocabulary

    Examples:

    Pronounce commonly used words shown in print

    Identify printed words upon hearing them pronounced

E. Use context for word identification

    Examples:

    Use rhyme or meter to determine the pronunciation of words

    Pronounce a word based on its function or usage in a sentence

    Select a word based on its function in a sentence

III. Possess skills for reading comprehension

There are times when it is necessary to grasp only the literal or obvious meaning of what is read. On other occasions readers must determine meaning by drawing inferences from what they read. Knowledge of written language conventions aids readers in either case. Some of the skills necessary for reading comprehension are presented in this section.

A. Utilize written language conventions as comprehension aids

   1. Understand the relationship of word order to meaning

      Examples:

      Recognize that word order may indicate interrogative or declarative statements

      Recognize differences in meaning when the words of a sentence are ordered in different ways

   2. Use punctuation marks as an aid to understanding

      Examples:

      Explain the function and purpose of various punctuation marks—e.g., quotation marks, apostrophe, question mark —when they are presented in sentences

      Demonstrate knowledge of the function and purpose of punctuation by their intonation pattern when reading passages aloud

B. Demonstrate literal understanding of material read
 1. Identify the literal meaning of a word, phrase, or longer passage
 Examples:
 State the denotative meaning of a given word
 Identify a fact or other obvious piece of information presented in a phrase, sentence or longer passage
 Follow a set of clearly stated directions
 2. Recognize prefixes and suffixes as meaningful units
 Examples:
 Comprehend the meanings of prefixes and suffixes apart from the meaning of the root word
 Recognize ways in which the addition of prefixes or suffixes may change the meaning of a word
 3. Use function words as an aid to understanding
 Examples:
 Determine the effect of a given function word on meaning
 Select the appropriate function word to achieve a given meaning
C. Demonstrate inferential understanding of material read
 1. Derive implied meaning of a word, phrase, sentence or longer passage
 Examples:
 Explain how the meaning of an unknown word can be determined from the context in which it appears
 Identify the appropriate meaning for a word with multiple meanings when it is presented in a sentence
 Determine the general idea or theme of a given passage when it is not clearly stated
 2. Use the connotation of a word as an aid to comprehension
 Examples:
 Distinguish between the emotional or affective meaning of a word and its explicit or denotative meaning
 Indicate how the selection of a word for its connotation affects meaning
 3. Use style or manner of expression as an aid to comprehension
 Examples:
 Identify the mood conveyed by a particular passage
 Determine the author's attitude toward the subject of his passage
 4. Understand the relationship of organization to meaning
 Examples:
 Identify the organizing principle of a passage, e.g., chronology, general to specific, specific to general

Identify reasons behind the location of particular sentences or particular information in given passages

5. Identify the writer's intent
   Examples:
   Recognize whether the intent is to entertain, persuade, inform, etc.
   Determine the intent of statements in advertisements, editorials, campaign literature, etc.
   Identify the audience for which certain information is intended

6. Identify the underlying assumptions of the writer
   Examples:
   Explain the beliefs that the writer used as a basis for attacking a problem
   Recognize the assumptions on which statements and claims are based

7. Make qualitative judgments about what is read
   Examples:
   Identify phrases and statements which are not internally consistent or do not make sense
   Evaluate clarity of various passages
   Evaluate sufficiency of information given in passages as a basis for drawing conclusions
   Recognize sentences or phrases which do not fit the context or style of the passage in which they are found

8. Relate what is read to other reading
   Example:
   Compare passages on the same topic for the purpose of generalization, verification, refutation or classification

9. Relate what is read to reality
   Examples:
   Distinguish between fact and opinion
   Compare what is read to personal experiences
   Assess relevance of given reading material to their own lives and/or to the lives of others
   Cite an instance from their own experience relating material they have read to their own life and/or the lives of others

IV. Use a variety of approaches in gathering information
   Successful readers possess a variety of approaches for gathering information. Study skills, efficient use of reference materials and flexibility in adapting reading rate to their purpose and the type of material are examined in this section.

   A. Demonstrate flexibility in adapting their rate of reading to suit their purpose(s) and the nature of the material

1. Scan to locate specific information
   Example:
   Adjust reading speed to search rapidly through a passage to find a specific piece of information
2. Skim for an overall impression
   Example:
   Adjust reading speed to obtain a general impression of the content
3. Read for maximum comprehension
   Example:
   Adjust reading speed to carefully comprehend the meaning(s) of a passage

B. Possess reading study skills
   1. Demonstrate efficient study techniques
      Examples:
      Identify main topics within a designated chapter of a non-fiction book
      Demonstrate ability to pre-read, take notes, ask questions about material, survey and summarize
   2. Use various parts of a book as study aids
      Example:
      Demonstrate use of title page, preface, introduction, table of contents, footnotes, index, charts, glossary, bibliography, appendix, and taglines to locate various kinds of information

C. Use reference materials efficiently
   1. Demonstrate dictionary skills
      Examples:
      Locate words in a dictionary
      Use a dictionary to determine the correct pronunciation of a word
      Know that the plural spelling of a word is found in the dictionary
      Use a dictionary to determine the meaning of a word
      Use a dictionary to determine the part of speech of a word
   2. Demonstrate skills in using an encyclopedia
      Examples:
      Identify key words in a passage that can be used to locate additional information in an encyclopedia
      Select the correct volume of an encyclopedia in which to find information on a given subject
      Use the index volume of an encyclopedia to locate information on a given topic

   3. Know other source materials and how to use them, e.g., card catalog, newspapers, directories, bibliography, abstracts, periodicals, indexes
Examples:
Explain the meaning of entries on a card from a library card catalog
Locate particular sections of a newspaper by using the index
Select the appropriate source materials for a given reference task

Adult Performance Level Study—
Objectives for Functional Competency*

Of particular value is this statement of APL Objectives for Functional Competency. The general goal and specific objectives are specified for each of the general knowledge areas. For example, the goal for *Occupational Knowledge* is the development of a level of occupational knowledge that will enable adults to secure employment in accordance with their individual needs and interests. Ten specific objectives, then, are defined for this goal. The goals and objectives for the other areas—consumer economics, health, government and law, and community resources—as well as occupational knowledge, may be used by librarians to identify subjects and types of materials for library collections.

Occupational Knowledge

Goal: To develop a level of occupational knowledge which will enable adults to secure employment in accordance with their individual needs and interests

Objectives:

   1. To build an oral and written vocabulary related to occupational knowledge

   2. To identify sources of information (e.g., radio broadcasts, newspapers, etc.) which may lead to employment

   3. To define occupational categories in terms of the education and job experience required, and to know minimum requirements of given occupations

   4. To be aware of vocational testing and counseling methods which help prospective employees recognize job interests and qualifications

   5. To understand the differences among commercial employment agencies, government employment agencies and private employers

---

* Source: Northcutt, Norvell, and others, *Adult Functional Competency: A Summary* (Austin: The University of Texas at Austin, Division of Extension, Industrial and Business Training Bureau, 1975).

6. To prepare for job applications and interviews
7. To know standards of behavior for various types of employment
8. To know attributes and skills which may lead to promotion
9. To know the financial and legal aspects of employment
10. To understand aspects of employment other than financial which would affect the individual's satisfaction with a job

Consumer Economics
Goal: To manage a family economy and to demonstrate an awareness of sound purchasing principles
Objectives:
1. To build an oral and written consumer economics vocabulary. This should be an ongoing process through each objective
2. To be able to count and convert coins and currency, and to convert weights and measures using measurement tables and mathematical operations
3. To understand the concepts of sales tax and income tax
4. To be aware of the basic principles of money management, including knowing the basics of consumer decision-making
5. To use catalogs, consumer guides and other reference documents to select goods and services
6. To be aware of factors that affect costs of goods and services and to determine the most economical places to shop
7. To be aware of the principles of comparison shopping, and to be aware of the relationship of price to quality among brand names, and between "firsts" and "seconds" and to be able to substitute economy for quality according to individual needs
8. To know the various methods by which goods are packaged and to know which methods are most cost-effective in terms of quality and storage
9. To be able to take advantage of sales by knowing where to find them, by planning for their eventuality, and by being able to determine which are of worthwhile value to the individual
10. To be aware of advertising techniques and to recognize appropriate and inappropriate forms of selling and advertising
11. To know how to order food and to tip in a restaurant
12. To be aware of different stores where home furnishings can be purchased and to determine the best buys for essential and luxury items based on individual needs and resources
13. To determine housing needs and to know how to obtain housing and utilities based on those needs
14. To know how to buy and maintain a car economically
15. To know basic procedures for the care and upkeep of personal possessions (home, furniture, car, clothing, etc.) and to be able to use resources relating to such care

16. To know the various media of exchange and to be familiar with banking services in the community
17. To develop an understanding of credit systems
18. To collect information concerning the types of insurance available and to be able to select the best insurance for the individual and his family
19. To know the resources available to the consumer in the face of misleading and/or fraudulent product/service claims or tactics
20. To understand the implication of consumption vis-a-vis finite world resources and to recognize that each individual's pattern of consumption influences the general welfare

Health

Goal: To ensure good mental and physical health for the individual and his family

Objectives:

1. To develop a working vocabulary related to health, especially as it relates to basic medical and physiological terminology, for accurate reporting of symptoms and following a doctor's directions in applying treatments
2. To understand how basic safety measures can prevent accidents and injuries and to recognize potential hazards, especially as such hazards relate to home and occupational safety
3. To know medical and health services in the community
4. To understand the physical and psychological influences of pregnancy as well as the need for proper prenatal care
5. To understand the importance of family planning, its physical, psychological, financial and religious implications and to have knowledge of both effective and ineffective methods of birth control
6. To understand general child rearing practices and procedures for guarding the health and safety of a child and to apply proper action in accordance with needs and resources
7. To understand the special health needs and concerns of the adolescent (and his parents) and to become acquainted with some ways to ease the transition from childhood to adulthood
8. To understand what contributes to good mental and physical health and to apply this understanding toward preventive care and health maintenance
9. To understand the interaction of self as a member of small groups (family, work, club, class) and to use this understanding to promote effective interpersonal coping skills
10. To be able to apply first aid in emergencies and to inform proper authorities of sudden illnesses, various accidents or natural disasters
11. To plan for health or medical insurance and to be aware of available financial assistance for medical or health problems

12. To understand what constitutes a proper diet and to plan meals according to individual needs and resources
13. To understand federal control of various drugs and items for health protection and to understand how public reaction influences this control

Government and Law

Goal: To promote an understanding of society through government and law and to be aware of governmental functions, agencies and regulations which define individual rights and obligations

Objectives:

1. To develop a working vocabulary related to government and law in order to understand their functions in society and in the personal life of the individual. This should be an ongoing process as each objective is covered.
2. To develop an understanding of the structure and functioning of the federal government
3. To investigate the relationship between the individual citizen and the government
4. To understand the relationship between the individual and the legal system
5. To obtain a working knowledge of the various legal documents which the individual will need as a member of society
6. To explore the relationship between government services and the American tax system

Community Resources

Goal: To understand that community resources, including transportation systems, are utilized by individuals in society in order to obtain a satisfactory mode of living

Objectives:

1. To build an oral and written vocabulary pertaining to community resources and to define community resources in terms of (a) services to community members and (b) services to persons outside the community or non-self-supporting members of society (unemployed, criminals, insane, etc.)
2-3. To know the types of community services provided for members of society including the purposes of and how to gain access to these services
4. To understand how and when to apply for community services, such as Social Security, and Medicare
5. To know various recreational services available in the community
6. To be able to utilize information services of the community
7. To be aware of the people and agencies in the community whose job it is to register and act upon citizen complaints

Subset: Transportation

8. To build an oral and written vocabulary of transportation terms, including car insurance terms
9. To be able to recognize and utilize signs related to transportation needs
10. To develop a familiarity with transportation schedules, and to calculate fares
11. To be able to find and utilize information facilities
12. To learn the use of maps relating to travel needs
13. To recognize time zone boundaries and understand the concept of daylight saving time
14. To request information on and make verbal and written travel and overnight accommodations/reservations
15. To understand the relationship between transportation and public problems
16. To understand driving regulations, including safety, courtesy, and rules such as having a driver's license, car license plates, etc.

Acronyms

AAEC	Appalachian Adult Education Center
ABE	Adult Basic Education
ABS	American Bible Society
ACE	American Council on Education
ADC	Aid to Dependent Children
AEA	Adult Education Association of U.S.A.
AEC	Adult Education Clearinghouse
AFDC	Aid to Families with Dependent Children
AIL	Adult Independent Learner
ALA	American Library Association
APL	Adult Performance Level
CAC	Community Action Committee
CAEO	Coalition of Adult Education Organization
CETA	Comprehensive Employment and Training Act
CLEP	College – Level Examination Program
CWU	Church Women United
EDL	Educational Development Laboratories
EHS	External High School Diploma Program
EOP	Educational Opportunity Program
ERIC	Educational Resources Information Center
ESL	English as a Second Language
GED	General Educational Development (Program, Tests, Certificate; also refers to the High School Equivalency Examination)
HEP	High School Equivalency Program
HSE	High School Equivalency
HumRRO	Human Resources Research Organization
IRA	International Reading Association
IRI	Informal Reading Inventory
LARK	Literacy for Adults and Related Knowledge
LCW	Lutheran Church Women
LSCA	Library Services and Construction Act
LVA	Literacy Volunteers of America
MAC	Materials Analysis Criteria

NACAE	National Advisory Council on Adult Education
NACED	National Advisory Council on the Education of Disadvantaged Children
NAEP	National Assessment of Educational Progress
NALA	National Association for Literacy Advance
NAPCAE	National Association for Public Continuing and Adult Education
NCVA	National Center for Voluntary Action
NEA	National Education Association
NICOV	National Information Center on Volunteerism
NIE	National Institute of Education
NRC	National Reading Council
NRO	National Rural Opportunity
OE	Office of Education (also USOE)
READ Project	Reading Efficiency and Delinquency
	Reading for Everyone—to Achieve and Develop
R-2-R, or R-to-R	Right to Read
RIF	Reading Is Fundamental
T-NAT	Test that's Not a Test
TESL	Teachers of English as a Second Language
TESOL	Teachers of English to Speakers of Other Languages
UNESCO	United Nations Educational Scientific and Cultural Organization
USOE	United States Office of Education (also referred to as OE)
VAC	Voluntary Action Centers
WIN	Work Incentives Program
YMCA	Young Men's Christian Association
YMHA	Young Men's Hebrew Association
YWCA	Young Women's Christian Association
YWHA	Young Women's Hebrew Association

Glossary

Adult: A person 14 years of age and older who usually has some adult responsibilities—a job, earning a living, family responsibilities, military service, voting.

Adult Basic Education (ABE): (1) A federally funded program established by the Economic Opportunity Act of 1964 and the Adult Education Act of 1966 and its amendments, to combat poverty and support educational opportunities for adults whose education was deficient. Supports Adult Basic Education and General Education Development. (2) Also used in a general way in referring to programs involving an elementary level of reading, writing, computing, or vocational skills.

Adult education: Includes the broad range of programs by which adults seek to gain knowledge and acquire or increase their skills. May include studies taken for credit, from ABE to Ph.D., or informal studies taken merely for pleasure.

Adult Education Act: Landmark legislation in 1966, with subsequent amendments, which greatly broadened and strengthened the Adult Education Program through federal support.

Adult Education Association of the United States of America (AEA): National professional organization for adult educators whose primary purpose is to "further the acceptance of education as a process continuing throughout life." Supports relevant research and distributes information in all of the many diverse areas of adult/continuing education. Publications include *Adult Education* and *Adult Leadership.* Address: 810 18th St., N.W., Washington, D.C. 20006.

Adult Education Clearinghouse (AEC): Acquires and abstracts materials for the National Multimedia Center for Adult Education at Montclair State College, Upper Montclair, N.J. Publishes the *AEC Newsletter*, an excellent source for current information.

Adult Functional Competency: The title of a report published in 1975 by the University of Texas, concerned with the ability of adults to apply skills and knowledge in practical situations. Measuring adult functional competency in terms of performance levels, the study is also known as the APL study.   (See also Adult Performance Level.)

Adult Independent Learner (AIL):   An adult who pursues a course of study independently, under his own motivation, rather than in a classroom or tutorial situation.

Adult Performance Level (APL):   A two-dimensional concept of literacy defined in the 1975 University of Texas report *Adult Functional Competency*, which defines literacy competency in terms of five basic skills and in five broad areas of knowledge.

Aid to Families with Dependent Children (AFDC):   Portion of the Social Security Act administered by the Social and Rehabilitation Service of the Department of Health, Education, and Welfare which provides income maintenance, medical, social, and other services to families in need.

American Bible Society (ABS):   Founded in 1816, with a present membership of 275,000 and representing over 70 supporting religious denominations.   Activities include providing information, translations in various formats and languages, volunteer activities, and world service.

American Council on Education (ACE):   A council of institutions of postsecondary and education organizations and related groups. Advances education and educational methods through comprehensive voluntary action on the part of American educational associations, organizations, and institutions.   It also sponsors the GED Testing Program. Address: One Dupont Circle, Washington, D.C. 20036.

American Library Association (ALA):   A nonprofit education association with the primary goal of promoting libraries and librarianship to assure the delivery of user-oriented library information service to all.   Headquarters: 50 East Huron Street, Chicago, Illinois 60611.

Appalachian Adult Education Center (AAEC):   Located at Morehead, Kentucky, the Center has been a leader in developing Adult Basic Education materials based on life-coping skills categories.   Has also had outstanding involvement in demonstration projects of library services to ABE programs.

Bilingual education: Education in one's native language, as well as in a second language.   The term is often combined in a cultural as well as linguistic sense as "bilingual-bicultural education."

Chicanos: Mexican Americans.

Church Women United (CWU):   An ecumenical organization which encourages church women to witness their faith through such activities as Volunteers in Community Service, Citizen Action, and international relations.

Clearinghouse for Offender Literacy Programs, American Bar Association: Project focuses on developing literacy programs and improved basic education technology to help reduce the high functional basic reading and literacy skills that are essential for enabling offenders to cope with modern society and achieve a lasting rehabilitative adjustment. Through this program correctional educators are trained to recruit, train, and evaluate literacy volunteers who will work with functionally illiterate offenders.

Client: A person for whom a particular service is intended.

Clientele: A group or groups of individual clients having some common characteristics.

Collaboration: Working jointly or cooperatively, with authority or decisions being shared equally or delegated by a consensus of those involved.

College-Level Examination Program (CLEP): Administered by the College Entrance Examination Board, these examinations enable individuals who have acquired their education in nontraditional ways to demonstrate their academic achievement and receive college credit for it. Used also by many businesses, industries, government agencies, and professional groups to meet their educational requirements for advancement, licensing, admission to further training, and other benefits.

Continuation Schools: Small high schools operated for adolescents who for any reason are unable to continue in the five-day, thirty-six-week high school of the average school system. They permit change in the form of education with varied opportunities for students, both adolescent and adult, to complete their studies. The General Educational Development diploma is awarded upon successful completion of the GED examination.

Continuing education: A term used to describe all opportunities available to adults of all ages who want to "pick up their education where they left off." Courses may be of any sort: academic, vocational, for enjoyment; formal or nontraditional; and pursued in classrooms, by independent reading, by correspondence, television, or telephone.

Coping skills, or life-coping skills: Skills necessary for successfully meeting the demands of daily living. A number of such areas have been defined, with implications for relating literacy studies and materials to these practical needs.

Declaration of Persepolis: A unanimous statement of the International Symposium for Literacy meeting in Persepolis September 3–8, 1975, at Shivaz, Iran, affirming that literacy is a fundamental human right.

Delivery system: The manner in which a program is brought to its intended users and made to work.

Educational Opportunity Programs (EOP): Program for educationally disadvantaged students.

Educational Resources Information Center (ERIC): A network of clearinghouses under the United States Office of Education that collect massive amounts of information in the field of education and make it available through catalogs, abstracts, indexes, and computer bases. Research findings are listed in *Resources in Education* (RIE), published monthly by the Government Printing Office.

Educational Testing Service (ETS): Designs tests and provides testing services, including those for the CLEP examinations. Operates centers for the College Entrance Examination Board.

Eighth-grade equivalency education: The level at which a person is considered literate by the Office of Education.

English as a Second Language (ESL): Specialized literacy programs for those who do not speak English as their primary language.

Exploratory Committee on Assessing the Progress of Education (ECAPE): Plan for conduct of the assessment of Reading National Assessment of Educational Programs.

External High School Diploma Program (EHS): The General Educational Development or High School Equivalency Program.

FORCAST: An easy-to-administer formula for estimating grade level, designed by HumRRO.

General Educational Development (GED): Refers to the program, tests, and diploma or certificate that one may pursue to obtain high school certification outside the usual school system. Interchangeable terms are "High School Equivalence Program," "High School Equivalency Certificate," and "External High School Diploma."

Head Start: Progam administered by the Department of Health, Education, and Welfare for poor children aged 3–6, to help them develop the preliteracy skills necessary for successful development during their school years.

High School Equivalance Program (HEP): Program outside the usual school system that leads to the High School Equivalency Certificate (General Educational Development).

High School Equivalency Examination (GED): Used interchangeably with the term "GED tests." The successful completion of these tests entitles one to the High School Equivalency Certificate.

Home Start: Like Head Start, is concerned with education, parent involvement, social services, and health. As part of the education component Home Start's "home visitors" encourage parents to interact verbally with their children, to read to them, and to involve children in daily activities around the home. Children show significant gains in school readiness. Mothers are involved in reading readiness activities, dramatization of stories, and other similar activities.

Human Resources Research Organization (HumRRO): An Air Force-related research organization that has produced considerable information about literacy in relation to job-related skills and performance.

In-kind funding: A system by which the dollar values for personnel or facility resources are provided by the sponsoring agency to match outside funding.

International Reading Association (IRA): Membership includes individuals engaged in teaching or supervising reading at any educational level. Purposes are to encourage the study of reading problems, to promote research in these areas, and to disseminate knowledge helpful in the solution of problems related to reading. Publications include the *Journal of Reading, The Reading Teacher, Reading Today,* and *Reading Research Quarterly.* Address: 6 Tyre Ave., Newark, Delaware 19711.

Language-experience approach: Teaches reading by having students dictate, or write with some assistance, their own stories or experiences and then read them. Because of the motivation involved, and the greater ease in reading what is already familiar, this method is often highly successful.

Languaging: Auding and reading.

Latinos: Term includes a number of different cultures and groups—Chicano, Mexican American, Mexicano, Hispano, Spanish, Spanish speaking, La Raza, Puerto Rican, Cuban, and others from Central and South America.

Laubach Literacy, Inc.: Founded by Frank C. Laubach, a pioneer in literacy education in this country and throughout the world, and based on the "each-one-teach-one" concept, this organization sponsors adult literacy programs in many foreign countries, in all fifty states, and in four provinces in Canada. Their publishing division, *New Readers Press,* has been in the forefront in providing materials written at an easy reading level. The National Affiliation for Literacy Advance (NALA) is the domestic arm of Laubach Literacy International. Address: Box 131, Syracuse, N.Y. 13210.

Library Services and Construction Act (LSCA): In 1956 Library Services Act (LSA) authorized federal financial assistance to the states and territories for library development. In 1964 coverage was extended to the construction of libraries by the Library Services and Construction Act (LSCA). Subsequent amendments were made; the implementation extended through 1976. The Act continues to authorize services in specific areas designated under Title I, Library Services, including services to the institutionalized and handicapped; Title II, Public Library Construction; and Title III, Interlibrary Cooperation. Emphasis is placed on providing library services to the disadvantaged in rural and urban areas, strengthening metropolitan public libraries that serve as national or regional resource centers, extending library service to state institutions and to physically handicapped, and improving and strengthening the capacity of state library agencies for meeting the needs of the people.

Lifelong learning, lifetime learning: A concept that is becoming an important commitment for educators, librarians, legislators, and the public in general because of the increased recognition of the value of education at every stage in life.

Literacy functional competency: The ability to use literacy skills in practical situations such as job performance, or any of the necessary activities of daily living.

Literacy Volunteers of America (LVA), *Inc.:* An organization with over sixty affiliates whose purpose is to foster and increase adult literacy in the United States and Canada through local volunteers. Training and supportive services are emphasized in helping tutors to be most effective. Materials and assistance in planning, organizing, and directing a volunteer reading tutorial program are provided. Address: 3001 James St., Syracuse, New York 13206.

Lutheran Church Women's Volunteer Reading Program: Trains volunteers to tutor illiterate English-speaking adults and teach non-English-speaking adults to speak, read, and write English. Helps communicator conduct assessments of needs and set up volunteer literacy programs. Upon request, trains persons in how to conduct literacy workshops. Assists already existing literacy groups. Develops and field tests "survival skill" materials written on beginning reading levels.

Manpower Administration: A branch of the United States Department of Labor, which administers the National On-Job Training program and provides money to trade associations, labor unions, and industries to train the disadvantaged.

Materials Analysis Criteria (MAC Checklist): Standards for measurement developed in Helen H. Lyman's study, *Library Materials in Service to the Adult New Reader.* These include a bibliographic analysis, analysis of content, the measurement of readability, appeal, and quantitative assessment and annotation.

National Advisory Council on Adult Education (NACAE): Composed of citizens and government officials with professional backgrounds or interest in adult education. Advises commissioner of education on adult education programs, and in policy matters arising in the administration of the Adult Education Act.

National Advisory Council on the Education of Disadvantaged Children: Established for the purpose of reviewing the administration and operation of the provisions of Title I of the Elementary and Secondary Education Act of 1965, including its effectiveness in improving the educational attainment of educationally deprived children.

National Affiliation for Literacy Advance (NALA): An extensive membership organization of 416 local groups and 17,500 volunteers throughout the United States and Canada, affiliated with Laubach Literacy, Inc. and providing training, coordination, and guidelines for local literacy operations. Address: Box 131, Syracuse, New York 13210.

National Assessment of Educational Progress (NAEP): An information-gathering organization surveying the educational attainments of various age groups in ten subject areas. See the General Bibliography following for a list of NAEP Assessment Reports.

National Association for Public Continuing and Adult Education (NAPCAE): An affiliate of the National Education Association, made up primarily of teachers and other professional educators active in continuing education for adults. Address: 1201 Sixteenth St., N.W., Washington, D.C. 20036.

National Education Association (NEA): Professional organization of elementary and secondary school teachers, college and university professors, administrators, principals, counselors, and others interested in American education. Address: 1201 Sixteenth St., N.W., Washington, D.C. 20036.

National Information Center on Volunteerism (NICOV): Promotes the exchange of ideas and information among volunteer programs in courts and correctional institutions in prevention and diversion. Address: 1221 University Ave., Boulder, Colorado 80302.

National Institute of Education (NIE): A major component of the Education Division, United States Department of Health, Education, and Welfare, provided for as part of the Education Amendments of 1972. Created to provide leadership in the conduct and support of scientific inquiry into the educational process, to provide more dependable knowledge about educational quality, and to improve education, including career education.

National Reading Assessment: An information-gathering project surveying the reading skills and attainments of several age groups in various subject areas. Part of the National Assessment of Educational Progress (NAEP).

National Reading Council (NRC): Federally funded project to assist in the achievement of the Right to Read program objectives. Operates the National Reading Center, and sponsored the "Survival Literacy" studies.

Native Americans: American Indians.

Nonformal education: The education one receives outside the classroom, as through practical experience, travel, television, independent study, or any of a number of nontraditional learning situations.

Nonliterate: Not literate; illiterate.

Office of Education (OE or USOE): A major component of the Education Division of the United States Department of Health, Education, and Welfare; administers programs at every level and for every aspect of education.

Open University External Degree Program: A form of nontraditional education in which universities carry out degree programs and students receive credentials. Programs follow various models of external degree programs—open university, university without walls, etc. Programs may include independent study, work experience, travel, courses, and structured or unstructured curriculum. New York State pioneered external degree programs in the 1970s.

Out-of-school: No longer enrolled in public school; often used in referring to young adults who have either finished their formal schooling, or have dropped out.

PACE: PACE Institute, Inc.: Programmed activities for Correctional Education (a private, not-for-profit corporation) for inmates at the Cook County Department of Corrections, Chicago, Illinois. Development Office Suite 1308, 220 South State Street, Chicago, Illinois 60608 (312-922-5598). Tests, trains, advises, and prepares inmates for life outside of jail.

Parenting: Parenting is a function shared by all individuals and organizations of individuals concerned with the development of children. It extends the responsibility for the functions of parents to embrace fully the personalities of both parents and as a function shared by other members of the child's community. It is the nurturing of the child's growth and development.

Preschool: Referring to the years before kindergarten or first grade, usually ages 0–5 or 0–6.

Programmed learning: Instruction utilizing a workbook, textbook, and/or mechanical or electronic device programmed to help students attain a specified level of performance by (a) providing instruction in small steps, (b) asking one or more questions about each step in the instruction and providing instant response regarding the accuracy of each answer, and (c) enabling students to progress at their own pace, either individually, through self-pacing, or as a team, through group pacing.

Public Library Association division of the American Library Association/Adult Literacy and Learning Committee (PLA/ALL):

Seeks to facilitate communication about learning and literacy in public libraries, and to strengthen and develop such programs.

Readiness: A developmental stage involving physical, mental, and psychological factors that must be reached by the learner at any age before he or she can master any of the broad spectrum of skills involved in listening, speaking, reading, writing, and computing.

Reading Efficiency and Delinquency (R.E.A.D.): A nationwide project supported by the Law Enforcement Assistance Administration (LEAA) National Institute for Juvenile Justice and Delinquency Prevention grant, and sponsored by the American Correctional Association. Provides teacher training in the areas of diagnosis and remediation of reading difficulties and provides paperback books for students in all participating juvenile training schools to increase the variety of reading material available. Publishes newsletter, *READ Resources,* and conducts workshops for teachers. Address: American Correctional Association, 4321 Hartwick Road, Suite 306, College Park, Maryland 20740.

Reading Is Fundamental (RIF): A program aimed at motivating children to read by allowing them to select and keep books for themselves. Operating from the Smithsonian Institution and working through local community organizations, RIF, Inc. has distributed millions of paperback books to children who would otherwise have no books of their own. Address: RIF, Inc., % Smithsonian Institution, Washington, D.C. 20560.

Regents External Degree Program: External degree program presented by New York State Regents Governing Board of Education.

Right to Read (RTR, R-2-R): A national effort, under the United States Office of Education, which serves to coordinate and strengthen all literacy efforts in the nation, toward the elimination of illiteracy in all age groups and all segments of society.

Survival literacy, survival thresholds: Terms used by Louis Harris & Associates in their studies for the National Reading Council to denote degrees of functional illiteracy. Low-survival, questionable, marginal, and likely-survival were the terms used to describe these stages.

Teachers of English to Speakers of Other Languages (TESOL): An organization based at the School of Language and Linguistics at Georgetown University, which publishes research reports, bibliographies, and other materials concerned with the methodology and practice of English as a second language.

Test that's Not a Test (T-NAT): An informal assessment of reading ability, intended for initial placement, available through Basic Education Trade House in Greeley, Colorado.

Tutor: One who teaches another, the tutee, in a one-to-one relationship.

United Nations Educational, Scientific and Cultural Organization (UNESCO): A specialized agency of the United Nations operating as an independent, cooperative body whose purpose is "to contribute to peace and security by promoting collaboration among the nations through education, science and culture in order to further universal respect for justice, for the rule of law, and for the human rights and fundamental freedoms" for all. Its distinct services include programs of education, natural sciences, social sciences, cultural activities, mass communication, and exchange of persons, on an international and worldwide basis.

Visual literacy: A term used to explain a person's level of visual awareness or capabilities in dealing with visual materials. This ability is being increasingly recognized because of its importance in modern communication.

Work Incentive Program (WIN): A program administered jointly by the Labor Department, Manpower Administration, and the Department of Health, Education, and Welfare to provide social support services such as child care and medical care for welfare recipients so they can look for and hold jobs.

General Bibliography

See also References at the end of each chapter and Suggested Readings within the text.

Abraham, Willard. *Living with Preschoolers.* Phoenix: O'Sullivan Woodside Co., 1976.

Adult Learning (It Can Happen in the Library, Too). Austin: University of Texas, Division of Extension, 1974.

Appalachian Adult Education Center, Morehead State University, Morehead, Kentucky. Library Service Guides. Chicago: American Library Association.

Assessing Community Information and Service Needs

Audiovisual Materials in Service to Disadvantaged Adults

Bookmobile Services: Moving the Library to Disadvantaged Adults

Books by Mail Services: Moving the Library to Disadvantaged Adults

Deposit Collections for Disadvantaged Adults

Evening and Weekend Library Services for Disadvantaged Adults

Expanding Library Services to the Elderly

Expanding Library Services to the Institutionalized

Group Library Tours for Disadvantaged Adults

Inservice Training in Service to Disadvantaged Adults

Interagency Cooperation in Expanding Library Services to Disadvantaged Adults

The Library Advisory Committee

The Library as a Community Information and Referral Center

Materials Selection for Disadvantaged Adults

Planning Expanded Library Services to Disadvantaged Adults

Public Library Services to Young Disadvantaged Adults

Reader Guidance Services for Disadvantaged Adults

Recruiting Disadvantaged Adults

Using Pamphlets with Disadvantaged Adults

Utilizing Volunteers in Expanding Library Services to Disadvantaged Adults.

Bailey, Stephen K., and others. *Alternative Paths to the High School Diploma.* Prepared by the Policy Institute, Syracuse University Research Corp. for the Ford Foundation. Reston, Va.: National Association of Secondary School Principals, 1973.

Baratta-Lorton, Mary. *Workjobs for Parents.* Reading, Mass.: Addison-Wesley Publishing Co., 1975.

A Bibliography of Easy Reading, Coping Skills Materials for Adults. Library/ABE Project, Memphis/Shelby County Public Library and Information Center, Spring 1975.

Brazziel, William F. *Quality Education for All Americans: An Assessment of Gains of Black Americans with Proposals for Program Development in American Schools and Colleges for the Next Quarter-Century.* Washington, D.C.: Howard University Press, 1974.

Burmeister, Lou E. *Reading Strategies for Secondary School Teachers.* Reading, Mass.: Addison-Wesley Publishing Co., 1974.

Carsetti, Janet K. *Literacy: Problems and Solutions: A Resource Handbook for Correctional Educators.* Project READ. Washington, D.C.: Clearinghouse for Offender Literacy, American Bar Association, 1975.

Casey, Genevieve M., and others. *Public Library Service for the Urban Disadvantaged.* [Detroit, Mich.]: Wayne State University, Department of Library Science, December 1972.

——— ed. *Public Library Service to the Illiterate Adult.* Proceedings of a Seminar, March 9–11, 1972. [Detroit]: Wayne State University, Office of Urban Library Research, 1972.

Colvin, Ruth J. *I Speak English. A Tutor's Guide to Teaching Conversational English.* Syracuse, N.Y.: Literacy Volunteers of America, Inc., 1976.

———, and Root, Jane H. *READ: Reading Evaluation—Adult Diagnosis. A Test for Assessing Adult Student Reading Needs and Progress. Administrative Guide.* Syracuse, N.Y.: Literacy Volunteers of America, Inc., 1976.

———*Tutor: Techniques Used in the Teaching of Reading. A Handbook for Teaching Basic Reading to Adults and Teenagers.* Syracuse, N.Y.: Literacy Volunteers of America, Inc., 1976.

Cullinan, Bernice E., ed. *Black Dialects and Reading.* Urbana, Ill.: ERIC Clearinghouse on Reading and Communication Skills, National Council of Teachers of English, 1974.

Establishing Library Learning Centers for Adult Basic Education. Austin: University of Texas, Division of Extension, 1974.

Gillette, Arthur. *Youth and Literacy: You've Got a Ticket to Ride.* Paris/New York: UNESCO/UNCESI, 1972.

Glass, J. Conrad, Jr., and Hoffman, Lee M., "Hunting the SNARK in ABE (The Search for Needed Adult-Related Knowledge)," *Adult Leadership* 24, no. 2 (October 1975): 58-61.

Gotsick, Priscilla, and others. *Information for Everyday Survival.* Chicago: American Library Association, 1976.

Haendle, Connie. *Organizational Management Handbook.* Syracuse, N.Y.: Literacy Volunteers of America, Inc., 1976.

Hagemeyer, Alice. *Deaf Awareness Handbook for Public Librarians.* Washington, D.C.: Public Library of the District of Columbia, 1975.

Hall, MaryAnne, and Coley, Joan D., "Needs in Reading Instruction in Adult Basic Education," *Adult Leadership* 24, no. 3 (November 1975): 103-4.

Johns, Jerry L., ed. *Literacy for Diverse Learners: Promoting Reading Growth at All Levels.* Newark, Del.: International Reading Association, 1973.

Johnson, Laura S., "Bilingual Bicultural Education: A Two-Way Street," *The Reading Teacher* 29, no. 3 (December 1975): 231-39.

Kelly, Marguerite, and Parsons, Elias. *The Mother's Almanac.* Doubleday & Co., 1975.

Klein, Howard A., ed. *Quest for Competency in Teaching Reading.* Newark, Del.: International Reading Association, 1972.

Lipsman, Claire K. *The Disadvantaged and Library Effectiveness.* Chicago: American Library Association, 1972.

Literacy Volunteers of America, Inc. *Basic Reading Tutor Training Workshop Leader's Handbook.* Syracuse, N.Y.: Literacy Volunteers of America, Inc., 1975.

————*Community Relations Handbook.* Syracuse, N.Y.: Literacy Volunteers of America, Inc. [1976].

MacDonald, Barbara J. *Bibliography of Reading Materials for Basic Reading and English as a Second Language.* Syracuse, N.Y.: Literacy Volunteers of America, Inc., 1976.

Mackay, David, and Simo, Joseph. *Help Your Child to Read and Write, and More.* New York: Penguin Books, Inc., 1976.

Markun, Patricia Maloney, ed. *Parenting.* Washington, D.C.: Association for Childhood Education International, 1973.

Marzollo, Jean, and Lloyd, Janice. *Learning through Play.* New York: Harper & Row Publishers, 1972.

Monahon, Robert. *Free and Inexpensive Materials for Preschool and Early Childhood.* 2d ed. Belmont, Calif.: Fearon Publishers, 1977.

National Assessment of Education Progress *Reports.*

   Functional Literacy: Basic Reading Performance: A Brief Summary of an Assessment of In-School 17-Year-Olds in 1974. 1975.

   General Information Yearbook: A Description of National Assessment's Methodology with Special Attention Given to Reading and Literature: May 1972 (#02-GIY)

   Reading Objectives: 1970.

   Reading Objectives: Second Assessment. 1974.

   Reading: Understanding Words and Word Relationships (Theme 1). April 1973 (#02-R-01)

   Reading: Graphic Materials (Theme 2). June 1973. (#02-R-02)

   Reading: Written Directions (Theme 3). May 1973. (#02-R-03)

   Reading: Reference Materials (Theme 4). July 1973. (#02-R-04)

Reading: Gleaning Significant Facts From Passages (Theme 5). May 1973. (#02-R-05)

Reading: Main Ideas and Organization (Theme 6). July 1973. (#02-R-06)

Reading: Drawing Inferences (Theme 7). August 1973. (#02-R-07)

Reading: Critical Reading (Theme 8). May 1973. (#02-R-08)

Reading: Reading Rate and Comprehension. (Theme 9). December 1972. (#02-R-09)

Reading: Released Exercises. July 1973 (#02-R-20)

Reading: Summary Data. July 1974. (#02-R-00)

Recipes, Wrappers, Reasoning and Rate: A Digest of the First Reading Assessment. April 1974. (#02-R-30)

Newman, Mayrelee F. *Cooperative Planning to Maximize Adult Basic Education Opportunities Through Public Library Extension in Appalachian North Carolina.* Final Report. Project no. R02-0560. Washington, D.C.: U.S. Department of Health, Education, and Welfare, Office of Education, 1975.

The Right to Read and the Nation's Libraries. Chicago: American Library Association, 1974.

Roufberg, Ruth B. *Your Child from Two to Five Years: Today He Can't, Tomorrow He Can* (The Learning Child Series). New York: Fountain Publishing Co., 1971; distributed by Thomas Y. Crowell Co.

Smith, Edwin H. *Literacy Education for Adolescents and Adults: A Teacher's Resource Book.* San Francisco: Boyd & Fraser Publishing Co., 1970.

Swarm, Christine C., "The Role of School Libraries in a Continuing Education Program," *Adult Leadership* 24, no. 3 (November 1975): 105–6.

Tests of Functional Adult Literacy: An Evaluation of Currently Available Instruments. Portland, Ore.: Northwest Regional Education Laboratory, n.d.

Thompson, Frances Coombs, ed. *Guide to Continuing Education in America.* New York: Quadrangle Books, 1973.

Ward, Martha Coonfield. *Them Children: A Study in Language Learning.* New York: Holt, Rinehart & Winston, Inc., 1971.

Whipple, Gertrude, and Black, Millard H., eds. *Reading for Children Without—Our Disadvantaged Youth* (Reading Aid Series). Newark, Del.: International Reading Association, 1966.

Wilson Library Bulletin. Issue "Librarians and the First R," 50, no. 9 (May 1976): 704–41.

––––––– Issue "The Librarian and the Teaching of Reading," 45, no. 3 (November 1970): 239–307.

Yearbook of Adult and Continuing Education 2d ed., 1976–77. Chicago: Marquis Academic Media, 1976.

Index